Class and Conservative Parties

CLASS AND CONSERVATIVE PARTIES

Argentina in Comparative Perspective

EDWARD L. GIBSON

The Johns Hopkins University Press / *Baltimore and London*

This book has been brought to publication with the generous
assistance of the Karl and Edith Pribram Fund.

The Johns Hopkins University Press
2715 North Charles Street
Baltimore, Maryland 21218-4319
The Johns Hopkins Press Ltd., London

ISBN 0-8018-5172-6

Library of Congress Cataloging-in-Publication Data
will be found at the end of this book.
A catalog record for this book is available from the British Library.

Para Rita y Eduardo Gibson

Contents

Figures and Tables

Figures

Tables

Preface and Acknowledgments

Will the propertied and socially privileged in Latin America be represented in political parties? As democratic governments spread throughout the region, this question grows in significance. In this second decade of democracy, the short-term fears of elite subversion of democratic rule have receded to a great extent. Leftist and popular challenges have subsided, and governments throughout the region have embraced free-market reforms. However, important questions of institutional development remain. One of these is the organizational forms that the representation of upper-class interests will take in the region's new democracies. In any democratic regime, the organizational forms of upper-class political representation will have a profound effect on the structure of decision making and the relevance of democratic institutions. It is precisely because the arenas for upper-class representation are multiple that the question of their relationship to political parties is important to the study of democratization. Stable democracy in Latin America, as everywhere else, has historically been linked to strong party systems. Strong party systems have historically been linked to the existence of parties that represent and are supported by the socially privileged strata of society. In this book such parties are defined as *conservative* parties.

This is a book about conservative party politics. It has three overarching objectives. The first is to propose concepts and ideas for the comparative study of conservative parties and party development, and to provide a theoretical understanding of the relationship between conservative parties and democratic politics. This goal is guided by the assumption that conservative parties are a comparative political phenomenon. They possess coalition-building dynamics that are unique to them, and that are replicated across historical and regional contexts. A minimal definition is provided in this book: conservative parties are parties that draw their core constituencies from the upper strata of society. This definition provides the basis for distinguishing conservative parties from other types of parties, and offers a starting point for analyzing the interaction between social constituencies, party leaders, and institutions that shape conservative party development over time.

The book's second objective is to detail and explain the historic patterns of conservative party development in one country, Argentina. Between 1880 and 1930, Argentina was ruled by civilian constitutional regimes. In 1916, an oligarchic regime was succeeded constitutionally by a regime of universal male suffrage. This successful transition was, however, followed by a massive failure of conservative party organization, and was brought to an abrupt end in 1930 by a conservative-led military coup. Thereafter, conservatives ruled by electoral fraud, coercion, and military government, initiating a pattern of social conflict and recurrent authoritarianism that dominated Argentine politics until 1983. This book will turn to the early phases of conservative party formation during the advent of mass politics to trace the historic causes of the country's failed conservative party development. It will also detail the burst of conservative party building that took place during the democratizing period between 1983 and 1989, and the equally sudden collapse of conservative party organization that followed. The argument presented is that the failures of conservative party organization in Argentina are to be explained by dynamics at the elite level: patterns of upper-class division and collective action and patterns of political action by party leaders. Upper-class divisions, specifically regional economic divisions, have historically hindered conservative party unity at the national level. In the contemporary period, conservative party development has also been shaped by an additional factor: the relationship between elites and the state. As opportunities for direct access by conservative party elites to state power or policy making emerged, they abstained from party-building efforts. Similarly, business elites remained aloof from party politics because of continued opportunities for access to state policy-making institutions and patronage. Conservative party development thus advances or retreats in response to the relationship of party leaders and their core constituencies with the state.

The third objective of this book is to provide answers to the question, What factors promote or hinder the development of conservative parties in Latin America? The analytical framework developed in the book and the insights drawn from the Argentine experience are also applicable to other countries in the region. The stress on interaction between core constituencies, party leaders, and the state can serve as an analytical thread for generalizations about problems and patterns of conservative party development in Latin America.

The book is organized into seven chapters. Chapter 1 provides a discussion of conceptual and theoretical problems in the study of conservative party politics and outlines an analytical framework that shapes the analysis in subsequent chapters. Chapter 2 provides a comparatively framed historical interpretation of the problem of conservative electoral organization in Argentina from the advent of mass politics through the twentieth century. Chapter 3 provides a study of the failed 1976–82 attempt by military leaders to use the authoritarian power of the state to engineer a conservative transition to democracy. Chapter 4 details the Argentine conservative leadership's struggle to reorganize for democratic competition in the "founding elections" of 1983 after the ignominious collapse of the authoritarian regime. Chapter 5 looks at a local experiment in conservative party building in Argentina. It examines the growth of the Unión del Centro Democrático (UCEDE) in Argentina's most important urban region, the city of Buenos Aires, during the 1983–89 period. Statistical analyses will give a glimpse of how the social bases of a new conservative electoral coalition were forged. Chapter 6 analyzes the collapse of the conservative party-building experiments of the 1980s after the advent of the Peronist government of President Carlos Menem. It also speculates on possible outcomes for Argentine conservatism of the current coalitional and institutional fluidity of party politics in Argentina. All empirical chapters in the book situate the Argentine case in a broader comparative perspective. However, the final chapter explicitly shifts its comparative emphasis to the problems of conservative party development in Latin America, and explores the generalizability of findings on Argentina for other democratizing countries in the region.

No book is an individual project. I do not see how anyone could make it through the long research and writing process without drawing on a large reserve of support from loved ones and friends. Judith Swartz Gibson was there at the beginning of this task and was my closest friend and critic through the years of graduate school, field research, and writing. Together we shared the joys of living in Argentina, traveling to its remotest corners, and becoming immersed in its culture and politics. Our three sons, Patrick, Alex, and Henry, were also participants in that experience, and added little doses of wonder and mystery.

The earliest origins of this book lie in the often passionate arguments about politics that were a regular part of my household during my childhood and adolescence in Latin America. My parents, Rita and Eduardo Gibson, to whom this book is dedicated, have always been a major source of inspiration. Their unconditional financial, moral, and emotional support sustained me through the years of study, research, and writing. It is hard to see how this project could have been completed without so much help from such a selfless and loving family.

Alfred Stepan communicated his enthusiasm for the study of politics — particularly its "ideologically inconvenient" dimensions — to me early in my academic career. I owe him a great intellectual debt. Blanca Heredia and Hector Schamis devoted countless hours to critical reviews and discussions of my manuscript, despite geographic distances and exorbitant telephone bills. At Columbia, I am also indebted to Margaret Crahan, Robert Kaufman, Maria do Carmo Campello de Souza, Douglas Chalmers, William Nylen, Brian Ford, Katie Roberts-Hite, Douglas Blum, Paul Haber, Todd Shapera, Tim Christenfeld, and Philip Mauceri.

In Argentina, I was associated with the Centro de Investigaciones Europeo-Latinoamericanas (EURAL), which provided me with a congenial and supportive environment for research. Thanks go to Atilio Boron, director of EURAL, as well as to Maria de las Mercedes Puga Marín, Deborah Norden, Thomas Scheetz, Aldo Vacs, and Rut Diamint. I also benefited from the criticism, assistance, and friendship of several individuals outside EURAL, including Ezequiel Gallo, Enrique Zuleta, Torcuato Di Tella, Carlos Acuña, Catalina Smulovitz, Rosendo Fraga, Ricardo Sidicaro, Gabriel Negretto, José María Ghio, and Ana María Mustapic. María Victoria Murillo was the best research assistant anyone could have hoped for.

The Juzgado Electoral de la Ciudad de Buenos Aires made available a great many unpublished electoral and party membership data. I am grateful to Judge Juan Edgardo Fégoli, Leonor de Montagna, Lelia Rodriguez de Bascarám, Pablo Aragón, and Alberto Chareca. Several political activists and politicians made themselves available for long conversations and interviews. They are far to many to mention by name, but special thanks go to Alvaro Alsogaray, who gave me time and complete access to his personal archives, as well as to Armando Ribas, the late Congressman Federico Clérici, and Congressman Francisco de Durañona y Vedia. Oscar Jimenez Peña and Lisandro Echenique gave endless hours of their time over a two-year period. In Peru, former President Fernando Belaúnde Terry, Enrique Ghersi, Alexander and David Grobman, and Pedro Planas gave time and support.

Field research and writing were supported by an Aaron Diamond Dissertation Fellowship from Columbia University's Center for the Study of Human Rights, and a grant from the Organization of American States. I was also awarded a two-year appointment as an Academy Scholar at Harvard University's Academy for International and Area Studies between 1990 and 1992. During that period, Jorge Domínguez was a valuable critic and advisor, Roberto Sokol assisted with the statistical data, and Jennifer Gibson Miller and Philip Miller were pals, babysitters, and anything else we needed.

Don Herzog and Rebecca Scott at the University of Michigan generously read and commented on the entire manuscript. I am also indebted to Daniel Levine, Douglas Dion, and Jacqueline Stevens. Jane Mansbridge, Jeffrey Winters, Ben Ross Schneider, and Ernesto Calvo at Northwestern University provided badly needed advice and perspectives in the final phases. Two anonymous reviewers gave very helpful comments, which structured the final revisions.

Naturally, I alone am responsible for any errors of fact or interpretation.

Acronyms

AP	Acción Popular (Peru)
ARENA	Alianza Republicana Nacionalista (El Salvador)
CFI	Confederación Federalista Independiente
CGE	Confederacion General Economica
CGT	Confederacion General de Trabajadores
CONADEP	Comisión Nacional de Desaparecidos
COPEI	Partido Social Cristiano COPEI (Venezuela)
FREDEMO	Frente Democrático (Peru)
FREPASO	Frente del País Solidario
FUFEPO	Fuerza Federalista Popular
GOU	Grupo de Oficiales Unidos
MAS	Movimiento al Socialismo
MID	Movimiento de Integración y Desarrollo
MODIN	Movimiento por la Dignidad e Independencia
MOLIPO	Movimiento Linea Popular
MON	Movimiento de Opinion Nacional
MPJ	Movimiento Popular Jujeño
MPN	Movimiento Popular Neuquino
MRyC	Movimiento de Renovación y Cambio
PAN	Partido Autonomista Nacional (Argentina)
PAN	Partido Acción Nacional (Mexico)
PCI	Partido Cívico Independiente
PCN	Partido de Conciliación Nacional (El Salvador)
PDN	Partido Demócrata Nacional
PDP	Partido Demócrata Progresista
PDS	Partido Democratico Social (Brazil)
PF	Partido Federal
PI	Partido Intransigente
PJ	Partido Justicialista (Peronist Party)
PPC	Partido Popular Cristiano (Peru)
PRI	Partido Revolucionario Institucional (Mexico)

PRN	Proceso de Reorganización Nacional
PSA	Partido Socialista Argentino
PSI	Partido Socialista Independiente
SRA	Sociedad Rural Argentina
UCEDE	Unión del Centro Democrático
UCR	Unión Cívica Radical (Radical Party)
UCRI	Unión Cívica Radical Intransigente
UCRP	Unión Cívica Radical del Pueblo
UDELPA	Unión del Pueblo Argentino
UDI	Unión Democrática Independiente (Chile)
UIA	Unión Industrial Argentina
UPAU	Unión para la Apertura Universitaria

Class and Conservative Parties

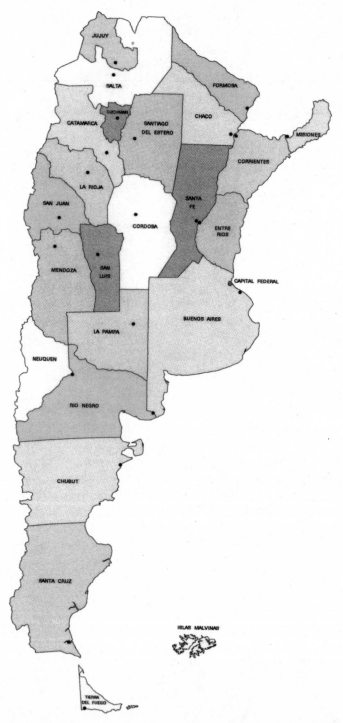

Argentina: Provinces. *Source*: Instituto Nacional de Estadísticas y Censos (INDEC).

Chapter One

Conservative Parties and Democratic Politics

Above all else, [parties] vary according to the structure of domination within the community . . . it is impossible to say anything about the structure of parties without discussing the structural forms of social domination per se.

MAX WEBER

One unexpected event in the wave of democratization that swept Latin America in the 1980s was the emergence of conservative electoral activism. Few could have predicted this development from past historical experience, especially in countries that had recently emerged from authoritarian rule. In those countries, democratic activists worried that powerful sociopolitical actors incapable of effectively organizing themselves for the electoral struggle would exercise the many options for exit from democratic politics available to them in authoritarian realms. The Right was thus seen as a force to be "pacified" or "neutralized" while democratic agendas were consolidated. This view also shaped the theoretical perspectives that dominated research on Latin American democratization in the 1980s. In one of the most influential texts in the field, Guillermo O'Donnell and Philippe Schmitter wrote at the time:

> Put in a nutshell, parties of the Right-Center and Right must be "helped" to do well, and parties of the Left-Center and Left should not win by an overwhelming majority. . . . The problem is especially acute for those partisan forces representing the interests of propertied classes, privileged professionals, and entrenched institutions. . . . Unless their party or parties can muster enough votes to stay in the game, they are likely to desert the electoral process in favor of antidemocratic conspiracy and destabilization.[1]

Surprisingly, conservatives did well in the electoral game without much help. In the 1980s, as democratic transitions spread throughout the region, the Right won power outright through the electoral process in Brazil, Uruguay, Ecuador, and El Salvador. It also shaped the political debate, as well as the policy-making process, in Peru, Mexico, Chile, and Argentina.

The conservative electoral movements in all these countries shared strikingly similar characteristics,[2] indicating that they were being driven in part by regionwide developments. They were also, however, separated by important differences. They operated in different national contexts, which gave rise to contrasts in their appeals, social bases, and organization. The conservative electoral activism that began in the 1980s therefore poses a challenge to the field of comparative politics: to study conservative electoral movements in ways that grasp the complexities of specific country-cases while at the same time shedding light on their theoretical relevance to democratic politics in the region. For this, a minimal consensus is needed on key concepts and analytical frameworks, a consensus that has always eluded the study of conservatism as an electoral force.

This chapter attempts to provide a first step in that direction. In it I propose a conceptualization of conservative parties for comparative analysis and outline a broad framework for the study of conservative party politics. This framework provides the analytical structure of subsequent chapters of the book. My broader objectives, however, are to supply a basic road map for the comparative study of conservative parties and to provide common points of reference for the growing number of country studies that will, in all likelihood, shape future research on Latin American politics. In this way the perspectives generated by such studies may be more readily interpreted in light of the broader theoretical issue of Latin American conservatism's relationship to contemporary democratic politics in the region.[3]

Conservative Parties and Comparative Politics

The first step in any effort at comparative research lies in the realm of conceptualization. "We can have a concept of A (or of A-ness) when we are able to distinguish A from whatever is not-A," Giovanni Sartori writes.[4] So it should be with conservative parties. In order to come to grips with the role they play in democratic politics, we must at a minimum have a clear understanding of what conservative parties are, and more to the point, what makes them different from other parties. Without such a concept, that "basic unit of thinking," as Sartori puts it,[5] the study of conservatism as an electoral force will remain shrouded in confusion. One need only look at the study of conservative parties in Europe and North America, where most comparative scholarship on the subject has taken place, to perceive the pitfalls of such a situation.

"Conservatism," Clinton Rossiter has written, "is a word whose usefulness is matched only by its capacity to confuse, distort, and irritate."[6] Thus one of America's preeminent conservative intellectuals summarizes the denotative quagmire of one of the most contested concepts in the social sciences. "Conservatism" has been used as an analytical concept at several levels of meaning. It has denoted a variety of ideological traditions, clusters of ideas, temperaments, attitudes, and political movements. By far the most systematic efforts at definition and conceptualization have taken place at the ideological level. It is here that one finds the most extensive terminological and typological treatments of the concept, as well as the most interesting debates on the ideological nature of conservatism, its variants, and its evolving political meanings. The result of this systematic treatment of conservatism at the ideological level has been a loose consensus (very loose, at times) among scholars on the basic meaning of the concept as a political ideology.

Unfortunately, the same cannot be said for the study of conservatism at the level of collective action, or, more specifically, in the study of conservatism as an electoral force. In spite of the widespread use of the term at this level of meaning, the study of conservative parties is characterized by a virtual absence of consensus on what, exactly, the term *conservative* denotes in the realm of electoral politics. The bulk of this scholarship has relied on the ideological tradition to carry the burden of conceptualization, a practice that has made confusion one of its most prominent qualities. This confusion has emerged with full force when scholars have wanted to go beyond the idiographic country study (where the tasks of selection and definition can be accomplished via arbitrary and locally specific criteria) and study conservative parties as a political phenomenon transcending national boundaries. The difficulties they have encountered are captured nicely in the frustration expressed by R. A. H. Robinson, the author of a country case study in a collaborative volume on conservative parties:

> The present writer feels it incumbent upon him to make clear from the first his distaste for the use of the concept. . . . After focusing on the Spanish case through a "conservative" lens, this writer remains convinced that the terms "conservative" and "conservatism" should be sparingly used. . . . Indeed, attempts to use it to describe it a trans-

national political phenomenon would seem to make relatively simple things unnecessarily complicated.[7]

Robinson is not alone in his dismay. An indication of the woeful conceptual state of the study of conservative party politics can be gleaned from the following statements, taken from the opening pages of scholarly articles in three of the most recent edited volumes on conservative parties in Europe:

> General definitions of conservatism are difficult and, ultimately, fruitless, since conservatism is a national phenomenon.[8]

> Any discussion of conservatism immediately entails problems of definition.[9]

> Any analysis of contemporary German conservatism is confronted with a serious methodological difficulty: it has to define its subject theoretically.[10]

> The problem of defining conservatism in the United States since 1945 is a complex one.[11]

> ... the bedeviling imprecision of the conservatism concept as an analytical tool.[12]

> Various uses of the term are widely employed and accepted by men in the street as well as by Conservatives and scholars, ... but this has not lessened the frequent ambiguity and confusion in the use of the term.[13]

> What is conservatism?[14]

Such confusion might be a good argument for purging the term *conservatism* from the lexicon of comparative politics. This is the suggestion put forth by Robinson, who proposes substituting the "admittedly imprecise" terms *Right* and *Center-Right*.[15] Attempting to do that formally, however, would not stop its continued use. Furthermore, as Clinton Rossiter suggests, there is little sense in jettisoning a contested concept that can be "an extremely useful tool when properly handled."[16] As shown further on in this chapter, there are compelling reasons to use *conservative* to denote a specific type of political party. When effectively formulated, the concept can possess greater denotative and analytical power than the "admittedly imprecise" terms *Right* and *Center-Right*. First, however, it is useful to review the main points of consensus in the literature on conservatism as an ideology that have found their way into the conceptualizations that today shape the comparative study of conservative parties.

The "Conservatism as Ideology" Literature

Most scholars on conservatism agree with the suggestion by Russell Kirk that "conservatism offers no universal pattern of politics for adoption everywhere."[17] In fact, the absence of doctrine or prescription appears to be the one characteristic of conservatism as an ideology on which all scholars on the subject converge. This is a major element of consensus in the literature. Furthermore, the conservative aversion to stable structures of abstract political thought has been used by scholars to explain the wide varieties of ideologies that have manifested themselves among theoretical and political exponents of conservatism over time. Conservative ideology, the argument goes, is in permanent evolution; its concrete manifestations are a product of individual circumstance. They vary from context to context depending on the nature of the political struggle and the threat to the existing sociopolitical order.

Yet in spite of this lack of doctrinal specificity, most scholars of conservatism agree that its many ideological variations over recent centuries of human conflict are loosely held together by one unifying thread. This is summed up by Samuel Huntington as "the articulate, systematic, theoretical resistance to change."[18] Furthermore, scholars of conservative ideology converge in identifying an intellectual fountainhead for this varied universe of ideological traditions: the thought of the eighteenth-century politician and political philosopher Edmund Burke. "All the analysts of conservatism," writes Huntington, "unite in identifying Edmund Burke as the conservative archetype and in assuming that the basic elements of his thought are the basic elements of conservatism."[19] This view is echoed in various texts. Robert Nisbet writes that "rarely in the history of thought has a body of ideas been as closely dependent upon a single man and a single event as modern conservatism is on Edmund Burke and his fiery reaction to the French Revolution."[20] In the same vein, Russell Kirk asserts that "almost by definition . . . the principal conservatives in the Western world have been conscious or unconscious disciples of Burke."[21] The substance of conservative political thought has thus been loosely specified by this body of literature. Burke's preference for the guidance of concrete experience over abstract political thought, his emphasis on the value of religion, community, and natural hierarchies in the maintenance of the social order, and his advocacy of evolutionary change over purposive reform are the building blocks of conservative political thought.[22] "Normative underpinnings, but no doctrine" sums up one of the major points of scholarly consensus on the substance of conservatism as an ideology.

Another important element of consensus in this literature is its rejection of a link between social class and conservative ideology. While most scholars in this tradition agree that social groups with a high stake in the existing socioeconomic order will tend to embrace the conservative ideology as part of their defense of that order, there is great resistance to formally conceiving of conservatism in terms of its relationship to specific social forces. For Russell Kirk, conservative principles are a matter of "will and intelligence," and thus can be found among "all classes and occupations."[23] In this view, the multiclass appeal of conservative principles over the centuries is proposed as a counterargument to conservatism's asserted formal connection to specific social classes. Scholars who conceive of conservative ideology as a product of defense of the status quo also reject a class connection. Huntington, for example, suggests that conservative ideologies arise from conflicts whereby groups seek to defend established institutions from specific threats. He argues that each historical situation will determine which social actors become protagonists in that struggle, and that the conservative ideology they articulate will be determined by the specificity of the struggle in question. Conservatism as an ideology, therefore, "does not reflect the continuing interests and needs of a particular social group."[24] Rather, it is a relational phenomenon, determined by the interaction of social and political forces, whose substance changes in response to the evolution of conflict in different historical periods.

These points of consensus in the literature on conservatism as an ideology—the nature of conservatism as an essentially ideological phenomenon, its lack of transferable doctrinal structure, and its theoretical separation from specific social forces—have dominated the comparative literature on conservative parties. Small wonder that confusion reigns. As a concept, conservatism in the ideological sense is inherently undenotative. By definition it lacks specificity. This has suited the scholarship on conservatism as an ideology, because its object of study is a moving target. Without flexible definitional approaches, there would be no way to link the variety of ideological traditions associated with it as a single transnational and historical phenomenon.

What works for the historical study of ideas, however, does not necessarily work for the comparative study of political parties. As a result, the conservative party literature for the developed world has struggled to establish any basis of comparison between parties labeled "conservative" and to develop common points of reference for studying what most scholars and observers know intuitively to be an important and definable political force. The problem has therefore generally been settled by leaving the definitional question unresolved. Where the task has been to study a single conservative party, the selection of the party has been based on arbitrary criteria. Where the task has been to study parties comparatively, attempts have been made to establish loose ideological criteria for the selection of country cases.[25] Consequently, the field has been characterized by single-country studies, where the difficult task of establishing a theoretical basis for comparison can be dispensed with. The result of this has been to make the conservative party literature rich in empirical studies but poor in theory.

In the following pages I provide an alternative conceptualization of conservative parties for their study as a comparative phenomenon. The thrust of this, and what sets it apart from the conceptualizations that have dominated the literature, is a shift in the search for defining characteristics — from the level of ideology to the level of social structure. Specifically, conservative parties are defined, not in terms of their relationship to ideology, but in terms of their relationship to society. This relationship provides a minimal definition for the concept — a starting point for analysis, not a comprehensive description of what conservative parties are. Nevertheless, it is a step that permits us to "seize the object" in the real world, and, most important, sets the stage for developing a broader framework for analyzing conservative parties and their relationship to political conflict.

Defining Conservative Parties

Among a political party's many tasks is the act of social coalition building. It is this activity that provides the basis for defining conservative parties in this book. What sets conservative parties apart from other parties is the composition of the social coalitions that support them. Stated as a minimal definition, *conservative parties are parties that draw their core constituencies from the upper strata of society.*[26]

The concept of core constituencies is simple; it is also central to the analytical approach developed in this book. A party's core constituencies are those sectors of society that are most important to its political agenda and resources. Their importance lies not necessarily in the number of votes they represent, but in their *influence* on the party's agenda and capacities for political action. A party's core constituencies shape its identity; they are necessary to its existence. However, given the competitive imperatives of mass politics, they are usually not enough. A party's political leadership must usually forge alliances between its core constituencies and other social sectors if it is to succeed at the polls. This is especially so when, as is the case with conservative parties, their core constituencies constitute a small share of the population. The study of conservative party politics is, therefore, the study of the construction of polyclassist coalitions.

Ideology and Conservative Parties

The approach outlined in this chapter does not include ideology among the defining characteristics of conservative parties. The reasons for this have to do with the needs of comparative analysis. The ideologies of movements vary in different historical periods and social settings. Defining conservative movements ideologically makes comparison difficult when ideologies vary across time and contexts. Equally important, it hinders the study of ideological diversity and struggle *within* conservative movements. The study of conservative electoral movements thus requires a more enduring basis of comparison than that found in the fluid universe of ideas.

This is not to say that ideologies do not matter. Quite the contrary. However, a conceptualization that is clear and useful to comparative research must establish a hierarchy among those characteristics that are defining and those that are descriptive. In the minimal definition presented above, I have focused on the former. Going beyond this minimal definition, we can resolve the relationship between ideology and conservative movements by distinguishing between "defining properties" and "variable properties."[27] The former define the concept; they provide the basis for excluding specific cases from the pool of cases being compared. Variable properties are characteristics associated with the concept, but their absence from a specific case does not provide grounds for removing it from the pool of cases being compared. In the definition proposed here, ideologies are placed among variable characteristics. We can thus define conservative parties as parties that draw their core constituencies from the upper strata of society, and can enumerate the ideologies with which they have been associated (e.g., economic liberalism, Catholic social thought, or developmentalism). Yet the presence or absence of such ideologies is a matter to be settled by research. It is not a necessary characteristic of our definition.

I would also like to introduce a caution against teleological conceptions of conservative political action, particularly those that see the purpose of such action as defense of the status quo. Such conceptions can lead to misleadingly static and monolithic views of conservative political action. There is nothing inherently static or monolithic about conservative party

politics. As with all political organizations, conservative parties are crea-
tures of social change and internal struggle. They are affected by the
evolution and internal contradictions of their constituencies and shaped
by interaction with their political environments. As political contexts and
socioeconomic structures change, the political agendas that mobilize conservatism's core constituencies change, their resources change, and so do
the composition and objectives of conservative electoral coalitions. My
plea for agnosticism on ideology is thus joined by a caution against a
priori assumptions about the objectives of conservative electoral movements. Resolving such questions lies in the realm of investigation, not in
the realms of definition and conceptualization.

Studying Conservative Parties: The Social Base

Core Constituencies

The influence of ideological conceptions of conservative parties is one
reason why scholars have resisted defining them in terms of their relationship to the upper strata of society. There is, however, another reason for
this resistance. It lies in the multiclass nature of electoral coalition building, which in the "catch-all" age of party politics has diluted the class
homogeneity of political parties.[28] This has made it more difficult than in
the past to disentangle the protagonism of a single social force from the
web of alliances and political projects that make up a political party.
Perhaps more than other types of parties, conservative parties have successfully adapted to the catch-all nature of modern electoral coalition
building.[29] This has made scholars wary of studying them in their role as
vehicles for upper-class collective action.[30]

The polyclass nature of conservative parties should not be a reason to
avoid studying their relationship to class conflict. Quite the contrary. As
the imperatives of coalition building obscure power relationships that lie
beneath the surface of political life, it becomes even more important to
uncover those relationships. We therefore need to develop a framework
that helps us accomplish a seemingly contradictory objective: to empha-
size the relationship of a party to a specific class while simultaneously
affirming its multiclass nature. The main obstacles to this endeavor lie, not
in our object of research, but in the conceptual tools we use to study it.

The relationship between class and electoral movements can be clar-
ified if we introduce the notion of core constituencies to the study of party
politics. As already mentioned, all parties aspiring to power must be poly-

classist. Their relationship to certain social constituencies will, however, be more significant than their relationship to others. A party's core constituencies will be more important to the shaping of a party's political agenda, particularly for high-stake issues, than noncore constituencies. They will also play a more important role in the provision of financial and ideological resources. Amid the many social and political relationships that must be nurtured by the leadership of a party, its relationship to its core constituency is the most important to its capacities for becoming a viable power contender.

The notion of core constituencies recognizes the fact of hierarchy among members of a coalition. All coalitions are characterized by some type of hierarchy, and the social coalitions that support political parties are no exception. While quite evident to most people, this fact has remained woefully underutilized in the formal study of political parties. Viewing them through such a lens, however, can give us a clearer perception of the social dynamics of electoral coalition building, as well as the impact of those dynamics on the evolution of party politics.

A conservative party (or any other party) can afford to lose segments of its mass base outside its core constituencies without imperiling its survival. In fact, regular fluctuations in the social composition of conservative coalitions are to be expected over time and contexts. Their policy agendas will reflect these fluctuations. Over the past century, the U.S. Republican Party has shifted its positions on key social issues repeatedly as its broad coalition has evolved, most noticeably with the addition of the largely lower-middle-class Christian Fundamentalist movement to that coalition in the late 1970s. However, its essence as a multiclass alliance led by the upper social strata has not been affected. Certain dimensions of the alliance were modified, with attendant consequences for vote-getting, policy orientations, and internal conflict, but the core constituency has remained unchanged.

Structural change within a party occurs when its relationship to its core constituency changes.[31] British Conservatism's absorption of the Liberal Party's commerce and manufacturing constituencies at the turn of the century crystallized the alliance between landed nobility and bourgeoisie behind the Conservative Party. This development transformed both parties and gave impetus to the Conservative Party's evolution as the most important electoral expression of Britain's dominant social strata in the twentieth century.

Argentine Radicalism in the early twentieth century provides another instance of structural change within a party. In this case, a struggle between social constituencies for primacy within the party precipitated the party's transition from conservative to nonconservative party. Although today the Radical Party is the most important electoral expression of the Argentine middle classes, the historian David Rock considers mistaken "the traditional notion that the party was from the start an organ of middle class interests." Instead, Rock concludes, in the late nineteenth and early twentieth centuries, the party resembled a "democratic conservative" party, "a mass movement managed by upper-status groups, rather than a grass-roots movement operating in terms of pressures from below . . . a coalition of landowners and non-industrial middle-class groups."[32]

The stability of this coalition was undermined by the explosive growth of urban patronage networks and middle-class participation in the party structure after its presidential electoral victory in 1916. To Rock, these developments unleashed "a struggle for control of the party between middle-class groups and the elite wing, which had supported Radicalism since the 1890's." Radicalism's first experience in power was characterized by "its difficulties in steering a balance between the party's middle class and elite-based groups."[33]

In other words, the internal conflict wracking the party during its formative stage was over whether the upper class or the urban middle class would make up the core constituency of Argentine Radicalism. Ultimately, the struggle was decided in favor of the urban middle class, and shortly thereafter the Radical government of Hipólito Yrigoyen was overthrown by a conservative coup. Since that period, and in spite of its ever-shifting multiclass alliances as a catch-all anti-Peronist electoral force, the Radical Party's strategic relationship to its middle-class constituency has remained its most important structural feature.

Introducing the notion of core constituencies to the study of conservative electoral movements allows us to highlight the protagonism of the upper social strata without reducing such movements to mere instruments of class or sectoral representation. We can thus conceive of conservative parties as vehicles for linking the upper social strata to other social sectors in a common political project. A conservative party's leaders seek to unite their upper-class core constituency with other social sectors in search of an electoral majority. Conservative party politics can thus be seen as a multi-layered process, in which interaction between the party's political leadership and its core constituencies, and between the core constituencies and other social forces in the coalition, open and close possibilities for political action.

Identifying and Measuring Core Constituencies

The notion of social stratification advanced here is Weberian.[34] It combines Marxist notions of "class" based on market-generated control over economic resources, and more general notions of social "status," based on nonmarket and traditional criteria of social standing. While recognizing that income and control over economic resources are the most important shapers of social stratification, this approach also leaves open the possibility that factors not rooted in market relations shape the "life chances" of individuals, their position in the social hierarchy, and thus their stake in the outcomes of social conflict. Measurements used in later chapters of this book in the Argentine case reflect both class and status dimensions of social stratification.

Thus, in most Latin American electorates the potential core constituencies of a conservative party would include the owners and managers of major business firms, large landowners, and finance capitalists. They would also, however, include individuals and groups that by virtue social status or income belong to the upper echelons of the system of social stratification. These might include descendants of aristocratic or socially prominent families, rentier groups, and high-income members of the liberal professions.

It should be stressed that this approach looks exclusively at the party's relationship to social power. The defining groups or individuals are those whose authority is derived from the socioeconomic order. They are not those whose authority or power is derived primarily from control over coercive, political, or institutional resources. Thus, the support of the armed forces or the Catholic Church for a conservative party would not be considered part of a core-constituency relationship. While such individuals or groups may be among the party's supporters and allies, their support is theoretically contingent, not defining.[35]

To identify a party's core constituencies, we need first to recognize the different ways in which it relates to its constituencies. The most obvious way is as an aggregator of individual voters. The "coalitions" in a party's electoral base can thus be imputed to the party by aggregating individual supporters in the electorate with common social characteristics into specific social categories. A party's constituencies, however, also relate to the party as organized collectivities — namely, as interest groups that bring support and resources to the party. The coalitions behind a party can thus also be inferred from the party's relationship to specific interest groups. Where possible, an analysis of the core-constituency dynamics of conser-

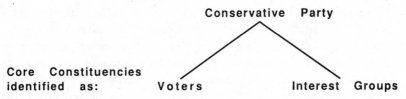

Fig. 1.1. Conservative parties and core constituencies.

vative party politics should take both the aggregate electoral and the interest group dimensions into account.

The separation of the electoral and interest-group realms also permits a
richer analysis of intra-core-constituency dynamics. Electoral data may
show that a given conservative party mobilizes the lion's share of upper-
class votes, thus confirming a core-constituency hypothesis. However, an
analysis of party–interest group ties may show that it fails at generating
business support. These findings would indicate problems in the party's
efforts at consolidating core-constituency support, shedding light on vital
factors affecting the party's development.[36]

In what other ways could a party's core constituencies be measured?
Here I offer four levels at which this composition can be gauged. Ideally,
these forms of measurement should be used together, but selection often
depends on the availability of data, as well as on the deductive processes
and analytical questions involved.

The social composition of electoral coalitions. Analysis of electoral
data and survey research can provide a profile of the social composition of
a party's electoral coalition. These techniques would measure the inten-
sities of support that different social groups give to the party, which can
provide the basis for inferences about them as core or noncore constituencies. These stratifications can provide broad outlines of the social bases of
a party's electoral support. If a party consistently scores highest among
"upper-strata" voters relative to other social strata, a basis can be established for asserting a core-constituency relationship between upper-strata
voters and the party.

The object here is to focus, not on the number of votes that different social groups provide, but on the differing intensity of support received by the
party from these groups. Even if a conservative party mobilizes the overwhelming majority of upper-income voters, most of its votes will nonetheless come from other social strata. Intensity of support indicates the party's
core constituencies. The number of votes indicates the party's mass base.

Resources. The sources of a party's financial support are one of the most telling indicators of a core-constituency relationship. The distribution of financial contributions received by a party from interest groups or individuals often provides an indication of the party's relationship to social power and conflict. Measuring core-constituency relationships with this type of information generally requires reliable financial reporting systems or campaign finance disclosure laws.

Programmatic convergences and links between the party and interest groups. The revealed preferences, actions, alliances, and policy statements of interest groups also provide one of the most forthright ways of assessing core-constituency relationships. Open alliances or endorsements of parties by business groups or other interest groups representing privileged strata, as well as regular convergences between the revealed preferences of such groups and those of the leadership of a political party, would provide strong indications of such relationships.

Identification of the social interests most consistently advanced by the party. This is one of the more difficult forms of measurement. It is achieved deductively, based on an evaluation of how the party's actions and statements fit in with interests imputed to different social groups. However, although quantitatively difficult to measure, it is also one of the more revealing indicators, especially where the party has a long history of actions and expressed goals that can be examined against the interests of different social groups.

Noncore Constituencies

A conservative party's fate is not dictated solely by its relationship to its core constituencies in the upper social strata. As important as they are to the party, these strata normally constitute a relatively small share of the electorate. A conservative party's mass electoral base thus lies outside its core constituencies. The study of conservative party politics must therefore focus on the process by which mass support is generated, and its impact on the party's evolution.

Most of the time, conservative parties mobilize support within core and noncore constituencies simultaneously. Nevertheless, the consolidation of core- and non-core-constituency support can be viewed as analytically distinct processes. The crystallization of support among core constituencies shapes the party's programmatic identity and provides it with vital resources for political action. It is the party's link to structural power. The crystallization of support among noncore constituencies provides the party with its mass base.

The process by which a conservative party builds mass support among noncore constituencies will feed back into the party and reshape its structure and ideological orientations. The search for mass support will spark changes and struggles within the political leadership. It will also force the party's core constituencies to adapt to new political agendas. Conservative mass coalition building is a story of harmonizing tensions between upper-class core constituencies and mass base, of reconciling the often conflicting imperatives of maintaining internal cohesion and pursuing external growth. These tensions apply as much to newly forming conservative movements as they do to parties with centuries of political experience. A conservative party's evolution is intimately tied to the way in which its political leadership mediates these tensions in its quest to build an electoral majority.

Studying Conservative Parties: The Political Dimension

The Question of Political Leadership

In the previous section, the social dynamics of party politics were addressed as a first step in developing a framework for the study of conservative parties. The picture is not, however, complete. A working assumption of this book is that social structures shape the boundaries and possibilities of political action. They are the skeletal structure of political conflict. As such, they are vital ingredients of any effort at causal explanation. However, they must interact with other factors before their ultimate impact on the political process is felt.

"No differentiation of life opportunities," wrote Max Weber, "no matter how deep, produces by itself 'class action.' "[37] The variety of "collective wills" manifested in the competitive struggles of politics cannot be understood without proper regard for the autonomy of political leadership. Social diversity creates possibilities for the political realm, but without political leadership even the deepest and most enduring cleavages can remain irrelevant to the political process. Joseph Schumpeter wrote that "collectives act almost exclusively by accepting leadership. This is the dominant mechanism of practically any collective action which is more than a reflex."[38] Schumpeter was an important modern critic of the notions of a *volonté générale* that permeated classical political thought and have become implicit in society-centered analyses of political conflict. He argued that group volitions were things to be shaped and created by leadership from the raw material of social differentiation, rather than autonomous forces driving the political process. The collective will was thus replaced in his analysis by a "manufactured will"; it was the primary task of the political leader, in his quest for mass support and political power, to call latent group volitions to life and turn them into forces relevant to the political struggle. The "will of the people," and, for our purposes, the political salience of class divisions, is thus "the product and not the motive power of the political process."[39]

Among the more interesting applications of this line of thinking to the contemporary literature on class and electoral behavior is the work of Adam Pzreworski and John Sprague. Their conclusions are similar to Schumpeter's: the organization of political conflict in terms of class and the collective identities that make such organization possible are themselves outgrowths of the actions and struggles of political leadership. Furthermore, they are the objects of permanently unresolved contestation, rising and falling in importance as the unending struggle to shape the terms of political conflict unfolds.

> "The counting of votes," wrote Antonio Gramsci, "is the final ceremony of a long process." This is a process of forming images of society, of forging collective identities, of mobilizing commitments to particular visions of the future. Class, ethnicity, religion, race, or nation do not happen spontaneously, of themselves, as a reflection of objective conditions in the psyche of individuals. Collective identity, group solidarity, and political commitments are continually forged — shaped, destroyed, and molded anew — as a result of conflicts in the course of which political parties, schools, unions, churches, newspapers, armies, and corporations strive to impose upon the masses a particular vision of society.[40]

In this light we can begin to address the role played by political parties in shaping the collective visions that make electoral coalition building possible. In the absence of a spontaneous "collective will," we can recognize that in the electoral process, social groups or classes do not themselves forge alliances. This is a role assumed by political parties and their leaderships — the "social communicators" and "political architects" who articulate messages and build institutions that generate cross-class loyalties to a specific party or electoral movement. By observing the role of parties in generating such loyalties, we can begin to understand how class, leadership, and ideology intersect in the realms of party politics. In addition, by returning to some of the concepts introduced earlier in this chapter, we can begin to uncover how the specific relationship of parties to different segments of society shapes the nature of their appeals and create different "logics" of electoral mobilization for conservative parties and parties of the Left.

Class, Parties, and the Logic of Conservative Electoral Action

Class and class politics are central to the appeal of parties of the Left. Appeals to broad class solidarity among workers, peasants, and salaried employees based on shared social subordination are the stuff of leftist political mobilization. Beyond ideology, there are practical reasons for this: the position of the Left's core constituencies in the social structure and the size of those constituencies in relation to the rest of the electorate. Given the electoral weight of the Left's core constituencies, class appeals represent the shortest route to winning electoral coalitions. Even in a multiclass alliance, its working-class core constituency will make up a significant share of the Left's total electoral support. For the Left, there tends to be a correspondence between the *influence* of its core constituencies in the party's political project and their *numbers* in the party's total electoral support.

Such is not the case with conservatism. Only a fraction of a successful conservative party's votes will come from the upper social strata. A conservative coalition draws its support from virtually all social sectors: it builds majorities by slicing up the social spectrum. In some cases, the Thatcher and Reagan coalitions being prime examples, it may even draw half its support from the working class. A conservative party is, in fact, the most polyclassist of parties.

And such a party is built precisely through denial of the importance of class as a salient source of cleavage in social and political life. This is central to the logic of conservative electoral action and crucial to its polyclassist potential. In contrast to parties of the Left, a conservative party must build its mass base *outside* its core constituencies. Its appeals must thus transcend class differences and forge bonds of social solidarity on the basis of other sources of collective identification. Conservative electoral majorities are built in part by weakening class-based solidarity and replacing it with other sources of collective identity.

This strategy is shaped by the minority status of conservatism's upper-class core constituencies in political systems governed by majority rule. The distance between the number of votes conservatism's core constituencies provide and those needed for an electoral majority is far greater than for movements rooted in larger social strata. This numerical difference begets a qualitative difference in the strategy of conservative mobilization: *the Left seeks to slice society horizontally; conservative movements seek to slice it vertically.*

Religion, region, ethnicity, and "the nation" are some of the collective identities often counterposed by conservative movements to the class-based appeals of the Left. The Christian Democratic turn of much of Western European conservatism after World War II provides one example. So do the variety of regional conservative parties found in much of the world, such as the Bavarian Christian Social Union (CSU) in Germany and Argentina's many provincial conservative parties. British Conservatism's invocation of its role as guardian of "the nation" against the "socially divisive" appeals of Labour provides another historical example of the vertical, cross-class, nature of conservative electoral appeals.

The publicity and statements of political leaders provide the most vivid manifestations of this ongoing struggle for the hearts and minds of the masses. "Lula: A Class Option," beamed a Brazilian Workers' Party bumper sticker about the party's presidential candidate during the 1989 presidential campaign. Compare this with the announcement by Mario Vargas Llosa, Peru's conservative presidential contender in 1989: "The historic struggle in Peru has not been between classes, but between the people and the state." Similarly, George Bush, in a burst of presidential cosmopolitanism, stated that "class is for European democracies, not America."[41] He might have revised his statement had he consulted Margaret Thatcher, who on the first day of televised sessions in the House of Commons in 1989, announced the demise of class politics on her corner of European soil: "The old Labour order based on class is dead; the new order based on effort, opportunity, and merit is here to stay."

Przeworski and Sprague write that "the relative salience of class as a determinant of voting behavior is a cumulative consequence of strategies pursued by political parties of the Left."[42] The corollary to this proposition is that the weakness of class as a source of political cleavage is also a cumulative consequence of the effectiveness of conservative electoral mobilization. The Right, like the Left, is permanently shaping collective visions of politics and society in its quest for political dominance. Effective conservative electoral mobilization will undermine the relative importance of class as a determinant of voting behavior. By the same token, the weaker class-based sources of collective identity are in a society, the more fertile the ground for conservative electoral mobilization.

The Institutional Dimension

In addition to their role as social coalition builders, conservative parties are also, of course, organizations. As such, they possess internal structures, rules, and power alignments that shape their evolution and have a life independent of the social coalition that supports them. While both the behavioralist and the Marxist currents of the literature on electoral politics have tended to ignore such institutional dimensions, they have been a central focus of an important body of theoretical literature on political parties. In his classic study, Maurice Duverger turned the organizational structures and dynamics of political parties into the bricks and mortar of his "general theory" of parties.[43] Other theorists of party politics, such as Moisei Ostrogorski, Robert Michels, and Giovanni Sartori, have also made the organizational dimension of party politics the centerpiece of their conceptual approaches to the subject.[44]

Recently, the field of comparative politics has been influenced by "new institutional" approaches to the study of politics. In the literature on political parties, these approaches have been given a boost by Angelo Panebianco, who has argued forcefully against social-coalition-based explanations of party development. The evolution of political parties, he suggests, can best be understood by analyzing them as institutions, and subordinating social factors to the primacy of "organizational core" variables.[45]

In the opening pages of his book *Political Parties: Organization and Power*, Panebianco takes aim at a prejudice that he claims has been dominant in the literature on political parties. He labels this "the sociological prejudice" and describes it as "the belief that the activities of parties are the product of the 'demands' of social groups, and that, more generally, parties themselves are nothing other than manifestations of social divisions in the political arena."[46] Panebianco argues that this prejudice, by mechanically seeing the party's organization and politics as mirroring underlying social dynamics, obscures the importance that variables internal to its organizational core play in shaping a party's evolution. Society's struggles only find their way into the internal life of political parties after being "filtered through the barriers and structures of organizational mediation."[47]

There is not a great deal to disagree with in these propositions. That institutional factors exert a powerful effect on a party's evolution is undeniable. However, there are reasons for taking Panebianco's call for organizational primacy with a dose of caution. The first is methodological. An organizational approach renders it difficult to make any distinction *be-*

tween parties that is relevant to broader social or political struggle. This can hinder the theoretical study of interparty conflict. Competition between parties may well be influenced by internal institutional interests, but it is also embedded in a social context that creates different conditions for each party according to its relationship to that context. Panebianco argues that differences between parties at the organizational level cannot be traced to the social composition of their electoral bases. Thus, distinctions between parties must be made along institutional lines (e.g., institutionalization, factionalism, fund-raising structure, and so on) that are specific to the organizational realm. If our concern is the study of parties as a specific category of political organization, this will suffice. If, however, our concern is to distinguish between parties in ways that are relevant to the broader conflicts of society, an organization-centered approach provides little to work with. We must shift our sights to another level of analysis in order to determine what makes certain parties different from other parties, as well as their relevance to the underlying conflicts of society.[48]

Another reason for not making institutional factors the centerpiece of a framework for the study of conservative party politics is provided by the Latin American political process. While organizational factors may play a constant and important developmental role in the institutionalized party systems of Europe — from which Panebianco's empirical data are drawn — it is difficult to maintain that assumption for the less-institutionalized polities of Latin America. In fact, it can be asserted that the one fluid and inconclusive dimension of party politics in the region is its institutional dimension. In many ways, therefore, the linkage between social structure and electoral politics is more direct in Latin America than in Panebianco's cluster of European party cases. The lack of institutionalized procedures for fund-raising makes Latin American political parties far more vulnerable to the whims of individual donors than parties with established membership subscription systems or stable relations to organized interest groups. Control of mass media by a conservative party's core constituencies in a context lacking guaranteed equal access to airtime or public campaign financing has a far greater impact on the outcomes of party politics than in contexts where such arrangements are available. The fluctuating support of business for party politics has a greater immediate impact on the fortunes of conservative parties in Latin America than in areas where stable relationships exist or where autonomous fund-raising capabilities allow parties to weather such fluctuations. In short, social structure dynamics often have important short- and medium-term effects on the uninstitutionalized context of party competition in Latin America. Any effort to analyze this competition should take that reality closely into account.

In sum, the issue should not be whether one level of analysis should, by methodological fiat, exclude another in a framework for the study of conservative electoral movements. The approach followed in this book is thus an interactive one. It seeks to join the conceptual insights into the social dynamics of conservative party politics developed in the earlier parts of this chapter with the organizational insights provided by the works of Panebianco, Duverger, Sartori, and others. The main unit of analysis is the conservative party, and factors of leadership and organization figure prominently in the arguments advanced. However, developments in those areas are always examined in terms of the party's relationship to its social base, shedding light on the connections between social reality and political agency that are the moving parts of the structures of collective action.

Political Leadership and "Polity Arenas" in Latin America

The focus so far in this chapter has been on conservative political action in the electoral realm. Nevertheless, it is important to bear in mind that when speaking of electoral politics in Latin America, we are speaking of a very tentative political arena. Participation in the electoral process involves a choice by both leaders and their constituencies. It is made in relation to the existence of other alternatives, to the types of political resources available, and to the existence of opportunities to employ them. In most of Latin America, this changing configuration of opportunities, rather than any fixed set of institutional procedures, has shaped the political process.

It is therefore necessary to integrate the fluidity of electoral politics into a conceptual approach to conservative parties in Latin America. Specifically, we need to factor in how the continuous movement of political leaders and constituencies between alternative political arenas shape conservative party politics in the region.

One place to begin is the distinction made by Alfred Stepan between three separate political realms that coexist in any democratic or democratizing polity. These three "polity arenas" are civil society, the state, and political society.[49] Stepan defines civil society as that arena in which social forces and movements (such as labor movements, business groups, intellectuals, religious organizations, womens' groups, etc.) constitute themselves for the political advancement and expression of their interests and ideals.[50] In his definition of the state, Stepan includes both "the government" and the "continuous administrative, legal, bureaucratic, and coercive system" that manages and executes public power. The state and its component parts are viewed here as actors that, like other participants in the political struggle, are endowed with political interests and objectives of their own.[51] Finally, political society is defined as "that arena in which the polity specifically arranges itself for political contestation to gain control over public power and the State apparatus." The core institutions of political society include parties, legislatures, political leadership, and elections.[52] Of the three polity arenas, only political society is specifically organized for the capture and exercise of power through formal democratic institutions.

Where do the leaderships of different social forces reside? This is an important question for the study of democratization in Latin America. If our concern is the consolidation of democratic regimes, we would want the most important leadership to be concentrated in political society. Yet in Latin America, social groups constantly shift their support from one arena to another. So do political leaders, as they redeploy their political actions and resources between arenas in response to changing political environments. In sum, the balance between the three polity arenas is constantly changing as organized forces in the polity seek to shift the political struggle to arenas where their political resources are most effective.

Max Weber suggested that as political systems evolved, individuals possessing a "a vocation for politics" would become subject to the imperative of specialization. Technocratic and administrative public functions would increasingly be handled by administrative officials, while party organization and political competition would become increasingly the domain of political officials.[53] Mass democracy in particular would require growing specialization in the tasks of political organization and mobilization, and, as such, would require cadres of leaders dedicated to the full-time pursuit of these activities.

In contemporary Latin America, however, political leaders tend to straddle polity arenas rather than to specialize in them. This is true for most types of leaders, but it is especially true for conservative leaders. The conservative party leader of today is often yesterday's technocrat. The military dictator of yesterday becomes tomorrow's presidential candidate or congressional leader. The business leader of yesterday, finding his privileged access to state power blocked, becomes tomorrow's conservative party politician. The ubiquity of the conservative political leader reflects the fluid relationship between polity arenas in Latin America. More important, however, it reflects the position of his constituencies in the system of social stratification. Their privileged social status endows them with the flexibility to shift their resources and support from one arena to another in response to changing circumstances. When social forces are constantly able to shift their support in this way, the most successful political leaders will tend to be those who "travel well" between arenas and are skilled in varied currencies of political power. Argentina's Alvaro Alsogaray, Brazil's Paulo Maluf, Chile's Hernán Büchi, El Salvador's Roberto D'Abuisson and Alfredo Cristiani, and Peru's Javier Silva Ruete stand out as some of the more prominent examples of Latin America's ubiquitous conservative leaders.

The ease with which conservative leaders and their constituencies shift from one political arena to another is one of the most important obstacles to the consolidation of conservative party politics in Latin America. Electoral politics is not the only game in town for the leaders and core constituencies of Latin American conservatism. Where mobility between polity arenas characterizes conservative political action, the relationship between polity arenas will be fluid and the institutionalization of party politics will remain problematic.

Conservative Parties and Democratic Stability in Latin America: The Historical Evidence

Stable democracy in Latin America, as everywhere else, has historically been linked to the existence of strong national party systems. Strong national party systems have historically been linked to viable conservative parties. Logically, this should not be surprising. The importance of conservative parties to democratic stability lies in the pivotal social position of their constituencies, and in the fact that they will inevitably be important participants in the struggle for power. The organizational forms of their political participation will have major consequences for the relevance of political institutions. If the organizational forms of upper-class power are weakly linked to political parties, regimes — or the major decision-making arenas of regimes — will be structured accordingly. Conservative parties help to mobilize the political action of powerful social strata into democratic channels. They improve the ability of those strata to influence political outcomes through the democratic process, thus enhancing the probability that they will submit to the binding authority of democratic institutions.

The argument here is not that conservative parties have made democracy "better" or more representative — only more stable. In fact, for most of this century, party-based elite control over the political process in Latin America has served as a buttress against the substantive demands of underprivileged strata on national political life. Democracy survived as long as elites controlled it, and as long as popular challenges could be neutralized through elite-controlled democratic institutions. Yet while limiting its scope, elite representation in the electoral process has also provided democracy with greater institutional continuity and opportunities for development over time.

This proposition is supported by evidence from a growing number of comparative historical studies of social conflict and political development in Latin America. Reviewing the evidence collected in her comparative study of turn-of-the-century party competition in Argentina and Chile, Karen Remmer concluded that "the consolidation of liberal democratic institutions depends not upon their effectiveness in equalizing the distribution of political power, but upon their acceptability to the propertied and powerful."[54] Dietrich Rueschemeyer, Evelyn Stephens, and John Stephens summarize their finding about the link between conservative parties and democratic politics similarly in a study of the social determinants of democracy in Europe and Latin America:

> A strong hegemony of conservative (rather than reactionary) upper classes can actually strengthen formal democracy as it can serve to defend the interests of the upper classes within the system and to keep the substantive demands of the lower classes off the immediate political agenda. This is one of the primary reasons for the positive contribution of the existence of a strong party of the right for the survival of democracy, which proved important in a number of our Latin American cases, but also can be seen as one factor in the gradual and stable nature of suffrage extension in Britain.[55]

The positive contribution of conservative parties to the development of democracy in Latin America can be gleaned from the data presented in table 1.2. The table compares two groups of countries with different historical legacies of conservative party organization. In the first group, national oligarchic competitive party systems had been established when political competition was restricted to the socially privileged—that is, prior to the advent of mass politics. As a result, conservative party structures were in place to deal with the challenge of mass participation when the expansion of popular participation took place. In the second group of countries, such legacies of oligarchic competitive parties were largely absent, and national conservative party organization during the advent of mass politics tended to be weak or fragmented. Taking the initiation of mass politics as the historical point of departure, we can see that the durability of democratic regimes during the twentieth century was af-

Table 1.1

Democratic and Authoritarian Regimes in South and Central America from the Advent of Mass Politics to 1990

	Oligarchic	Democratic (full or restricted)	Authoritarian
Argentina	until 1912	1912–30	1930–46
		1946–51	1951–55
		1958–62	1955–58
		1963–66	1962–63
		1973–76	1966–73
		1983–90	1976–83
Bolivia	until 1930	1952–64	1930–52
		1982–90	1964–82
Brazil	until 1930	1945–64	1930–45
		1985–90	1964–85
Chile	until 1920	1920–24	1924–32
		1932–73	1973–89
		1990	
Colombia	until 1936	1936–49	1949–58
		1958–90	
Costa Rica	until 1940	1940–48	1948–50
		1950–90	
Ecuador	until 1925	1948–61	1925–48
		1978–90	1961–78
El Salvador	until 1931	1931–32	1932–84
		1984–90	
Guatemala	until 1931	1944–54	1931–44
		1986–90	1954–86
Honduras	until 1948	1948–63	1963–81
		1981–90	
Mexico	until 1911	1982–90	1920–82
Peru	until 1930	1939–48	1930–39
		1956–62	1948–56
		1963–68	1962–63
		1980–90	1968–80
Uruguay	until 1903	1903–19	1933–42
		1919–33	1973–84
		1942–73	
		1984–90	
Venezuela	until 1935	1945–48	1935–45
		1958–68	1948–58
		1968–90	

Table 1.2

Conservative Parties and Democratic Rule in South and Central America from the Advent of Mass Politics to 1990

	Competitive national conservative party(s) prior to mass politics?	Years of democracy (restricted or full)	Years of authoritarian rule	Ratio of years democratic/ years authoritarian
Chile	yes	45	24	1.9
Colombia	yes	45	9	5.0
Costa Rica	yes	48	2	24.0
Uruguay	yes	67	20	3.4
Average				8.6
Argentina	no	40	38	1.1
Bolivia	no	20	40	0.5
Brazil	no	24	36	0.7
Ecuador	no	25	40	0.6
El Salvador	no	6	53	0.1
Guatemala	no	14	45	0.3
Honduras	no	24	18	1.3
Mexico	no	8	62	0
Nicaragua	no	0	54	0
Peru	no	30	30	0.5
Venezuela[a]	no	35	20	1.8
Average				0.7

[a]The Social Christian Party COPEI played a crucial role as the founding conservative party in interparty agreements for the democratic regime inaugurated in 1958. Thereafter, upper-class representation was gained in the two major parties, Acción Democrática and COPEI.

fected by this "genetic legacy" of conservative party organization. Countries where national conservative parties were in place during the expansion of participation tended to experience significantly longer periods of democratic rule than those where conservative party organization was weak.

The data in Table 1.2 indicate the importance of historical legacies of conservative party organization to the continuity of democratic institutions. Countries that had viable, competitive national conservative parties in place at the start of democratic politics exhibited far greater democratic stability during the twentieth century than countries that did not. The average ratio of years under democratic rule to years under authoritarian rule for the four countries with strong legacies of conservative party organization was almost 9 to 1. For countries with weaker legacies of national conservative party organization at the start of mass democracy, the average ratio was 0.7 to 1.[56]

The existence of a strong tradition of conservative party politics has involved a trade-off for the development of democracy in the region. While limiting the rate of growth and scope of democracy, it has also given it greater institutional continuity. While helping to secure the interests and representation of the socially privileged, it has also helped stabilize democracy, and thus provide spaces for the gradual (and often quite autonomous) political organization of the underprivileged.

It is beyond the scope of these pages to provide an evaluation of the normative merits of this trade-off. The point is only to suggest that, regardless of the multiple arenas available for the organization of elite interests, one of the massive facts of democratic development in Latin America has been its positive association with stable upper-class participation in party politics. Conservative party development is therefore a key issue in the consolidation of contemporary democratic regimes and should have a visible place in the study of comparative political development in Latin America. The following chapters provide a step in that direction.

Conservative Party Development in Argentina: The Argument

This book attempts to explain the puzzles posed by Argentina's troubled patterns of conservative party development. It examines the Argentine case through the theoretical lenses provided in the preceding pages and provides answers through an analysis of dynamics at the social, institutional, and leadership levels. In addition, the analysis places the Argentine case in comparative perspective. Conservative party development in other parts of Latin America provides a comparative backdrop against which the Argentine case can be analyzed, both historically and in light of the wave of conservative electoral mobilization that occurred in the 1980s.

The following chapters start out by providing a historical argument. The causes of contemporary dilemmas of conservative party organization in Argentina are traced to the origins of conservative party formation. The argument is that core constituency dynamics during the period of oligarchic rule prior to the advent of mass politics were paramount in shaping early conservative party formation. Specifically, regional cleavages in the Argentine upper social strata became crystallized in a regionally fragmented pattern of party organization that impeded the development of national, cross-regional, competitive party networks. This event acted as a historical cause of the institutional fragmentation of conservative parties along provincial lines, a fragmentation that has characterized national conservative party organization during this century.[57]

Causes of a more constant nature are also examined to explain conservative party development in contemporary Argentina. The argument is that the primary determinants of party development operate at the core constituency and leadership levels. The key incentives for participation in electoral arenas by conservative leaders and their constituencies are determined by their relationship to the state. In the uninstitutionalized context of Argentine conservative party politics, when opportunities exist for direct access to state power or policy making, conservative politicians will tend to neglect or retreat from party-building efforts. Similarly, when opportunities exist for business elites and organizations to gain access to state policy making and patronage through corporatist channels or direct links to the state, they will not actively support party politics. Conservative party development will thus advance or retreat as a function of the relationship between conservative politicians and their core constituencies with the state.

Chapter Two

Region, Class, and Conservative Parties:
The Trials of Argentine Conservatism, 1880–1976

We have nothing to fear from the democratic social struggle if there are compensatory forces and means to restrain its excesses. Any extremist push will fail if the conservative classes, today discordant and apprehensive, organize a united defense.

CARLOS IBARGUREN, speech before the Argentine congress, 1912

Regionalism and Conservative Party Development in Latin America

Conservative party development has followed divergent paths in Latin America. In some countries conservative parties have long been a major presence in electoral politics, with historic traditions of voter loyalty, regular participation in political power, and relevance as avenues for the career advancement of politically ambitious individuals. In other countries they have been an ephemeral affair, rising and dissolving with each election, exerting little influence on policy making, and serving as marginal vehicles for the upward mobility of politicians in national politics.

These patterns have generally been consistent within each country for most of this century. Countries with well-established conservative parties today tend to have had such parties in place when the advent of mass politics transformed political competition. Furthermore, when civilian democratic rule was interrupted by authoritarian interludes, conservative party politics returned full strength after the fall of authoritarianism, either in the same institutional form, as in Colombia in 1958 or Uruguay in

1985, or as viable electoral coalitions with recast institutional labels, as in Chile in 1989.

Countries without stable conservative parties have similarly been marked by their condition since the advent of mass politics. The absence or weakness of national conservative party organization prior to mass politics generally meant the absence or weakness of conservative party organization throughout the twentieth century. Only in rare instances have new conservative electoral coalitions crystallized into stable political parties in countries without previous legacies of conservative party organization. The most notable of these cases was the rise of COPEI as a conservative electoral alternative to Acción Democrática in Venezuela in the 1940s and 1950s, and the subsequent institutionalization of elite representation in both COPEI and Acción Democrática through the 1960s, 1970s, and 1980s. Venezuela has, however, been an exception. The historical legacy of inchoate national party formation during the oligarchic period bequeathed an uphill struggle for subsequent generations of political leaders committed to strategies of conservative party building.

The importance of these variations transcends conservative parties per se. It speaks to the long-standing relationship between socially privileged actors and democratic politics, and to the relevance of democratic institutions in national political decision making. As the discussion in Chapter 1 attempted to show, countries with legacies of conservative party organization enjoyed markedly longer periods of democratic rule than countries without such legacies. In the former cases the ability of elites to control political outcomes through electoral politics institutionalized a central role for political parties in national political life. In this sense, the formation of national party systems is an issue inseparable from the formation of conservative parties.[1]

Chile, Colombia, and Uruguay have long historical legacies of conservative party organization. Elite-controlled parties competed with one another prior to the expansion of the suffrage and were firmly in control of national political life during the transition to mass politics. In Chile, this process reaffirmed the centrality of democratic institutions as political participation expanded, and opened the way for the later integration of working-class parties into a democratic regime in which elite interests were strongly represented. In Colombia and Uruguay, it paved the way for the development of party systems dominated by the old institutional expressions of upper-class interests during the oligarchic phase of politics.

In all of these countries the continuity of civilian rule and democracy was predicated on a party system that protected elite interests and allowed for the controlled mobilization of the masses. The prior construction of national conservative parties was the vital ingredient of this formula. Their existence paved the way for democratic regimes that gave elites control, not only over the substantive outcome of social conflict, but also over the institutional shape of political competition.

In other countries these goals had to be achieved through other institutional means. In Brazil, Peru, Argentina, and Venezuela, existing forms of party organization failed to crystallize into national party organizations capable of protecting elite interests, checking or incorporating newly enfranchised sectors, or structuring political competition during the era of mass politics. Eventually, party organizations declined in importance as elite reliance on the coercive and bureaucratic institutions of the state took center stage in national politics. Conservative electoral weakness at the national level made party politics a precarious arena for the protection of elite interests, and political regimes were structured accordingly.

These contrasting patterns of conservative party development present a puzzle. What factors account for the simultaneous emergence of strong national conservative party organizations in some countries and weak national conservative party organizations in others? For answers to this question, we now turn to core-constituency dynamics during the crucial phase of early party formation. Specifically, we shall look at the upper-class cleavages that shaped early partisan alignments and became crystallized institutionally in the region's first political parties during the period of oligarchic rule. Divisions of interest among socioeconomic elites gave rise to certain institutional arrangements for intra-oligarchic bargaining and contestation. What was crucial was whether such divisions promoted the formation of national political parties, or whether the state would emerge as the most important arena for elite bargaining and contestation.[2] Once these institutional arrangements were in place, they had continuing effects on the subsequent development of political institutions. This interaction between social cleavage and institutional development operated as a historical cause of conservative party formation and would shape patterns of upper-strata involvement in politics, as well as the evolution of political regimes, for years to come.[3]

Regionalism and the Origins of Conservative Party Development

The paramount issue to be resolved during the period of oligarchic rule was the regional issue. If anything characterized the oligarchic period, it was the transition from the politics of regionalism to the politics of centralized authority. *Caudillo* structures of power, under which personalistic local rulers operated beyond the reach of central government, were broken down and subordinated to the national authorities. Sectionalist challenges were subdued as national boundaries were consolidated, and political control by central governments was exercised throughout the territory.[4]

It was a period of consolidation for national political institutions. Politics, once localist, now had a national stake, and even those forms of political organization rooted in local power forged links to the national arena. Political authority expanded, either from the center outward, as elites in control of the state absorbed regional rivals, or from the periphery inward, as networks of regional oligarchies were knit into alliances that covered the nation. Just as power now had a national reach, so would institutions designed to capture state power. Political parties had to become national if they were to be relevant players in the political process. If not, state institutions would emerge as the primary mediators of conflict between national oligarchic factions.

In a context of postcolonial regional fragmentation, the chief catalyst for national party formation was the struggle between the city and the country. Rural-urban conflicts tended to be the driving force of party alignments in countries that saw the emergence of national conservative parties prior to the advent of mass politics. Parties representing agricultural elites, generally adopting the ideological label "conservative," tended to come into partisan conflict with "liberal" parties representing urban commercial and financial elites.[5] Ideological conflicts, such as those revolving around church-state issues, were drawn along these rural-urban alignments. Political leaders representing rural oligarchies from one region of the country reached out to rural oligarchies from other regions in common cause against urban liberals. The urban liberals likewise reached out to their brethren in other urban areas. The first national-level oligarchic party networks were thus formed.

The conflict between the city and the country created the first possibilities for cross-regional oligarchic alliances. As national party networks spread, mutual penetration occurred, with each side exploiting divisions within the other camp and gaining support in the other's stronghold. Liberals, therefore, succeeded in gaining support in sectors of the rural elite, often through appeals on the church-state issue or more specific conflicts. Conservatives gained footholds in liberal urban strongholds, as the search for electoral supremacy similarly expanded their reach. Nevertheless, the driving force of the city-country cleavage continued to dominate the spatial dimensions of support for each party.[6]

In Colombia and Uruguay, the evolution of conflict during most of the nineteenth century led to the expansion of clientelistic partisan networks linking the urban-based liberals (or Colorados, as they were called in

Uruguay) against the rural-based conservatives (Blancos in Uruguay). Through decades of civil war, fratricidal violence, and electoral competition, strong partisan loyalties were established in the population. These loyalties ran deep, not only among the upper strata that benefited most from the policies advocated by the parties, but also among the lower strata that manned the front lines of armed partisan conflict and depended upon the patronage benefits offered by the parties.[7]

In Chile, upper-class involvement in party politics also had its origins in the nineteenth century. Parties facilitated the domination of national politics by agricultural interests in the country's fertile central valley. In the mid-nineteenth century, these elites battled urban-based liberals over such issues as state intervention in the economy and church-state relations. Conservatives possessed elaborate networks of clientelistic control in the countryside, which gave them a ready-made electoral base for gaining control of the national parliament. The defense of parliamentary supremacy thus became the centerpiece of conservative efforts to check the expansion of state prerogatives by urban liberals.

As parties expanded in the second half of the nineteenth century, new opportunities arose for coalition building between elite factions. Party politics were particularly important in permitting agricultural elites and mining elites in northern Chile to form a common front in the parliament against the centralizing and state-expanding urban liberals. The tool used by this alliance to counter the liberals was suffrage expansion. In 1874, conservatives joined the Radical Party, which represented emerging northern mining interests, in a parliamentary coalition that passed an electoral reform law doubling the number of eligible voters.[8] This expansion of suffrage allowed the Conservatives to make full use of the large "captive" electorate provided by patron-client networks in the countryside. This, and other measures in the reform bill, weakened the Liberals electorally and advanced the Conservative-Radical cause of limiting the power of the state.[9]

The culminating point of oligarchic party rule in Chile came during the "Parliamentary Republic" of 1891–1920. In 1891, a parliamentary insurrection against the liberal president led to a brief civil war. The defeat of the Liberals led to the demise of the presidential regime and the inauguration of a regime in which the supremacy of congress over the executive was firmly established. The power of the conservative oligarchies was thus protected in the parliament against liberal encroachments. As Federico Gil writes, during this period of parliamentary rule, "political parties were to multiply rapidly, and the oligarchs in Congress were to wield unrestricted power."[10]

Conflict in Colombia, Uruguay, and Chile during much of the nineteenth century was thus often shaped, caused, and ultimately mediated by elite-dominated party networks that covered the national territory. Party politics, and in the Chilean case, party politics *and* parliamentary institutions, were integral components of the structure of national oligarchic domination in the nineteenth century. When the expansion of male suffrage occurred in the twentieth century, conservative parties dealt with the challenges from below. The integration of newly mobilized groups took place through the party system. Elite control of the major political parties mitigated the threat the newly mobilized groups might otherwise have posed.[11]

In the two-party systems of Colombia and Uruguay, the incorporation of lower-class groups generated considerable conflict within the party system. Maverick liberal factions took the lead mobilizing lower strata into their parties as part of their electoral struggle against the conservatives. The maverick liberals, however, had to contend with conservative factions in their own parties, whose regional bases were largely in the countryside, and who were determined to prevent a power shift in the party's constituencies toward the newly mobilized lower-class groups. At the national level, elite liberal factions also often made common cause with their conservative party counterparts to thwart the radicalization of the liberal party. In these struggles over the core-constituency alignment of the liberal parties, the elite factions ultimately prevailed, and prevented the parties' shift to more radical electoral mobilization. Subsequent pact-making between party leaders ultimately stabilized elite control over the political process.[12]

In Chile, the Radical Party took the lead in incorporating middle-class sectors into the electoral process toward the end of the nineteenth century. In later years, working-class mobilization in the electoral arena was carried out through socialist and communist parties. Here, too, strong representation of the upper social strata in the major political parties, and the importance of coalition building between parties, ensured the integration of newly mobilized sectors into an elite-controlled political system.

In other countries, however, regional divisions hindered the national expansion of oligarchic parties along city-rural alignments. In these cases, particularly where sectional divisions coincided with economic divisions, the crystallization of party alignments was regional. Party politics and electoral mobilization were thus primarily local, and aimed to capture executive positions at the regional or provincial level. While effectively maintaining local oligarchic power, regionally divided party systems failed to bring coherence to oligarchic domination at the national level.

National unity was, therefore, made politically effective by other institutional arrangements, particularly regularized deal making between provincial governors that was subsequently enforced by the national executive. State-mediated consociational arrangements between regionally organized oligarchic groups, not party competition, became the organizing principle of national politics.

In Brazil, firm oligarchic control of politics was maintained locally through clientelistic party networks in the countryside. In this sense, the local bases of oligarchic power were similar to those existing in Chile, Colombia, and Uruguay. In Brazil, however, party networks and coalitions did not transcend regional boundaries. Rather, they were organized as instruments of local control and defense of regional economic interests. National institutions during the period of oligarchic rule known as the "Old Republic" (from the 1890s to 1930) were organized in a weak federal system where power resided at the regional level. This was a period known as the "politics of the governors."[13] A national governing party, the Republican Party, existed as an umbrella alliance of state parties, but power resided in the independent regional parties. These parties organized elections for state governors, who subsequently negotiated with one another on matters of national policy, the selection of presidents, and the regional distribution of the benefits of economic growth. Agreements and decisions reached by the governors were subsequently enforced by the national state. State institutions, both regional and national, played a central role in mediating regional elite conflicts and organizing national oligarchic domination.[14] This regional fragmentation and dependence on the state for the exercise of national power would shape conservative politics for the next few decades.[15] As discussed in detail later in this chapter, this system of decentralized national oligarchic rule resembled Argentina's own Liga de Gobernadores, which provided Argentina's regionally divided oligarchies with an institutional formula for national governance between 1880 and 1916.

In such Andean countries as Peru and Venezuela, regional oligarchic conflict, aggravated by the geographical dispersion of major export sectors, prevented even the establishment of Argentine- and Brazilian-style decentralized formulas of oligarchic civilian rule. In both countries elite dependence on systematic repression and military intervention to overcome regional conflicts marked the periods preceding the advent of mass politics. In Venezuela, the regional deadlock was finally broken by the installation of the highly repressive dictatorship of Juan Vicente Gómez, which ruled the country from 1908 until his death in 1935.[16] In Peru, political parties were somewhat more developed, but remained regional in orientation. The most important among them, the Civilista Party, failed to reach out beyond its base in the prosperous coastal elite, in spite of repeated control of the executive branch between 1872 and 1919.[17] Its turns in government were hampered by repeated regional oligarchic challenges backed by military intervention.[18]

The sectional cleavages that shaped oligarchic partisan alignments in these countries prevented the emergence of national competitive party systems during the period of oligarchic rule. Conservative reliance on the state for the mediation of elite conflict and the maintenance of political power would thus be forged during this period. This would have important consequences during the advent of mass politics. Labor, populist, and middle-class challenges would find expression in new national electoral coalitions and mass organizations, while conservative political capabilities would be constrained by the legacies of regional core constituency division and national electoral fragmentation.

Historical Scenario I: Successful Conservative Party Formation

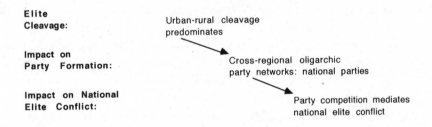

Elite
Cleavage: Urban-rural cleavage
                 predominates

Impact on
Party Formation: Cross-regional oligarchic
                        party networks: national parties

Impact on National
Elite Conflict: Party competition mediates
                       national elite conflict

Historical Scenario II: Incomplete Conservative Party Formation

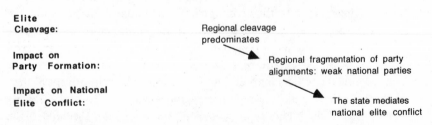

Elite
Cleavage: Regional cleavage
                 predominates

Impact on
Party Formation: Regional fragmentation of party
                        alignments: weak national parties

Impact on National
Elite Conflict: The state mediates
                       national elite conflict

Fig. 2.1. National conservative party formation in Latin America during the oligarchic period.

Argentina: The Regional Origins of Conservative Electoral Failure

Between 1880 and 1930, Argentina was ruled by civilian constitutional regimes. In 1916, an oligarchic regime was succeeded constitutionally by a regime based on universal adult male suffrage. This successful transition was, however, followed by a massive failure of conservative party organization, and was brought to an abrupt end in 1930 by a conservative-led military coup. Thereafter conservatives ruled by coercion and electoral fraud, initiating a pattern of social conflict and recurrent authoritarianism that dominated Argentine politics until 1983.[19]

The sudden collapse of conservative political organization under democratic rule would not have been readily predicted by most observers prior to the advent of mass suffrage. Between 1880 and 1916, Argentina was ruled by an oligarchic regime that has become legendary among mythmakers and historians alike for its success at state building, wealth creation, and political innovation. The regime's leaders, celebrated collectively in the country's historical annals as the "Generation of 1880," brought an end to several decades of almost continuous armed conflict among the country's fractious provinces. They also established a powerful presidential regime that ensured the representation of the once belligerent provinces in national decision making. In the economic sphere, the Generation of 1880 gave full rein to an economic development model based on the export to European markets of beef and agricultural commodities produced in the country's large and fertile Pampas region. Agricultural exports firmly integrated Argentina into the world economy and produced an economic boom that by the early twentieth century placed Argentina among the wealthiest countries in the world.

The country's growing population was largely excluded from political life during this period. Yet the balm of ever-expanding economic opportunity, particularly for the European immigrant population living in the Pampas region, kept popular challenges to oligarchic power to manageable levels. Until the end of the nineteenth century, the serious challenges to political stability came from intra-oligarchic struggles, which were as a rule settled by the regime's intricate practices of deal making and co-optation.[20]

By the early twentieth century, however, the leaders of the oligarchic order were under growing pressure from something new in Argentine political life: the phenomenon of mass organization. A new political party, the Unión Cívica Radical (henceforth usually referred to as the Radical Party) had built extensive party networks among the urban middle classes, and established itself as the standard bearer of middle-class demands for the right of participation. The Radical Party itself was of aristocratic origin, a splinter from an earlier dissident elite movement that had challenged incumbent governments at the turn of the century. However, with the Radical Party leadership's subsequent discovery of the power of mass mobilization, the intra-elite conflict of earlier years had mushroomed into a serious challenge from below to the Generation of 1880's continued hold on power.

The Radical Party challenge sparked a reform movement within the oligarchic leadership, which in 1912 successfully enacted a universal adult male suffrage law. With this new law, the reformers sought to open up the political system to middle-class participation in order to preserve stability and establish new bases for continued conservative rule. The Radical challengers, after all, did not question the basic socioeconomic order or the agricultural-exporting model of development. Their demands were for a greater say in decision making and for a larger middle-class share of the country's ever-expanding wealth from agricultural exports.

To the conservative reformers, it was clear that politics could no longer be controlled by the small oligarchy that sat astride the pinnacles of state power. For conservatives to remain in control of the government, they would have to emulate the Radical Party's strategies of mass organization. "Power was no longer located as before, in the government," wrote a prominent member of the oligarchy. "It had to be sought in the masses."[21]

Argentine conservatives had reason to be confident of their abilities in this department. They were the architects of Argentina's "century of gold." Introducing competitive politics would permit them to deploy the political resources gained from thirty years of economic growth and conservative control of state institutions to the task of electoral mobilization. Electoral reform would compel conservative forces to unify these formidable resources in a national electoral alliance, defeat the Radical challengers on their own turf, and add a measure of popular consensus to the conservative structure of political power. President Roque Sáenz Peña, architect of the universal male suffrage law, expressed the conservatives' optimism in a message to his followers: "The Radicals may take power by assault, by means of the coup they have always been trying, but this would be difficult in free elections. The National Autonomist Party [the official party], which is a tradition and a historic force, rules without opposition throughout the country."[22]

This optimism, however, would be dashed by the experience of electoral competition. Conservatives would lose the first presidential election held under conditions of universal male suffrage in 1916. They would never win a cleanly held presidential election after that. In fact, to this day

Table 2.1

Argentine Presidential Elections, 1916–1928

%

	1916	1922	1928
UCR	45.5	54.4	57.4
Conservatives[a]	42.0	31.1	16.9

Source: Darío Cantón, *Elecciones y partidos políticos en la Argentina: Historia, interpretación y balance, 1910–1966* (Buenos Aires: Siglo XXI Editores, 1973), 119, 268.

[a]Totals are the sum of all conservative parties and alliances that ran national or local slates for the presidential race.

no conservative party's presidential vote in a free and fair election has ever exceeded the 16 percent won by the largest conservative party, the Partido Demócrata Progresista, in the presidential elections of 1916.

Tables 2.1 and 2.2 trace the conservative electoral decline between the enactment of universal adult male suffrage and the 1930 coup against the Radical government of Hipólito Yrigoyen. This coup inaugurated the armed forces' role as a major player and important conservative ally in Argentine politics, and initiated a half-century of recurrent authoritarian rule. Table 2.1 shows the decline of conservatism as an electoral force in presidential elections during the 1912–30 period:

Another indication of conservatism's electoral decline is its gradual loss of seats in the national congress, the most important democratic institution, which might have served as a conservative base for checking the power of a Radical-controlled executive. The conservative decline in this arena was also dramatic. After the elections of 1912, conservatives controlled 77 percent of the seats in congress. Following the elections of 1930, which took place shortly before the overthrow of Yrigoyen, that figure had dropped to 19 percent.

The following pages explore some of the historical factors that proved the optimism of the 1912 conservative reformers wrong. The main argument is that the collapse of conservative party politics in the early years of mass democracy can be explained by the impact of regional cleavage on conservative party formation. Regional cleavage served as the primary shaper of upper-class partisan alignments during the nineteenth century. As such, it obstructed the development of cross-regional party networks, which in other countries facilitated institutionalized competition between elite-dominated national parties. Given the absence of national conservative parties, the oligarchic order was dependent on state mediation in

Table 2.2
Composition of the Argentine National Chamber of Deputies 1912–1930

	1912	1914	1916	1918	1920	1922	1924	1926	1928	1930
UCR	11	28	44	56	86	91	72	60	92	98
Dissident Radicals[a]			4	8	12	10	17	27	19	10
Socialist	2	9	9	6	10	10	18	19	4	1
Independent socialist									6	15
Conservative[b]	14	25	28	19	14	14	14	15	14	12
Demócrata Progresista[c]	1	3	8	14	19	14	14	9		3
Other conservative[d]	29	55	23	12	12	11	18	21	21	15
Total conservative	44	83	59	45	45	39	46	45	35	30
Total	57	120	116	115	153	150	153	151	156	154
% Conservative	77%	69%	51%	39%	29%	26%	30%	30%	22%	19%

Source: Darío Cantón, *Materiales para el estudio de la sociología política en la Argentina*, vol. 1 (Buenos Aires: Centro de Investigaciones Sociales Instituto Torcuato Di Tella, 1968), 33–51.
[a]Includes conservative dissident splinters from the UCR that opposed Yrigoyen in several interior provinces.
[b]Predominantly Buenos Aires, although occasionally represented in other provinces.
[c]Until 1916 named Liga del Sur, in Santa Fe province.
[d]Includes various provincial parties and occasional small parties with multiprovincial representation.

Argentina before the advent of mass politics. National conservative party building was only attempted subsequently. This effort was to be hindered by core-constituency divisions and the attendant "genetic defect" of conservative party organization: the fragmentation of existing conservative party organizations along provincial lines.[23] These legacies of upper-class division and institutional fragmentation would continue to shape conservative party politics throughout the twentieth century.

Patterns that conform to comparative analytical frameworks only tell part of the story, however. The accidents of history and the actions of political leaders tell the rest. As we shall see later in the chapter, efforts by conservative leaders to organize party-based oppositions after their loss of the presidency were repeatedly thwarted by the hostile institutional environment created by a Radical president bent on destroying the remaining organizational bases of conservative power. These events gave rise to an incentive structure for political action that discouraged conservative leaders, already burdened by social and institutional divisions, from embarking upon sustained strategies of conservative party building.

Regional Cleavage and Political Conflict in Argentina

Regional cleavage in Argentina was driven by a basic incompatibility between the interests of dominant socioeconomic strata in the coastal Pampas region and those of the interior provinces. Argentina is characterized by a socioeconomic dichotomy between the coast and the interior, a dichotomy that emerged with full force during Argentina's integration into the world economy in the mid nineteenth century.

The regional inequalities fostered by the country's integration into the world economy were striking. Between 1857 and 1884, a period in which the Argentine economy quintupled in size, wealth per capita in the province of Buenos Aires grew by an average of U.S. $54 per year, while the average rate for the rest of the country, including the relatively prosperous adjoining Litoral region, was only $20 per annum.[24] By 1884, 61 percent of total fixed investments were located in the province and city of Buenos Aires, and the region was generating 50 percent of the national income.[25] Table 2.3 compares levels of investment by province in the main economic activities.

Other socioeconomic indicators provide further evidence of regional

Table 2.3
Fixed Investment by Province in Argentina, 1884 (U.S. $ millions)

	Land	Cattle	Buildings	Public works	Other	Total	Per capita (not in millions)
Buenos Aires	301	202	303	98	231	1,135	1,245
Santa Fe	45	18	24	8	24	119	628
Córdoba	26	20	25	18	22	111	346
Tucumán	14	6	13	6	10	49	272
Santiago	6	11	11	4	8	40	252
Catamarca	10	5	8	4	7	34	333
Salta	11	5	11	4	8	39	234
Jujuy	3	2	4	1	3	13	198
La Rioja	5	3	6	1	4	19	219
San Juan	13	3	8	3	7	34	374
Mendoza	19	4	10	5	10	48	485
San Luis	9	3	6	4	6	28	373
Entre Ríos	39	31	24	4	25	123	652
Corrientes	26	17	19	4	17	83	405
Total	527	330	472	164	382	1,857	656

Source: Oscar E. Cornblit, et al., "La generación del 80 y su proyecto: Antecedentes y consequencias," in Argentina: Sociedad de masas, ed. Torcuato Di Tella, Gino Germani, and Jorge Graciarena (Buenos Aires: Editorial Universitaria de Buenos Aires, 1965), 30.

disparity. In 1913, 72.1 percent of industrial capital was located in the Buenos Aires and the Litoral region.[26] The population of the city and province of Buenos Aires grew from 500,000 to 3.6 million between 1869 and 1914, increasing the region's share of the total population from 28 percent to 46 percent. During the same period, the interior's share of the population fell from 40 percent to 19 percent. The immigration flow from Europe was also destined overwhelmingly for Buenos Aires and the Litoral region. In 1914, according to that year's census, 39 percent of the population of the city and province of Buenos Aires were European-born; for the Litoral province of Santa Fe, the figure was 34 percent. In contrast, the northwestern provinces of Jujuy and Salta registered only 5 percent of their populations as European-born. In the province of Catamarca, the figure was 2 percent; in Santiago del Estero, 3 percent; and in San Luis, 8 percent.

The disparity in economic growth reflected a marked conflict of interest between the dominant socioeconomic groups of each region over the position of Argentina in the world economy. By virtue of its resource endowments, geographic location, demographic structure, and culture, the Buenos Aires region was overwhelmingly committed to a model of growth led by agricultural exports. The political and economic prominence of this region helped to ensure that the lion's share of infrastructural development credit went to supporting that model of growth. In contrast, the economies of the interior were primarily oriented toward the domestic market, either supplying stagnant local demand or meeting the consumer needs of the large urban markets of the metropolis with local manufactures and primary products. These endeavors were constantly threatened by outside competition, both from abroad and from the more prosperous coastal regions. From very early on, the interior provinces concentrated on strategies of regional economic self-defense. Writing about the immediate postindependence period, the historian Miron Burgin noted that

> ever since the opening of the country to foreign commerce and the virtual cessation of commercial intercourse with Peru, the provinces were anxious to protect their industries and trade against outside competition. And from the point of view of each province outside competition implied not only foreign capital and trade, but also those of the other provinces. Each province endeavored to attain as high a degree of economic self-sufficiency as possible, hoping thereby to make itself politically and financially independent of other provinces and especially of the government of Buenos Aires.[27]

Nowhere is the conflict of interest between economic elites more apparent than in the dynamic poles of agricultural production in the two regions. In the Pampas region, cattle and temperate agricultural production prospered in an environment of free trade and export-oriented production. In the interior, the situation was quite different. The two most important poles of agricultural production there were the sugar and wine industries. The first was located in the provinces of Salta and Tucumán; the second in the western province of Mendoza. Both of these industries experienced a boom in the 1880s that was a product of the inter-regional oligarchic bargains typical of the post-1880 regime. Among the benefits received by the interior from these bargains were high levels of tariff protection for the sugar and wine industries and almost exclusive access for these industries to the growing urban markets of the metropolis. Thus, while the Buenos Aires region grew wealthy under a system of free international exchange, the pockets of prosperity in the interior owed their very existence to tariff protection negotiated with metropolitan elites.[28]

A result of these contrasting patterns of economic development was the formation of very different class structures in each of the regions. The Buenos Aires and adjoining Litoral regions experienced the emergence of a significant urban middle class, a growing, largely foreign-born working class, and, in some areas, an expanding free-holding agricultural population. Urbanization was also a phenomenon largely limited to the Buenos Aires and Litoral regions. In 1914, over one-half of the country's total population lived in cities, but the interior's rural population averaged between 70 to 85 percent of its total population.[29] In the interior provinces, these patterns produced only minor changes in the local class structures that had existed since colonial times:

> In the interior towns a traditionalist type of society continued to hold sway, untouched by the radical transformations taking place in the coastal region. . . . A mass of population which lived at little more than subsistence level topped by a tiny elite class provided neither producers nor consumers to swell the flow of trade through the interior. Perhaps the most resistant to change in these interior cities was the class structure. The descendants of the conquistadors still constituted the elite. For three centuries they had maintained a pure lineage, marrying only within their class and rejecting any introduction of new blood within their society. Here the immigrant or middle-class person found himself excluded from upper-class homes even more effectively than on the coast.[30]

Regional differences in the socioeconomic realm would inevitably make themselves felt in the realms of culture and politics. As Karl Mannheim has pointed out, the process of social differentiation "tends to draw the intellect along with it and forces it to develop along its own lines."[31] Thus, the Argentine regional dichotomy, while rooted in socioeconomic factors, had important political, cultural, and ideological ramifications for Argentine politics. In the interior provinces, traditionalist conservative ideologies prevailed, buttressed by the ideological and political power of the Catholic Church, which played a prominent role in local politics and social life. In contrast, the Buenos Aires region was a bastion of liberalism and anticlericalism. The leaders of the Generation of 1880 instituted free secular education, removed the Church's monopoly on civil registers, burials, and marriages, and, in the late 1890s, went so far as to break off diplomatic relations with the Vatican. In the face of liberal social reforms emanating from the nation's metropolitan region, the Catholic Church in the interior became "a conservative body struggling to preserve vestiges of its former glory."[32]

Elites in the interior found their most important cultural referents in their Hispanic roots. Buenos Aires looked to non-Iberian Europe. The nation's capital was lavishly built by the exuberant Generation of 1880 as a replica of Paris. They celebrated and promoted the massive inflow of European immigrants as part of a "civilizing" campaign that would eradicate the vestiges of traditionalism and *barbarie* entrenched in the country's remoter regions.[33] In the 1920s, tensions generated by this coexistence of diametrically opposed worldviews would fuel the clericalist and quasi-fascist *nacionalista* movement, which, affirming the Hispanic and Catholic roots of Argentine history, would rise up as a powerful countermovement to liberal dominance.

The political regime built by the Generation of 1880 was an institutional solution to interregional elite conflict. It brought relative peace to a war-torn country, permitted the consolidation of the nation-state, and provided mechanisms for reconciling the economic domination of the country by the Buenos Aires region with the demands of interior elites for political representation and a share of the wealth derived from agricultural exports. What the regime did not do, however, was to lay the institutional foundations for a national competitive party system. Given sectionalist divisions, free electoral competition would have threatened the country's precarious national unity. The state, not parties, thus emerged as the key mediator of national oligarchic conflict. This would haunt conservatives when the advent of mass politics compelled regional elites to seek formulas for conservative unity in the arena of electoral politics.

The 1880–1916 Oligarchic Regime and the Rise of Mass Politics

The Oligarchic Regime

In 1880 the province of Buenos Aires rebelled against the central government and was defeated decisively on the battlefield by an alliance of interior provinces. The military defeat of Buenos Aires put an end to a series of provincial wars that had marked the first century of Argentine independence. Regional conflict had been the most important feature of Argentine political life since the 1810–20 wars of independence. Early conflicts were expressed largely along city-country lines, whereby liberal elites from the major urban areas of the interior provinces, led by the city of Buenos Aires, struggled to unify the nation under their political domination.[34] With the development of Argentina's agricultural-export economy in the second half of the nineteenth century, however, intra-elite conflict acquired pronounced regional dimensions. Growth in the agricultural Pampas region of Buenos Aires province and the surrounding Litoral region exploded, relegating the interior to the status of socioeconomic backwater.[35] Furthermore, the port city of Buenos Aires, which served as the nation's capital, controlled the flow of most of the nation's agricultural exports and imported goods. The formidable port revenues these generated also came under the control of Buenos Aires province. The combination of these two factors — its status as the motor of growth in Argentina's agricultural exports, and its control over port revenues — gave the province of Buenos Aires enormous economic and political power over the rest of the country. Political alignments in the interior, both urban and rural, crystallized defensively against its hegemony.

The power of the province of Buenos Aires was finally undercut by its 1880 military defeat. The victorious provinces deprived it of its pivotal financial resource, the city of Buenos Aires, by placing the capital city directly under the control of the national government as a federal district. The enormous wealth generated by that port city would now flow directly to the national government, and would never again form part of the arsenal of resources used by the province to impose its hegemony on the rest of the country. The new regional power equilibrium thus established laid the bases for a new political order and decades of stability and growth.

The new political regime that emerged from the ashes of this conflict represented an institutional solution to the problem of interregional elite cleavage. Virtually every aspect of this new institutional order reflected a carefully structured balance between the dependence of the country on the

Pampas region's export-generated wealth and the demands of the interior for political influence. A statist bargain thus emerged between Argentina's regional elites, which left the agricultural-exporting development model intact, but made the state the central arena for negotiating the regional distribution of its fruits. The overrepresentation of the interior in national political institutions and a system of permanently shifting gubernatorial coalitions that kept the power of individual provinces in check became pillars of the national political system.

The basic outlines of the regime led by the Generation of 1880 was as follows: formally, Argentina was governed by a liberal constitution that established the separation of powers among the executive, legislative, and judicial branches. But its reality was the concentration of power in the executive branch. Decision making resided in a hierarchic power structure that linked the presidency to the provincial governorships. This was key to the formula for national unity devised by the regime's leaders: a presidency endowed with great powers over the national domain, and provincial governors with a virtual monopoly over local politics. Each level of executive power had tools with which to check the power of the other. The president required the backing of a majority of provincial governors for all major decisions, including those concerning presidential succession and the distribution of national revenues. This ensured a provincial voice in national politics. Yet the president also possessed the power of "federal intervention," which allowed him to remove provincial governments and replace local authorities with those of his own choosing should local developments threaten either the national political equilibrium or preexisting agreements between elites. This power would become an important tool for asserting national executive power over fractious provincial authorities.

The Generation of 1880 also organized a powerful political machine to organize national politics: the Partido Autonomista National (PAN), which functioned as the official party and integrated the landholding elites of Buenos Aires with provincial elites from the interior. While officially a party, PAN was in reality the political manifestation of the structure of state power forged between the presidency and the governorships. It served as a transmission belt of communication between local oligarchies, provincial governorships, provincial parties, and the presidency, and organized the election of presidential candidates previously selected by a majority of governors. Karen Remmer provides a succinct description of how PAN operated as an electoral machine:

> At the local level its chief agents were the tax assessor, municipal intendant, police commissioner, and justice of the peace. In some provinces

one or more of these posts were theoretically elective, but in practice governors ceded the power to appoint these officials to local *caudillos,* who in return ensured that the governor's partisans succeeded in all elections. A similar relationship prevailed between the president and provincial governors. Governors supported the PAN's presidential candidate and made certain that he won the election. In return they considered themselves entitled to choose provincial legislators, national legislators, and their own successors.[36]

In contrast to their counterparts in such countries as Chile, Uruguay, or Colombia, the Generation of 1880's leaders established, not a national network of competing parties, but a national single-party system that served as an umbrella for disparate provincial interests. Most national political decisions, from the designation of presidential successors to the allocation of credit, were made via a decision-making process known as the *acuerdo* — informal agreements between members of the executive branch and provincial governors. These agreements were subsequently ratified by the PAN and legislative institutions. Control by provincial governors of nominations to the Senate, as well as of the electoral machineries of provincial government, ensured that decisions made by acuerdo within the institutions of the state would be faithfully reproduced in the institutions of political society. Representative bodies existed, not to organize competition among rival currents or to check the power of the executive, but as ratifiers of decisions reached in the hierarchically organized structure of state power. The victors in intra-oligarchic power struggles asserted their will over all issues and policy arenas through their control of state institutions. The losers, lacking an autonomous political society into which they could retreat, remained excluded from the political process until such time as their ability to organize winning coalitions in the executive branch through negotiation or violence might return them to the levers of state power.

The "conservative order," as the historian Natalio Botana has labeled the 1880–1916 regime,[37] was a system designed to maximize oligarchic power amid extraordinary economic growth and social change, establish orderly mechanisms for allocating the unequal benefits of that growth, and minimize interregional conflict. In a system where parties were organized along regional lines, open electoral competition posed a major threat to national unity. It was thus subordinated to the shared interest among regional elites in maintaining this statist bargain. Bread-and-butter deal making among elites took precedence over ideological debate and electoral mobilization. All open competition that might have allowed un-

derlying intra-elite conflicts to come to the fore and threaten the pragmatic equilibrium that guaranteed institutional stability was systematically suppressed. Elections were held, but they were fraudulent. Congress
passed laws, but did not challenge the overarching decision-making authority of state institutions. The system helped guarantee order, but it was
predicated on what Peter Smith has called "a fundamentally passive relationship between politics and Argentine society."[38] At the turn of the
century this passivity could no longer be taken for granted. It would be
disrupted by the appearance of new opposition willing to introduce the
power of mass organization into the Argentine political system.

Radical Opposition and Political Reform

The rise of the Unión Cívica Radical, or Radical Party, produced a major
change in the modus operandi of Argentine politics. The UCR was born of
a revolt of sectors of the oligarchy against the presidency of Miguel Juarez
Celman in 1890. It emerged as a splinter from the Unión Cívica, the movement that had spearheaded the 1890 revolt. In contrast to most of the
Unión Cívica's leadership, which eagerly allowed itself to be co-opted by
the oligarchic regime shortly after the revolt, the UCR's leaders embarked
on a prolonged strategy of opposition to the regime. They concentrated on
a strategy of political organization aimed, not at strengthening intra-elite
political networks, but at recruiting among the large and theretofore unorganized urban middle class. In so doing, the UCR introduced a new currency of political power into Argentine politics: the power of organized
numbers. And it did this through what Natalio Botana has described as "a
new type of political organization, independent of state resources, structured around the base committee, the conventions (national and district-
level), and individual membership."[39]

In other words, the UCR was a modern political party, and its challenge, based on the concept of mass consensus, created serious problems
of legitimacy for the oligarchic regime. Specifically, it put the issue of the
economic elite's relationship to the large urban middle classes on the political agenda. The reform movement within the conservative oligarchy was
a response to this challenge — an attempt to recast both Argentine political
institutions and conservative ways of doing politics in order to cope with
the political innovations introduced by the UCR.

The conservative reformers of 1912 thus sought to devise ways to
integrate these powerful new opponents into the political system, but they
also aimed their reforms at the conservative movement. The reformers
firmly believed that the changes they were enacting would produce com-

mensurate changes in conservative political practices. For almost a decade there had been calls within the oligarchy to modernize conservative politics, to move from electoral restriction and backroom acuerdos to open electoral mobilization. One such call was made in 1905 by Carlos Pellegrini, one of the oligarchy's most eminent leaders, who, in the throes of an intra-elite political struggle exhorted his supporters to break with tradition and "organize a truly disciplined political force with a fixed objective, that is, a party with a banner."[40] In 1912, the reformers believed that the institution of free and universal suffrage would be the catalyst for the formation of such a party. True, at that moment the radicals possessed the organization—the party cells, the committees, the information networks—and commanded impressive support among the middle classes. But the conservative reformers saw little need for despair. They possessed formidable political resources of their own. They had presided over a time of economic growth that had made Argentina one of the richest countries in the world. They had fashioned a complex political system and controlled its most important levers of power. All these resources, when deployed in the realm of party politics, would allow them to deal with the UCR's extensive party organization among the increasingly mobilized middle classes. The existence of such organization was thus not a reason for further restricting electoral politics. Rather, it made the task of conservative replication imperative.

Regional Cleavage and the 1916 Presidential Election

The divisive effect of regional cleavage on conservative electoral capabilities was fully manifested in the 1916 presidential elections—conservatism's first national test in free elections. A group of prominent conservative leaders heeded the reformers' call to found a new party. Named the Partido Demócrata Progresista (PDP), it was intended as a national movement uniting the disparate provincial conservative parties under one flag. According to its founders, it was to be the Argentine standard-bearer of "a modern and innovative conservatism, characteristic of European conservatisms."[41] The leaders involved in this effort were prominent members of Argentina's political elite; many had served the oligarchic regime at the highest levels of government. The majority were members of, or descended from, the most socially prestigious families of the interior.[42]

It was this last fact that sparked the apprehension of the most important provincial conservative party in the country—a party without whose support no national electoral project could succeed: the Conservative Party of Buenos Aires. After much negotiation and recrimination, the

Buenos Aires Conservative Party, led by its iron-fisted caudillo, Marcelino Ugarte, refused to join the PDP-led conservative alliance. The Conservative Party endorsed no presidential candidate in the national election and asked its supporters to vote for its unpledged electors.[43] This decision made it quite likely that the UCR, facing a divided conservative opposition, would emerge triumphant from those elections.

The reasons for the Buenos Aires Conservative Party's reluctance to join the PDP-led alliance has been widely debated by historians and social scientists. The most influential interpretation of this event has been put forth by Oscar Cornblit, who argues that notwithstanding that it threatened to seize power from the conservatives, the UCR did not in fact pose a class threat to the interests of their constituencies. Its political platform was vague, and its political leaders were drawn from the same social strata as those of the conservatives. Cornblit thus looks for an explanation to personalistic and organizational rivalries within the conservative movement, which, in the absence of a genuine class threat from the radical opposition, remained paramount in shaping the structure of political alignments. "If the conservative formula had remained united, conservatism would have triumphed," he writes, "and if this did not happen, then it was due to the fact that there was nothing to fear from a radical victory."[44] The cost to Marcelino Ugarte of the PDP capturing the presidency, this argument goes, would have been to forever lose the possibility of establishing himself as the supreme leader of the conservative movement. Temporary loss of national power to the relatively unthreatening UCR was preferable.

This argument, however, overlooks the fact that there were very good reasons, beyond the petty and personal, for Buenos Aires to be apprehensive of the PDP's leadership. They can be found in the PDP's own political platform, which had been drawn up by Carlos Ibarguren, who two decades later was to devote his impressive literary talents to writing nacionalista and pro-fascist tracts. The platform called for a protectionist and nationalist economic policy. In his memoir *La historia que he vivido*, Ibarguren paraphrased the 1915 speech in which he made public the basic elements of the platform adopted by the PDP, describing it as "protectionist in economic matters; mutualist, cooperativist, and assistance-oriented toward the working masses in regard to social policy":[45]

> I pointed to the pressing need to increase our productive potential and to make ourselves independent of the foreigner. In this regard the policy we recommended was the intensive promotion of our industries, and the exploitation, processing, and utilization of our nation's products in order

to replace foreign products as much as possible. "In order to attain," I said, "our economic independence, it is indispensable to create a national merchant marine and, in addition, *to organize a system of foreign trade protected and fiscally controlled by the state.*" To realize this transformation, which will give us economic independence, I proposed these solutions: "Organize the most effective defense and exploitation of our petroleum reserves; create a banking system for the promotion of production that will distribute credit toward productive activities, as well as a regime that will control and regulate foreign exchange and monetary circulation." [emphasis added][46]

State control of foreign trade, diversion of credit to domestic industry, control of foreign investment, monetary and exchange controls. . . . This was not a platform that would have brought much joy to the landowning and commercial interests of the Buenos Aires region, which were still riding the wave of a long export-based boom. Nor was it a platform that the political leadership of Buenos Aires conservatism could have embraced without running into major problems with its core constituencies. Thus, in spite of the trepidation that the UCR leader Hipólito Yrigoyen and his middle-class "hordes" might have caused the conservative leadership, the basic commitment of the Radical Party to the existing model of development through agricultural exports might well have seemed preferable to Ugarte and his core constituencies than the protectionist and nationalist proclivities of the conservative parties of the interior.

It is in the light of upper-class regional divisions that the failure of Argentina's first conservative electoral project in the era of mass politics can best be understood. Regional cleavage overcame class cleavage as a determinant of core-constituency alignments in the first national electoral test of Argentine conservatism. This would, in varying degrees of change, remain an enduring feature of conservative party politics for the remainder of the century.

Regional Cleavage and Conservative Organizational Fragmentation

Had regional cleavage crystallized conservative alliance structures into two organizational poles, one for the interior and one for the Buenos Aires region, conservative party prospects would have been difficult enough. Once national unity proved elusive, however, atomization prevailed over bifurcation as the key structural characteristic of conservative electoral organization. The effect of this was to compound even further the divisive effects of regionalism on conservative party politics.

The guiding principles of conservative political organization after 1916 were the pursuit of provincial interests and strategies of local self-defense — political self-defense against a central government controlled by a hostile political party, and economic self-defense against other provinces. As such, it introduced a logic of political action that made regional differences paramount among the catalysts of conservative electoral organization. While effective at the local level, it stood in obvious conflict with the need for unity at the national level. It also concentrated conservative political resources at their weakest point vis-à-vis national governments controlled by other parties. By fragmenting conservative opposition, it allowed the central government to deal with its conservative opponents on a province-by-province basis, playing them off against one another through the arbitrary assignation of state resources, or attacking them directly through the power of federal intervention and other state prerogatives available for political use. Regional atomization, a structural characteristic of conservative party politics, thus also became a condition whose perpetuation was relentlessly pursued by central governments controlled by other parties.

An additional important factor was the dynamic of organizational fragmentation that regionalism bestowed on conservative party politics. This would also have negative consequences for national coalition building. Regionalist conservative strategies created a variety of independent provincial parties with *organizational* interests of their own. Each had an interest in perpetuating its existence. The proliferation of party institutions also fostered the proliferation of ideological and political agendas that different parties committed themselves to advance. As these became linked to the identities and interests of the individual parties, it further complicated the task of coalition building at the national level. Thus, any conservative project of national electoral unification had to deal, not only with real conflicts of interest between regions, but also with a constellation of organizational interests.

If a national conservative party were ever to have been built, it would have taken place through a process known in the theory of party development as "territorial diffusion." As Angelo Panebianco notes in his "genetic model" of party development, this process, which fuses preexisting parties with organizational interests of their own into a national federation, tends to produce weaker party organizations than development through "territorial penetration," in which the party's expansion is carried out and controlled by a defined leadership core.[47] Thus, to form a conservative party, the national leadership would have had to overcome the entrenched organizational interests of its parts. And even if such a party had been formed, its subsequent development would have been plagued by problems of discipline and disunity bequeathed by the legacy of its genetic origins.

In this sense, the origins of the UCR also worked against Argentine conservatism. Its development had taken place mostly through territorial penetration. Territorial diffusion had played a part in that party's development in some of the interior provinces, and it was in these areas that the weakest links in the UCR's organization (and the strongest opposition to Yrigoyen) were to be found. Yet the power of Yrigoyen's leadership and organization, which extended throughout the most populous regions of the country and many of its peripheral areas, was the party's dominant characteristic. Argentine conservatism was thus forced to compete with an established national party whose own genetic legacy endowed it with an inherent organizational cohesion that exceeded any that might have been aspired to by the conservative leadership.

These were the cards dealt Argentine conservatism by genetic legacies in the initial rounds of its political organization. They shaped the organizational context in which conservative leaders had to confront the advent of mass electoral politics. In a favorable institutional context, however, the obstacles they posed would not have been insurmountable. There was still room for the political leadership to overcome regional and organizational problems and build new forms of conservative electoral organization. Unfortunately, such a favorable context would not emerge in Argentina's first experiment with political democracy. It is to this subject that we now turn.

Institutional Dynamics, Leadership, and Conservatism's First Experience with Democracy, 1916–1930

The conservative reformers of 1912 had hoped that Radical participation in national politics following the electoral reforms would be gradual. They had envisaged the first decades of democratic politics as a period of apprenticeship in legislative and local politics for the UCR's leaders, after which, instructed in the arts of government, they would accede to the periodic exercise of national power. Radical capture of the presidency turned the tables on the conservative reformers. Electoral organization asserted itself as the dominant means to political power. Now it was conservatism that faced a period of apprenticeship.

The loss of the presidency, given the importance of that institution in the period of oligarchic rule, was a formidable blow. But on the surface, conditions might have actually seemed propitious for conservatives. The

UCR controlled the presidency, but both houses of the Argentine congress remained under conservative control after the 1916 elections. This, and conservatism's continued dominance in most of the provinces (where elections for legislative office were held), gave it control of important bases from which to check the power of the radical government, and considerable incentives to strengthen its role as an actor in the institutions of political society. Congress promised in this context to become both a stronghold from which regional elites could check the power of the central government, and an arena for new forms of conservative political action.[48] Strategies of congressional opposition and coalition building at the national level, buttressed by political power bases in the provinces, were the most sensible courses of action for Argentine conservatism after 1916. In the process, the congress would become invested with a relevance in national political life that it had never possessed before.

The legacies of the old order would, however, return to haunt Argentine conservatives. This time they were turned against them by their Radical opponents. Faced with a potential conservative veto of major policy initiatives from the congress, and with a check on the powers of central government from the conservative-controlled provinces, President Yrigoyen utilized the powers of the presidency to neutralize these institutional arenas. Furthermore, he made full use of the powers of the presidency to destroy the provincial bases of conservative political power.

The presidency had been used in this way during the previous period of oligarchic rule. In his bid to centralize power in the presidential institution, Yrigoyen went further, however, than the Generation of 1880 had ever dared. During the old regime, leaders had been careful to maintain a balance between the prerogatives of the presidency, the autonomy of provincial governments, and the representation of provincial interests in national decisions. Since the provinces were largely under conservative control after 1916, however, respecting preexisting norms of national-provincial relations would have compelled the Radical government to accept conservative veto power over its decisions and leave a potential source of political opposition intact. President Yrigoyen therefore decided to alter the national-provincial equilibrium by centralizing authority in the presidency, and to destroy his opposition using enhanced presidential powers.[49] His primary targets were the old regime's leadership and organizational structure. These would be undermined by two key methods: marginalizing the congress as an effective arena of decision making, and using the constitutional powers of federal intervention to dislodge conservative governments in the provinces from power.

The defense of constitutional norms became a public political crusade for Argentine conservatism after its defeat in 1916. Central to the conservative agenda was the affirmation of congressional powers. Now that its power was limited to the legislative branch, conservatism's embrace of parliamentary due process was vital to its political survival. The protection of conservative political interests was now intimately linked to the viability of democratic institutions.[50]

The Radical government's response was to circumvent the congress in key political decisions and to reject its constitutional powers of executive oversight. The president used the power of executive decree to enact major political measures. When challenged by the congress, or when his ministers were subpoenaed to appear before congressional committees to explain executive decisions, he rejected the legal bases for the congressional actions. Fixing his public stand in what proved to be one of his presidency's most bitter conflicts, President Yrigoyen recognized only the legislative functions of the congress, rejecting a constitutional basis for that body's claim to the prerogative of executive oversight. The congress, he stated in a 1918 message to that body, "does not possess the power to reproach nor correct the actions of the executive power."[51]

Even more ominous to his conservative opponents was Yrigoyen's strategy of wholesale federal intervention in the provinces. Federal intervention powers allowed the president to remove provincial governments and replace local authorities with others of his own choosing. They had been instituted by the framers of the Argentine constitution in the mid nineteenth century as an instrument for imposing order on a fractious nation. Prior to 1880, their use by the national government was intimately linked to the internal wars that pitted region against region and threatened the national government's authority throughout the territory.[52] After 1880, federal interventions became a more openly political resource. They were used by the national government primarily to settle local conflicts, either in favor of the local status quo, or against it, depending on the coalitional imperatives it faced at the time.

Prior to 1880, the overwhelming majority of interventions were carried out by simple presidential decree. Of thirty-five interventions decreed by the executive power between 1854 and 1880, only five were approved by congress. In the more institutionalized politics of the post-1880 period, however, the regional oligarchic power equilibrium placed normative and institutional checks on arbitrary presidential authority. Of forty interventions decreed between 1880 and 1916, twenty-five had congressional approval. Furthermore, nearly 44 percent of those interventions were carried out following a request for intervention by the provincial governors.[53]

This situation changed dramatically with the ascension of Hipólito

Yrigoyen to the presidency. In the first six years of his term, he decreed nineteen interventions (Argentina had fourteen provinces at that time). Only four of these interventions received congressional approval. All ten provinces under conservative control were intervened in — all but one of these during the first two years of his presidency.[54] Yrigoyen's main objective was to alter the composition of the conservative-dominated Senate, whose members were selected not by direct election, but by provincial legislatures, which usually operated under tight gubernatorial control. But Yrigoyen also sought to eliminate the key source of conservative electoral strength: the machinery of state patronage and electoral manipulation provided by control of provincial governments. By dislodging local conservative governments from power, he deprived these parties, unaccustomed to the exigencies of autonomous political and ideological mobilization, of their most important political resource.

The effect of these interventions at the local level was devastating. An example of their impact can be seen in the most important Argentine province, Buenos Aires. Governed under the tight-fisted rule of the conservative caudillo Marcelino Ugarte, this province was Yrigoyen's first target for intervention. The intervention was decreed in April 1917, one week before the congress was to convene for its regular sessions. In addition to the removal of the governor and senior elected officials, the intervention also removed from office all administrative personnel in the executive, legislative, and judicial branches. The provincial police force, an important political tool of the provincial government, was also subject to sweeping reforms and personnel changes. In all, more than three thousand public employees were removed from office as a result of the intervention.[55]

The impact of the intervention on the electoral performance of the Conservative Party of Buenos Aires between 1918 and 1930 can be seen in table 2.4. After the intervention, it never won another provincewide election. In the congressional elections of 1918, it suffered a 30 percent decline from the previous elections in 1916. Following a brief resurgence in the 1920 elections, the party embarked upon a steady decline throughout the rest of the decade.

A comparison of the data in table 2.4 with data in tables 2.1 and 2.2 reveals that the conservative decline in the province of Buenos Aires was reflected in a conservative decline nationwide. The actions of the Radical government thus created a serious dilemma for Argentine conservatism. By centralizing power in the presidency and marginalizing all other arenas in which conservatives were present, the Radical government made the presidency the only viable prize of Argentine politics. Given the concentration of power, and the potential arbitrariness of presidential actions

Table 2.4
Congressional Election Results, Province of Buenos Aires, 1914–1930 (%)

Parties	1914	1916	1918	1920	1922	1924	1928	1930
Conservative	47.3	48.9	35.5	42.9	32.7	27.0	17.4	43.3
Radical	44.2	45.5	59.7	48.8	60.6	64.6	58.1	47.4
Socialist	6.5	3.4	3.5	8.3	6.7	8.5	5.5	7.4

Source: Richard J. Walter, *La provincia de Buenos Aires en la política Argentina, 1912–1943* (Buenos Aires: Emecé Editores, 1987), 263–66.

against provincial governments, the potential fruits of capturing provincial governorships could be considered uncertain at best. Furthermore, the other potential benefit of provincial organization, the capture of seats in a national congress where conservative coalitions could be formed, was also limited by that body's displacement by the presidency. A strategy of political opposition based in the institutions of political society thus lost its relevance to the Argentine conservative leadership.[56]

For the conservative political leaders of the 1920s, therefore, the most logical political strategy was to focus on the recapture of the presidency. Here, however, the regional dynamics described earlier intervened. Again in 1922, the year of presidential elections for Yrigoyen's successor, the Buenos Aires–interior rivalry destroyed prospects for unity. This time it was the Partido Demócrata Progresista that refused to join the Concentración National, a conservative coalition supported by Buenos Aires province. The PDP's recalcitrance doomed whatever chances conservatives had of organizing a united front against the UCR in the 1922 elections.[57]

Without prospects for an autonomous electoral challenge to the Radicals, the conservative strategy shifted to seeking coalitions with dissident Radical factions. The opportunity for this strategy was provided by the ascent to the presidency of Marcelo T. de Alvear, son of an aristocratic Buenos Aires family, who only counted upon a limited base of support within Yrigoyen's party machinery. Within a year of his election, the UCR was rent by an internal conflict that became known as the personalist-antipersonalist split. Alvear's supporters, the antipersonalists, were Yrigoyen's conservative opponents within the party, and their main strength lay outside Buenos Aires province.

The conflict within Radicalism gave conservatives the opening they sought to regain some of the ground they had lost in the previous six years. The rift between personalists and antipersonalists, and the control of the presidency by the antipersonalists, opened up possibilities for a new national conservative strategy. It would rely on the exercise of federal intervention powers by conservatism's new ally, Alvear, to restore conservatism's earlier hold on the machineries of provincial government.

Although eminently logical, given the opportunities open to the conservative leadership, this strategy would in the long run prove deleterious to conservative party development. On the one hand, it placed the political initiative and conservative fate in a radical faction whose hold on the party was tenuous at best. The bulk of party patronage resources and middle-class support were under Yrigoyen's control. Furthermore, faithful to conservative tradition, the antipersonalist coalition was also plagued by regional tensions. Foremost among these was the resistance of antipersonalist leaders in the Santa Fe region and other parts of the interior to the leadership of the Buenos Aires–based Alvear.[58]

The alliance with antipersonalism also centered conservative strategies on the quick fix of federal intervention to regain control of provincial governments. In several provinces, the conservative strategy was entirely predicated on the possibilities of federal intervention. Most notable among these was the Conservative Party of Buenos Aires, whose leaders abstained from party-building activities — and even abstained from participating in the provincial elections of 1924 — pending the enactment of a pro-conservative federal intervention in their province.[59]

The interventions never took place. Alvear's own position within the UCR was not solid enough for him to have embarked upon such a course, and the growing Radical presence in the national congress, which was mostly supportive of the personalist wing, made congressional approval of wide-scale interventions so difficult to obtain that Alvear preferred not to attempt their implementation. The failure of the antipersonalist option, and the subsequent return of Hipólito Yrigoyen to the presidency in 1928, would leave conservatism with few cards left to play in democratic politics.

In a handful of cases, the collapse of the antipersonalist option actually forced the conservatives to dedicate themselves to local party building. In Buenos Aires province, the Conservative Party came under the control of leaders previously opposed to the strategy of alliance with the Radical antipersonalists. The new leaders embarked upon an impressive project of modernization and ideological revitalization which bore fruit in a relatively short period. In the congressional elections of 1930, the party increased its vote total from its 17.4 percent tally in 1928 to 43.3 percent, only four percentage points away from the incumbent UCR.[60] In Argentina's largest and most urbanized province, the Conservative Party's discovery of electoral mobilization and organization had converted it once again into a viable electoral alternative to the UCR. Its brief experience in this activity demonstrated that conservative coalition building between the upper strata and the large urban lower and middle strata was by no means an impossible task — given, of course, an adequate investment of manpower and resources.

Events at the national level would, however, overtake local developments. In 1928 and 1929, President Yrigoyen ordered federal intervention in the provinces of San Juan, Mendoza, Corrientes, and Santa Fe by executive decree, reigniting opposition fears of a new hegemonic bid. This, along other effects of Yrigoyen's increasingly erratic rule, led to a convergence among conservatives, antipersonalists, and the armed forces as to the desirability of his overthrow, resulting in the toppling of the Radical government in September 1930. The coup effectively gave control of the state back to the conservatives, ending the "formative phase" of conservative involvement in mass politics, and initiating thirteen years conservative rule that would become known in common Argentine parlance as the "infamous decade."

Rule by Electoral Fraud: Conservatives in Power, 1930–1943

Between 1930 and 1943, a coalition of conservatives and antipersonalist radicals known as the Concordancia ruled over Argentine politics. The Concordancia essentially helped to re-establish the old bases of state-centered conservative power via a new institutional alignment with antipersonalist radicals. With the carrot of guaranteed access to national state resources, conservatives found the wherewithal to unify behind a national political party. The Partido Demócrata Nacional (PDN) was founded after the 1930 coup as a national vehicle for multiple provincial parties to select candidates for the presidency, to administer the national government, and to negotiate on behalf of local conservative organizations with their antipersonalist partners in the Concordancia.

Beyond the new power-sharing arrangement between conservatives and antipersonalist radicals, however, the Concordancia was in many ways a return to the pre-1916 status quo. The state once again became the central arena for negotiation and political competition, and it also became the allocator and enforcer of national power-sharing arrangements between regional elites. Electoral fraud once again became the primary tool for enforcing decisions reached via elite-level negotiation in the executive branch, a procedure that became more blatant and cumbersome than in the pre-1916 period, given the much larger number of enfranchised voters.[61]

The conservative recapture of national power during this period, which reforged pre-1916 power-sharing arrangements between regional elites, did not provide a propitious context for conservative party-building efforts. Conservative incentives at the provincial level to mobilize popular support and build party networks were greatly reduced by assured access to power. Conservative electoral patronage networks were restored, but these were aimed more at control over an expanded electorate than at popular mobilization. With the national government under the direction of the Concordancia, abundant local resources for electoral fraud, and the certain futility of outside challenges through popular mobilization, the incentives for strategies of conservative party building withered away.[62]

At the national level, the Concordancia did not result in efforts to institutionalize a new electoral project, either between conservatives and antipersonalists or within the conservative PDN alliance itself. Rather, conservative leaders focused on maintaining the delicate equilibrium between regional elites that had been forged after the 1930 coup. Maintaining the lineaments of the new "statist bargain" took priority over long-term efforts to find new bases of electoral unity between members of a fractious conservative movement. As the historian Richard J. Walter has noted, the conservative strategy was predicated on preventing underlying sources of regional tension from coming to the fore and undermining the regime's stability:

> The problem resided in part in the fact that Buenos Aires conservatives felt that their opinions and positions should prevail in any alliance that they might join, by virtue of the superiority of their resources and the importance of their province in national affairs. This assumption frequently clashed with the positions of other important members of the conservative coalition, particularly Córdoba and Mendoza, who openly voiced their suspicion and hostility toward the aspirations of Buenos Aires conservatives (an attitude that was frequently reciprocated). The leaders of the conservative coalition were sensitive to these problems; because of this, most political arrangements were put together on the basis of vague federal plans that respected the individuality and autonomy of each participating member. They allowed each provincial party to conserve its particular characteristics and, in great measure, to pursue its own political paths. But they did little to provide the type of leadership and unity required to establish a lasting and cohesive national organization.[63]

This strategy, while important to the Concordancia's internal stability, would prove costly in the long run. The Concordancia's leaders had put significant transformations of the Argentine economy in motion. In response to the Great Depression, they launched Argentina's first import-substitution industrialization program, greatly expanded the role of the state in economic affairs, and presided over a period of significant economic expansion.[64] Conservative leaders did little, however, to harness the social changes put in motion by these policies for a national electoral project. No efforts were made to incorporate the expanding local bourgeoisie benefiting from the regime's industrial policies into the conservative political machinery. No efforts were made to capture the growing and politically unclaimed migrants who were pouring into the country's urban areas in search of economic opportunity. Demobilization, and the regional allocation of the fruits of state control, took precedence over the building of conservative institutions in political society.

The Rise of Peronism and the Conservative Electoral Diaspora

The nacionalista movement that gathered steam in the 1920s emerged initially as an elitist and clericalist movement. It provided an ideological alternative to the secular "liberalism" that had dominated conservative politics for decades.[65] The 1930 coup coalition against Hipólito Yrigoyen included members of the antiliberal nacionalista movement. One of them was José F. Uriburu, the coup's military leader and first president after Yrigoyen's ouster. The ideological agendas of the movement's leaders blended traditional currents of local conservatism with corporatist models imported from European fascism. But their intellectual roots were deeply set in the Hispanic, clericalist, and antiliberal soil of conservative thought that prevailed in the interior provinces of Argentina. In fact, several nacionalista leaders were actually prominent members of the Argentine interior's social elite and had organized the failed 1916 Partido Demócrata Progresista. Uriburu himself had been involved in that effort. He descended from a prominent family from the northwestern province of Tucumán and was the nephew of an Argentine president during the 1880–1916 oligarchic regime.[66] The nacionalista leaders involved in the coup of 1930 were apostates of the liberal Generation of 1880. They reproached the liberal leadership for failing to deal with the popular pressures of mass politics.

Shortly after taking office in 1930, President Uriburu presented a plan for the corporatist transformation of Argentina's polity and economy. His design was thwarted by a liberal counteroffensive within the new regime's coalition. Uriburu stepped down from the presidency in 1931. Juan B.

Justo, a military officer linked to liberal sectors, was inaugurated as president and swept all nacionalista designs from the elite's new political order.

During the period of rule by the Concordancia, however, *nacionalismo*'s influence spread. Prominent members of the conservative establishment embraced the nacionalista ideology, even in the liberal bastion of Buenos Aires province. Manuel Fresco, the conservative governor of Buenos Aires, integrated it into his program of government. During this time, nacionalismo also extended beyond its original elite boundaries. By the mid 1930s, it was more than an ideological alternative within the conservative movement. Its influence extended to virtually all parts of the political spectrum. Strong nacionalista currents emerged in the UCR during these years. They also spread throughout the armed forces, and by the early 1940s, they provided the glue that united a disparate array of opponents to the conservative regime. In 1943, a coup led by a group of nacionalista army colonels, among whose leaders was Colonel Juan Domingo Perón, overthrew the Concordancia-led government, and put an end to the last period of civilian conservative rule in twentieth-century Argentina.

The 1946 presidential elections, which inaugurated nine years of Peronist government, led to the virtual obliteration of conservatism as a national political force. The reasons for this development were twofold. In the first instance, the delegitimation suffered by conservative forces from their thirteen years of fraudulent political rule hindered their ability to present themselves as an electoral alternative to Perón's candidacy. The main anti-Peronist ticket, the Unión Democrática, was led by the UCR. Key conservative parties, such as the Buenos Aires Conservative Party, were not permitted to join in the alliance. Conservative fragmentation thus permitted radicalism to seize the leadership of the anti-Peronist movement.

The greatest blow to Argentine conservatism came, however, from the absorption of much of its mass base by the emergent Peronist movement. Throughout the country, Perón succeeded in recruiting local conservative leaders into his electoral alliance, both from the top leadership as well as from the cadres of local party hacks who controlled electoral machinery in rural areas and small towns.[67]

In the 1946 election, Perón forged the key pillars of his national coalition. In large urban areas, he mobilized the unincorporated working class as the primary constituency of his new political movement. Throughout the interior, and in towns and rural areas of the Pampas region, he captured the votes of town residents and the rural poor, many of which had been controlled by local conservative electoral machines.[68]

The ideological glue that held this disparate coalition together was nacionalismo. Its populist and corporatist variants attracted urban working-class support for Perón's candidacy. Perón's nacionalista roots were also, however, instrumental in attracting conservative leaders into the Peronist ranks. To elites from the interior, Peronism offered nationalist and protec-tionist economic policies that promised economic growth for their back-ward regions. They were also attracted by Perón's apparent adherence to many of the traditional and antiliberal ideological tenets of the na-cionalista movement, and to the potential they saw in Peronism for con-trolling popular mobilization. These factors were instrumental in splitting conservative loyalties and sparking the exodus of conservative votes to-ward the Peronist coalition.

In the national elections of 1946, the Peronist coalition obtained 52.4 percent of the vote, against 42.5 percent for the radical-led Unión Demo-crática. The smattering of conservative votes obtained nationally was less than 2 percent.[69] The rise of Peronism crystallized Argentine politics into a Peronist–anti-Peronist bipolarity. From the mid 1940s to the 1980s, the main anti-Peronist electoral vehicle was the UCR. With this development, the surviving remnants of conservatism retreated to their bases in the provinces. In some areas, most notably the city of Buenos Aires and the key provinces of Buenos Aires and Córdoba, conservative party organiza-tion virtually disappeared.

With the rise of Peronism, the fragmented conservative movement now faced two mass parties with nationwide organization. The electoral net-works of the Radical and Peronist parties covered the nation. Yet it was not merely the possession of vast electoral organization that these two movements had in common. The logic underlying their regional coalition building was nearly identical, in spite of the ideological differences that separated them. Both parties were in reality national umbrella organiza-tions, which harbored very different regionally based social coalitions. Their success in bringing these disparate social coalitions together was made possible by the regional division of Argentina's upper classes. It also compounded the political isolation of the powerful Buenos Aires upper classes, which saw potential allies in the interior absorbed by the Radical and Peronist movements.

The Effect on Conservative Alignments of Class and Regionalism in the Radical and Peronist Coalitions

In contrast to conservatism, both Radicalism and Peronism bridged re-gional differences and built national electoral alliances. The key to their success lay in the common antagonism of lower strata in and around the

Buenos Aires region and upper strata in the interior provinces toward those who sat at the top of the nation's social hierarchy: the Buenos Aires upper classes. The national, multiclass, and internally conflictual coalitions forged by both Radicalism and Peronism were held together by this common antagonism.

The Radical and Peronist success at national organization essentially meant bringing two very disparate social coalitions under one organizational umbrella. For the UCR of the 1910s and 1920s, it meant linking sophisticated urban party networks in the metropolitan regions with more traditional patrimonial networks in the interior, "where elections were still largely a matter of winning the support of the local *hacendado,* who could browbeat the peasants into voting whichever way he wished."[70] This represented a major feat of political engineering, but it also created a major and enduring source of internal tension. Conflict within the UCR has been strongly influenced by regional tensions, and even today Left-Right cleavages correspond strikingly to regional divisions.[71] During the early twentieth century, opposition to Buenos Aires dominance within the party led to its fragmentation in the interior.[72] The antipersonalist movement that arose in opposition to Yrigoyen had its strongest support in the interior provinces, from which most of its leaders were drawn. Peter Smith, writing about the UCR's troubled evolution during this century, highlights the regional aspect to its internal conflicts:

> First, and primarily, it was a regional conflict between Buenos Aires — both city and province, where Yrigoyen had most thoroughly developed his political machine — and the rest of the country. The lines of this division, pitting the coast against the interior, are strongly reminiscent of the nineteenth-century struggle between the unitarians and federalists. The issues appear to have changed, now being more political than economic, but the roots of regional antagonism continued to run deep. In a sense, the Radical movement failed as a party because it failed to overcome this fundamental and historic cleavage in Argentine society.[73]

A similar duality has characterized Peronism. The previous section of this chapter discussed the Peronist formula for national coalition building in the presidential election of 1946. An interprovincial statistical study of the Peronist vote in the 1973 elections by the sociologist Manuel Mora y Araujo revealed the continuity of this duality in the party's social base through subsequent decades. Mora y Araujo discovered an interesting paradox. In spite of the overwhelming support the urban working classes gave Peronism, there was a strong negative correlation between the Peronist vote and the economically advanced regions of the country where the urban proletariat was concentrated. The less developed the region, and thus the smaller the size of the industrial proletariat, the higher the Peronist vote. Peronism won, in fact, in regions with negligible proletarian populations. It lost in regions with large proletarian concentrations. To Mora y Araujo, this paradox was explicable in terms of the fundamental duality of the Peronist movement — a duality rooted in the regional duality of Argentina as a nation.

In the most advanced urbanized parts of the country, such as Buenos Aires and the cities of Rosario and Córdoba, Peronism was indeed an overwhelmingly proletarian movement. In fact, it was so proletarian that it exhibited one-class tendencies. Middle- and upper-class voters, apprehensive of Peronist working-class mobilization in these regions, gave their support to anti-Peronist parties. This explained the negative correlations at the aggregate level between economically advanced regions and the Peronist vote. In the underdeveloped regions in the interior, however, the Peronist coalitions were larger and more heterogeneous. While mobilizing the overwhelming support of the urban and rural lower social strata, these parties were multiclass, and in several provinces, they commanded strong upper-class support.[74] This led Mora y Araujo to assert that "Argentina is marked by an important structural divide, with acute inequalities on each side of this divide. These two Argentinas, one relatively modern, the other essentially underdeveloped, seem to generate two different political phenomena within the very movement that today governs and is majoritarian. One of the most surprising characteristics of this movement is its capacity to bring together under one political coalition such disparate social sectors."[75]

For both Peronism and Radicalism, this unity was forged on the basis of opposition to the Buenos Aires upper classes, which sat at the pinnacle of the national social structure. The Radical middle class and the Peronist proletariat in metropolitan areas both mobilized on the basis of opposition to the financial and landholding "oligarchies" of the Buenos Aires region. The same was true of the economic elites of the interior, who could be mobilized into multiclass alliances against the Buenos Aires upper classes under the banners of federalism and populism. By skillfully exploiting class cleavages in the major metropolitan regions and regional cleavages in the interior provinces, each of these movements was able to unify its disparate coalition under a common institutional umbrella.

The electoral fortunes of Argentine conservatism cannot be divorced from the dual nature of its most important electoral opponents. The effect of this on conservatism was double-edged: on the one hand it undermined the basis for unification of its national core constituency. The initial impulse toward such unification should have been a shared fear of the Radical and Peronist threat among the upper strata of the coast and the interior provinces. But the reality of regional duality created a situation of *threat duality* for the Argentine upper classes. Just as the UCR had meant different things to different regional elites in the 1920s, the meaning of Peronism for the Buenos Aires upper classes was quite different from its meaning to the upper classes of the interior. For the upper classes of Buenos Aires, Peronism constituted a clear working-class threat. To upper classes in the interior, lacking a proletariat in their own regions, and anxious for a state sympathetic to the development of the domestic market, the class threat from Peronism was less clear-cut. For emerging industrial interests, it provided a vehicle for pushing for a nationalist economic agenda. In many cases, traditional social elites also saw it as a convenient popular vehicle with which to consolidate their power locally.

Conservatives were thus deprived of a major catalyst of national core-constituency unity. Regional duality begat threat duality, and the unifying effect of a national class-based menace did not emerge. Faced with local class threats, Buenos Aires conservative leaders found it difficult to mobilize their counterparts in the interior against those threats, whether they came from Peronism's proletariat or from the Radical middle class. By dichotomizing the social threat to Argentina's elite, regional duality ensured that class cleavages at the national level would fail to overwhelm regional cleavages as the primary determinants of conservative political alignment.

"Federalists" and "Liberals":
Argentine Conservatism after 1955

After the overthrow of Juan Perón in 1955, Argentina entered a tumultuous period of alternating elected and authoritarian governments. The period was marked by military dominance over the political process and the 1955–73 electoral proscription of Peronism, the country's majoritarian political force.

Conservative political action during this period was divided into two fronts: "federalist" and "liberal." These were ideological labels, but they corresponded to the prevailing division between the interior and Buenos Aires. In the interior provinces, through local party organization, federalists focused on securing provincial bases of power, as well as on pragmatically shifting their support between Peronist, anti-Peronist, and military contenders in the national arena depending on local exigencies. The provincial parties of the interior often sought to gain influence in national affairs through the formation of national confederations. The most important of these during the 1970s and 1980s was the Fuerza Federalista Popular (FUFEPO), which included most of the interior's conservative parties. However, without the power of a Buenos Aires conservative party, these confederations by themselves added up to little more than the sum of local provincial organizations. Their ability to become national players depended on their success in influencing the political force in control of the national state, whether civilian or military. Under civilian governments, this often involved trading local pre-electoral support for high-level cabinet positions in the national government or ambassadorial appointments (beyond the usual pork-barrel benefits to provincial interests that they would extract in exchange for that support). Under military governments, a similar dynamic would take place, except that in these cases support for the national government often involved appointment to provincial gubernatorial positions that might not have been as accessible under democratic conditions.

In the Buenos Aires region, where there were no counterparts to the myriad conservative provincial parties of the interior, conservative political action became divorced from party politics altogether. No conservative parties existed in either Buenos Aires province or the capital city of Buenos Aires that were capable, by virtue of their electoral strength, of playing a significant role in the political process. This did not, however, mean the absence of conservative political leadership. It only meant that the arenas in which this leadership would appear would not, as a rule, be those of political society.

The conservative political leadership that emerged in Buenos Aires was technocratic. Its preferred arenas of political action were the institutions of the state. It used a claim to technical expertise, particularly in economic matters, and an array of contacts with circles of influence in the social elite and the armed forces, as its most important political currency. It tended to disdain the practice of mass mobilization and as a rule avoided party politics.[76]

Yet in spite of this aversion to *la política,* this cadre of technocrats were in every sense professional politicians. They in many ways resembled the earliest professional politicians, who, as Max Weber observed, "arose first in the service of a prince" and "unlike the charismatic leader, [did not wish] to be lords themselves, but . . . entered the *service* of political lords."[77] The most important "political lords" of this group of leaders were senior officers in the armed forces. However, the relationship between them was more one of alliance than of subservience. The armed forces provided a vital political resource for conservative political leaders to gain access to the institutions of executive power, whether the state was under the control of an elected civilian government or directly controlled by the military. As such, competition between members of the technocratic elite involved an intricate game of alliance building and lobbying with key individuals and internal factions in the military institution.[78] Factions were courted, individual contacts nurtured, position papers circulated, and internal conflicts monitored, as different members of the technocratic elite sought to position themselves as favorably as possible for impending allocations of state power by the military institution.

The social constituencies of these political leaders were the most important social sectors of the Buenos Aires region: the agricultural *gran burguesía* of the Pampas region, the larger and more transnationalized sectors of industry, and the most important sectors of banking and finance. It was this relationship, rather than agreement on ideological grounds, that most visibly identified this technocracy as a political group. They were known collectively as the "liberal" technocracy, but this common ideological label often masked important differences over economic models and policy measures to be pursued. What the liberal technocrats had in common were the socioeconomic forces whose support they courted.

As the most ambitious of party politicians, the liberals competed relentlessly with one another for the attentions of influential economic groups. They sat on the boards of major industrial and financial concerns, established economic think tanks and consulting organizations, published editorials in the most important conservative and business newspapers, and spoke regularly before business chambers and economic organizations. For a powerful regional upper class divorced from any real representation in the party arena, political representation resided in the liberal technocratic elite. It negotiated on behalf of its constituencies with the armed forces, staffed the highest economic policy-making institutions, and sought to reconcile the conflicting demands of different sectors of its social constituencies while in power.

As a group of political leaders, the liberal technocratic elite were remarkably successful in capturing political power. Save for the three-year interregnum of the government of Arturo Illía between 1963 and 1966, liberal technocrats served in the top economic policy-making institutions of every civilian and military government between 1955 and 1983. The

Revolución Libertadora that overthrew Perón in 1955 and ruled until 1958 served as the first major training ground for this technocratic elite. Alvaro Alsogaray, Roberto Alemann, José Alfredo Martinez de Hoz, and Adalbert Krieger Vasena, all future economy ministers in the 1958–83 period, cut their political teeth as senior economic policy makers in that government. Alsogaray would go on to serve as economy minister in the elected government of Arturo Frondizi in 1959, and returned as economy minister in the military-controlled government of President José María Guido in 1962. Alemann also served as economy minister to Frondizi and was General Leopoldo Galtieri's economy minister in 1982. Krieger Vasena served as economy minister to the military government of Juan Carlos Onganía between 1967 and 1969, and Martinez de Hoz became "super-minister" of the economy under the presidency of General Roberto Videla between 1976 and 1979.

In spite of the different structures of their political organization, the "federalist" forces in the interior, and their "liberal" counterparts in Buenos Aires shared a similar approach to gaining influence in national affairs. For both sets of actors, national influence was predicated on gaining access to a state controlled by other political forces. Occasionally, attempts were made to organize national electoral alliances for presidential elections, but these met with meager results. In 1963, a conservative alliance led by retired General Eugenio Aramburu, president during the period known as the Revolución Libertadora, gathered only 7.5 percent of the national vote. In the March 1973 elections, Alvaro Alsogaray's Nueva Fuerza, a liberal-led alliance, mobilized an embarrassing 2 percent of the vote. Far more successful in that election was a federalist alliance, composed primarily of interior provincial parties, called the Alianza Popular Federalista. Led by Francisco Manrique, a popular journalist who had served as minister of social welfare under the military government of General Alejandro Lanusse prior to the 1973 elections, the federalist alliance mobilized nearly 15 percent of the vote, as opposed to 21 percent won by the radical ticket.[79] This was the highest percentage ever received by a national conservative ticket in fair and open presidential elections since the advent of mass politics.

The appendix at the end of this chapter provides a list of the more important parties of Argentine conservatism between 1955 and 1976. This list covers the period after Perón's overthrow up to the military regime inaugurated in 1976. It is by no means intended to be exhaustive. Only those parties that have exhibited some continuity through much of this period, or that have played a discernible political role, are included.[80]

Conclusion

This chapter has identified regional cleavage as the most important historical variable shaping conservative electoral alignments in Argentina. Rooted in a basic incompatibility between the economies of the prosperous coastal Pampas region and the less-developed interior provinces, regional cleavage had a pronounced effect on conservative core-constituency dynamics. It made regional conflict the driving force of elite political alignments during the oligarchic period, and repeatedly undermined the development of national-level upper-class coalitions against electoral challenges from middle- and lower-class-based parties. Institutionally, it hindered the emergence national party competition prior to the advent of mass politics and bequeathed a legacy of fragmentation that marked conservative organization throughout the twentieth century. Conservative electoral organization, where it existed, was thus concentrated at the provincial level. National conservative responses to the challenges of mass politics became increasingly dependent upon the coercive and administrative power of the state.

This chapter has attempted a systematic examination of the impact of regionalism on the development of a vital sociopolitical force in Argentina. It may be hoped that it will spark some interest in one of the most understudied dimensions of Argentine politics. In part, the neglect of the regional question in Argentina is due to a general underappreciation of the impact of the interior on the development of Argentine politics by a scholarly community, both Argentine and foreign, more drawn to the pivotal importance of its metropolitan region. Yet a fixation on Buenos Aires politics is not the only factor at work here. The scholarship on Argentina has also fallen prey to a general underestimation of the importance of regionalism as a structural variable in the politics of Latin America. Contemporary literature on Latin American suffers from a particularly strong aversion to systematic analysis of the impact of regionalism on national political development. Yet renewed theoretical attention to the subject could cast considerable new light on the evolution of Latin American institutions, the growth of the state, the development of party competition, and patterns of ideological conflict. The case study provided in this chapter has attempted to shed light on how regional dynamics have influenced institutional development in earlier periods of Argentine history. As more recent periods of conservative party politics are addressed in the following chapters, we shall see how they have continued to be a powerful factor in the evolution of Argentine conservatism.

APPENDIX: ARGENTINE CONSERVATIVE PARTIES, 1955–1989

Parties of Conservative Origin

Partido Autonomista de Corrientes (Corrientes)
Partido Liberal de Corrientes (Corrientes)
Unión Provincial de Salta (Salta)
Partido Demócrata de Córdoba (Córdoba)
Partido Demócrata de Mendoza (Mendoza)
Partido Demócrata (City of Buenos Aires)
Partido Demócrata Liberal de San Luis (San Luis)
Defensa Provincial Bandera Blanca de Tucumán (Tucumán)
Movimiento Popular Provincial de San Luis (San Luis)
Partido Demócrata Progresista (Santa Fe)

All parties listed here save Defensa Provincial Bandera Blanca de Tucumán, and the Movimiento Popular Provincial de San Luis, have their origins in the pre-1916 period. The Tucumán party was the result of local conservative division in the 1920s. The Movimiento Popular Provincial de San Luis was founded in the early 1970s. The Partido Demócrata Progresista, which originated in Lisandro de la Torre's 1914 attempt to build a national conservative party, is actually officially registered as a national party, and has some presence outside the province of Santa Fe, especially in the city of Buenos Aires. Its primary base, however, is Santa Fe province.

Parties of Radical Origin

Partido Acción Chubutense (Chubut)
Partido Bloquista de San Juan (San Juan)
Movimiento Popular Jujeño (Jujuy)
Movimiento Federalista Pampeano (La Pampa)
Vanguardia Federal (Tucumán)
Movimiento Línea Popular (Santa Fe)

The Partido Acción Chubutense, from the country's Patagonian region, resulted from defections by local Radical leaders from the UCR in the 1960s, following an attempted intervention by the Radical-controlled federal government. The Partido Bloquista de San Juan was founded by anti-

Yrigoyenist UCR members in the early 1920s. The Movimiento Popular Jujeño, the Movimiento Federalista Pampeano, Vanguardia Federal, and Movimiento Línea Popular were founded by former provincial governors originally elected to office as candidates of Frondizi's Unión Cívica Radical Intransigente.

Parties of Peronist Origin

Movimiento Popular Neuquino (Neuquén)

Inclusion of the Movimiento Popular Neuquino (MPN) among the parties of Argentine conservatism may be somewhat controversial. It was created after the proscription of Peronism in the 1950s as a local electoral vehicle for the nationally banned Peronist movement. Its Peronist origins and its independent stand regarding alliances with conservative provincial parties have therefore generally led to its exclusion by analysts from parties usually grouped as "conservative."[81] However, given the conservative origins of much of the Peronist movement in the interior, and the fact that since its founding, the MPN has jealously defended its autonomy from efforts to reincorporate it into the Peronist movement, its Peronist origins should not disqualify it from being classified among the country's "conservative" provincial parties. In addition, over the years, the MPN has remained the province's strongest party, and it has become the most important electoral vehicle for the province's economic elite against the Peronist Party and the UCR. Until 1995 the MPN had never allied itself with Peronism either in national or local elections. Finally, its ideological agenda of provincial autonomy and regional development, and its pragmatic strategies vis-á-vis the national government, have not differed significantly from those of its counterpart provincial parties in the Federalist-conservative movement, particularly those in the country's southern region.[82]

Other Provincial Parties

Partido Renovador de Salta (Salta)
Partido Provincial Rionegrino (Rio Negro)
Fuerza Republicana (Tucumán)
Movimiento de Unidad Chaqueña (Chaco)
Unión Popular Fueguina (Tierra del Fuego)
Partido Cívico Independiente (Buenos Aires)

The Partido Provincial Rionegrino, the Partido Renovador de Salta, and Fuerza Republicana of Tucuman, were founded by former military governors of their provinces. The first was established in 1972 by General Roberto Requeijo, who had governed the province of Rio Negro between 1970 and 1972. The second was founded in 1983 by Navy Captain Roberto Ulloa, who governed Salta province during the 1976–83 military regime. Fuerza Republicana was founded in the mid 1980s by General Antonio Bussi, also military governor of the province during the 1976–83 military regime. The Partido Cívico Independiente was founded by Alvaro Alsogaray in 1957 and existed on and off until the mid 1960s. It had official recognition as a national party, but its real presence was in Buenos Aires.

National Conservative Parties and Electoral Alliances

Partido Federal
Fuerza Federalista Popular (FUFEPO)
Concentración Demócrata
Movimiento para la Nueva Mayoría
Unión del Centro Democrático
1958 elections: Federación Partidos de Centro
1963 elections: Unión del Pueblo Argentino (UDELPA)
1973 elections: Nueva Fuerza
                Alianza Popular Federalista
1983 elections: Alianza Federal
1989 elections: Alianza de Centro
                Confederación Federalista Independiente

The Partido Federal was a federalist party based in Buenos Aires, created in 1972 by Francisco Manrique. In national and presidential elections, it tended to form alliances with federalist parties in the interior. Fuerza Federalista Popular and the Movimiento para la Nueva Mayoría were two federations of existing provincial provinces from the interior. The first was active during the 1960s, 1970s, and early 1980s. Nueva Mayoría was created in 1986 by José Romero Feris, then governor of Corrientes province, in a bid to unite the nation's provincial parties for national congressional elections and presidential elections. It also sought to make the federalist parties of the interior the axis of such a movement, rather than the Buenos Aires–based liberal parties led by the Unión del Centro Democrático. Concentración Demócrata was a federation of the largely liberal provincial parties throughout the country labeled "Demó-crata." The Unión del Centro Democrático was founded by the veteran Buenos Aires liberal leader Alvaro Alsogaray. Previously, Alsogaray had also been the founder and leader of two other liberal parties, the Partido Cívico Independiente and Nueva Fuerza. In 1973 and 1989, two national conservative alliances, one federal and one liberal, competed against each other in the presidential elections.

Chapter Three

Authoritarian Crafting of Conservative Democracies:

The Failed Transition in Argentina, 1979–1982

It will be necessary to fill the political vacuum that appeared after 1945, when conservative forces ceased acting in an orderly manner and created a void that had to be filled by the armed forces.

GENERAL ALBANO HARGUINDEGUY,
minister of the interior, 1976–81

The endurance of an authoritarian regime's legacies is often a function of its success at political engineering. Nothing denotes failure more strongly for such a regime than to permit a return of the political status quo ante. In different ways, the authoritarian rulers of Spain, Brazil, and Chile succeeded in their political engineering and left a civilian polity in place that differed substantially from the one they had overthrown. Long periods of authoritarian rule, coupled with successful economic strategies, produced changes in these countries' social structures that altered the bases of national political coalitions and created new constituencies for the authoritarian project. The political impact of these changes was made effective by the redesign of political institutions or the creation of pro-official electoral movements.[1]

In Chile and Spain, the combined effects of repression and economic change transformed the social landscape. When events forced a transition to democracy, regime leaders were supported by important social sectors that owed their existence to their economic strategies. This gave government elites considerable influence over the transition process. It permitted state elites to control the agendas of the transition, to shape the institutional context of the subsequent democratic regimes, and to sponsor the formation of civilian electoral movements committed to continuing their policies.[2]

In Brazil, the 1964–85 military regime's leaders were realistic from the outset about an eventual return to democratic rule.[3] To prepare for that event, they sought to use their tenure in office to recast the structure of party competition. The Brazilian transition was long in the making. It had, from its origins, a plan (if imperfectly executed) for recasting the national electoral politics. State elites fostered the creation of a pro-official party, the Partido Democratico Social, that aimed to unify the regionally and organizationally fragmented electoral Right. They also initially passed laws inhibiting the multiplication of parties and forcing the coalescence of opposition into one organization. These measures were taken with a view to creating a "stabilizing" and "moderating" bipolar pattern of political competition to replace the chaotic and ideologically polarizing multiparty system of the pre-1964 period.[4]

The attempts at political engineering by these regimes were not the whims or fancies of isolated military leaders. They had their determinants in the evolution of social conflict in their countries. All of these regimes were conservative and came to power following conflictual periods of democratic rule. Their key bases of support were in the upper social strata, and they owed their very existence to the failure of those strata to counter the mobilization of popular movements in the electoral arena. The failure of civilian conservative leadership had prompted the emergence of authoritarian regimes, and authoritarian political engineering sought to rectify the structural causes of that failure. The goal was to use the power of the state to create new institutional bases for conservative rule. At different moments, and in different ways, each of these regimes succeeded in creating more propitious conditions for conservative electoral survival after the return to democratic politics. Each played a major role in shaping the rules and procedures that governed the transition process. Each also ensured that its closest supporters would be well protected and represented in the postauthoritarian regime. This was accomplished through such devices as the promulgation of new constitutions, the rigging of electoral laws, the malapportionment of legislative seats, the institution of indirect elections or "appointed" senate seats, the proscription of leftist parties, and the use of state patronage to favor supporters of the regime in founding elections.[5] One of the key legacies of each of these regimes was, therefore, to make politics safer for conservative leaders and their core constituencies once the return to mass electoral competition could not be forestalled.

This chapter looks at the failure to engineer such a conservative transition of the military regime that ruled Argentina between 1976 and 1983.

No less than their counterparts in other countries, the military leaders of Argentina's Proceso de Reorganización Nacional, as they named their regime,[6] also sought to refashion national coalitions and institutions. They viewed their seizure of power as a result of the failure by civilian leaders to build mass support for a conservative electoral movement. In 1979, following the example of their Brazilian counterparts, they initiated a transition designed to return civilian elites to power gradually, and to use state power to bequeath the "inheritance of the Proceso" to a new mass conservative party.

The conservative transition failed in Argentina because of deep conflicts within its two main protagonists: the military and the regionally fragmented conservative political leadership. As a result, Argentine conservative party development would have to proceed without the benefits of authoritarian political engineering. This chapter analyzes the failed conservative transition of 1979–82 through the lens of the military regime's relationship with its civilian interlocutors in the Argentine conservative movement. In contrast to most analyses, which situate the transition period in the brief and chaotic interlude between the June 1982 military defeat in the Falklands and the October 1983 elections, this chapter takes a much longer view.[7] It places the start of the transition in mid 1979, when the subject of a transfer to civilian rule was first put on the agenda by the military regime and negotiations were initiated with key civilian political leaders.[8]

In order to understand the evolution of Argentine conservatism after the 1983 democratic transition, we need to understand how its tangled relationship to the rise and fall of the Proceso fundamentally altered the structure of opportunities that had guided conservative political action over the previous half-century. The Proceso was a critical juncture in the historical evolution of Argentine conservatism. It was a dramatic attempt to engineer a solution to the conservative electoral dilemma under military auspices. Its collapse threw the tensions and contradictions of the conservative civil-military alliance into sharp relief and made clear to important sectors of the conservative leadership that the political basis for that alliance no longer existed. It was this rupture that made the search for autonomous forms of political organization necessary after 1983.

The 1976 Coup

The military officers who came to power on March 24, 1976, sought to change Argentine society forever by radically transforming the Argentine polity and economy. There were many competing visions within the military of what the new Argentina would look like. In the early years, however, the military leadership succeeded in overcoming these divisions by framing its objectives, not in terms of the new institutions it sought to create, but in terms of those it sought to eradicate. It is helpful here to bear in mind a point made by Alfred Stepan:

> In any regime, but especially in a BA [bureaucratic-authoritarian] regime, the capacity to lead the regime's political allies depends on the degree to which the regime has both "defensive" and "offensive" projects that potential allies consider to be feasible, crucial for the preservation and advancement of their own interests, and dependent on authoritarian power for their execution. Since coercion is a particularly important part of the regime's power, the degree of internal institutional cohesion of the repressive apparatus is also a key variable.[9]

The internal institutional cohesion of the military was forged around "defensive" objectives, and the key defensive objective of the regime was simple: to eradicate the legacies of "populism" from Argentina's social and political life. Armed subversion, economic inefficiency, class conflict, political demagoguery — all were products of the same populist contamination that had eroded civilian authority and compelled the military to seize power. In the military view, all civilian sectors of society were infected: business elites absorbed in zero-sum sectoral struggles, labor leaders bent on destabilization for political profit, intellectuals committed to subverting national values. These and similar indictments structured military interpretations of Argentina's political decline.[10]

The military's notion of "populism" was simple. It was democracy without conservatism. It was not only the cause of immediate problems but also the effect of a prior condition. "Populism" was what happened to democratic societies lacking the "equilibrating effect" of a conservative mass party. It led to party competition that widened class divisions rather than closed them, that induced party leaders to mobilize society on the basis of social conflict rather than multiclass harmony, and that led to politics based on the quest for sectoral gain rather than the collective good. Populism in Argentina was a consequence of conservative abdication in the age of democratic politics. In the words of one military analyst:

> Unfortunately, the exhaustion of the [Project of 1880] took place at a moment when tutelary leadership was vitally needed to absorb the eruption of the masses into Argentine political life. It was replaced by popu-

list demagoguery and the progressive evolution to collective tendencies that led the country to the precipitous collapse of 1973–76. During this long and dark period, political leaders . . . lacked the necessary serenity and responsibility to reformulate new political projects and enterprises capable of maintaining the momentum that carried the country to its past splendor.[11]

The military's most powerful indictments were reserved for the nation's professional politicians. Conservatives, Radicals, and Peronists shared equally in the failure to articulate a "national project" capable of forging national unity. No party or political current had risen above the fractiousness and partisan struggle of the previous turbulent decades of democratic politics. Demagoguery, not political leadership, had been the legacy of Argentina's political elite.

One of the Proceso's defensive objectives was thus to banish the existing party leadership from Argentine political life. What it would be replaced with was left unsaid in the Proceso's early years. No "offensive" plans for constructing a new political order were discussed. There was a civil war on: the task was not to build a new society, but to destroy the old one. Hostility to the political status quo was the glue that held the military together in the regime's early years, and there was little desire to undermine that unity with open discussion about what would replace the old order once it had been dismantled. Furthermore, the armed forces were so united on the subject of their defensive objectives that they could be implemented by the military alone. There would be no need in the early years of the Proceso to rely on civilian allies.

The coup of March 24, 1976, was thus not a merely a coup against the government of Isabel Perón. It was a coup against Argentine political and civil society. Upon displacing the Peronist Partido Justicialista from power, the military set out to govern to the almost complete exclusion of civilians. For the first time in Argentine history, the armed forces assumed complete control of the machinery of government. State power was divided equally among the army, navy, and air force; roughly one-third of cabinet posts and provincial governments were assigned to each branch, and territorial control of the country was also assigned equally in thirds to each of the armed services.[12]

The effect of these measures was to insulate the military government from societal pressure during its first years in office. This permitted it to carry out its "dirty war" against leftist and popular opposition free from public scrutiny, and to exclude the civilian political leadership from key circles of influence during that period. It also permitted it to shield its economic policy-making team from growing public opposition to its free-market economic reform program. This extended even to many of the regime's supporters in the business community, who eventually found themselves at odds with its economic policies, but found their traditional channels of access to state power closed. As David Pion-Berlin has noted, during the 1976–81 government of General Jorge Rafaél Videla,

> virtually every socio-economic sector of Argentine society, from la-borers and small shop owners to large industrialists and agriculturalists, opposed the economic policies . . . [but] by denying the dominant classes their traditional access to state policy-making circles (i.e. by limiting personal contact with the military elite), Videla created a pressure-free environment which allowed the government to function as if special interests didn't matter . . . the regime's very isolation from society con-tributed to its stability.[13]

The New Military Government and the Conservative Leadership: Liberals In, Federalists Out

The military government dealt with the two currents of the conservative political leadership very differently. It turned to the liberal technocratic elite to implement economic policy, making this the significant exception to the ban on civilian influence on policy making. It remained aloof from the eager overtures of the federalist leadership.[14] As party leaders, they were members of the despised "traditional political class" and were not considered "valid interlocutors" by hard-line sectors of the military hier-archy. Furthermore, as conservative politicians, they were particularly associated by the military with the conservative legacy of political abdica-tion that had brought on the era of populist politics. They were thus consigned during the first phase of the Proceso to a political purgatory of sorts: excluded from decision-making arenas while the internal debates of the armed forces decided their eventual fate as political actors.

Liberal Technocrats and Economic Policy Making

The Economics Ministry was entrusted to a team of technocrats headed by José Alfredo Martinez de Hoz, a prominent member of the liberal technocracy who descended from an economically and politically influential family.[15] During his career, he had developed extensive ties within the agricultural and business communities and had served in senior economic policy-making positions in previous military governments.[16] Martinez de Hoz was selected from the pool of competing technocratic candidates after his economic plan had been reviewed and approved by the military hierarchy in the weeks preceding the 1976 coup.

During Martinez de Hoz's tenure, the Ministry of the Economy attained the status of a "superministry." It became the locus of decision making for a wide-ranging crusade to reduce inflation and expose the Argentine private sector to the rigors of the free market. However, while the design and implementation of the program was ceded to civilian technocrats, it was not autonomous from the military's own project of political transformation. Martinez de Hoz's success at gaining the military government's support hinged on his ability to present his program to the armed forces as a vital component of their mission to eradicate populism from Argentine society. The senior officer corps accepted liberal economic reform following an intensive lobbying campaign by Martinez de Hoz, both before and after the coup. During this campaign, Martinez de Hoz reportedly framed free-market economic reform in terms of its affinities with the military's defensive objectives. In this way, he was able to make the liberal technocracy's economic prescription converge with the military bureaucracy's political vision:

> In 1976, the economy was conceived of as a fundamental instrument, together with repression, to radically transform the social and political morphology. But in contrast to the dominant conceptions of the 1960s, the economy became a means and not an end in itself. The economic program of the armed forces was perceived as a means to "restore health to political life" and to unearth what, in their vision, fed the recurring emergence of populism and "black parliamentarism."[17]

The political convergence of the liberals' economic reform program with the military's defensive project insulated the technocrats in the Ministry of the Economy from societal pressures and gave them enormous power during the first years of the Proceso. It also, however, established the limits of that power. It tied the fate of economic reform to the continuity of military unity around defensive objectives. The technocrats who made economic policy were not insulated from politics. Quite the contrary. They were chin-deep in politics. As events in subsequent years were to reveal, the eventual reach of the reform program would be constrained by military conflicts and by the fundamentally political definition given their mission by the Proceso's uniformed leaders.[18]

The Federalists Spurned

The coup of 1976 was warmly greeted by the Argentine provincial party establishment. By the final year of Isabel Perón's chaotic government, all conservative parties had moved into opposition, and several conservative leaders had gone on record as endorsing her forcible removal from office. It was therefore no surprise that Argentine conservatives were unanimous in support of the coup once it took place.

On March 25, 1976, the day following the coup, two of the main federalist party confederations, the Fuerza Federalista Popular (FUFEPO) and the Movimiento Línea Popular (MOLIPO) issued a joint declaration of support for the Proceso. The document was signed by Horacio Guzmán, FUFEPO's president and caudillo from Jujuy province, and MOLIPO's president, Silvestre Begnis. Ironically, Begnis had just been ousted from his position as elected governor of Santa Fe province by the military authorities.

With this declaration, FUFEPO linked itself indissolubly to the Proceso's fate. The federalist leaders embarked upon a strategy of unwavering support, which, they hoped, would give them the national influence that their fragmented provincial bases had proved incapable of securing. From the start, therefore, federalists presented themselves to the military as civilian partners in government and co-architects in the recasting of the country's political institutions.

The federalist overtures were sympathetically received at the highest levels of the military regime. General Jorge Rafaél Videla, the newly appointed president, and his army chief of staff, General Roberto Viola, favored collaboration with supportive sectors of political society. In fact, personal contacts between Videla, Viola, and the civilian conservative leadership extended back to pre-coup days. They were reflected in the joint FUFEPO-MOLIPO declaration, which outlined a number of agreements on policy reached between the leaders of those organizations and Videla and Viola in the months preceding the overthrow of the Peronist government.[19]

Federalist ambitions for access to power were held in check, however, by powerful hard-line elements in the armed forces. To military hard-liners, many of whom had long-term political plans of their own, civilianization was a threat to the Proceso's mission of radical political transformation. Opening the doors to the traditional political elite threatened, not only the military's plan to purge that elite from Argentine political life, but also the military institution's monopoly on the design of a future post-Proceso order. To the more conciliatory leaders in charge of the military government, the unity of the armed forces was vital to their ability to govern. In their first years in office, Videla and Viola thus chose not to threaten that unity in the interests of their civilian supporters. For the time being, the federalists would not be brought in from the cold.

Denied access to power by a suspicious and disdainful military, the federalists pursued a strategy of unqualified support from without between 1976 and 1979. These "friends of the Proceso," as they publicly labeled themselves, publicly proclaimed their devotion to the military authorities and quietly kept up their contacts with their allies in the government. They hoped that in this way, time and loyalty would eventually work to shift the internal power balance in favor of Videla and Viola's *aperturista* position and permit them to breach the impenetrable walls of the militarized state. They never wavered as to their ultimate goals: to gain access to state power, serve as the civilian buttress of the regime, and eventually be designated the natural "inheritors of the Proceso" in a postauthoritarian order.

The price of this strategy, which they were more than willing to pay, was complete subservience to the military regime. In June 1979, over three years into the Proceso, the ongoing federalist strategy was tactfully analyzed by the influential conservative daily *La Nación*:

FUFEPO will limit itself, until 1981, to supporting the government's actions whenever they reflect the spirit of the Proceso, and to induce the government to reflect that spirit in regard to other actions that it has failed to carry out because they have escaped its attention. . . . It appears that there is no intention on the part of FUFEPO to address governmental errors incurred by commission. . . .

The general idea would seem to be that the current governmental authorities represent a phase of the Proceso that will end in 1981, when a presidential succession is to take place [from Videla to Viola]. Thenceforth the Proceso will generate conditions of greater permeability to the participation of political leaders supportive of the principles in effect since March 1976. . . . In the judgment of the federalists, 1981 will open a chapter in which it will be possible to bring to the Proceso the power of assembly that they are now attempting to consolidate. . . . As of 1981, FUFEPO will seek to crystallize its support in a context of greater responsibilities, shared by the military government with civilian currents of opinion that have identified themselves with the Proceso.[20]

FUFEPO's contribution to the national debate was thus limited to sig-
naling the regime's sins of omission — and only those resulting from unin-
tended oversights. Not all sectors of the federal-conservative movement
were, however, as supportive of the military regime during this period as
the FUFEPO-led sectors. Francisco Manrique, a politician who had mobilized 14 percent of the national vote for a federal coalition in the 1973
presidential elections, took a stand more distant from the regime.

In 1976, Manrique had been a strong supporter of the coup against
Isabel Perón. Two days before the coup, in the name of his party, the
Partido Federal, he had published a long statement in *La Nación* that
essentially announced its willingness to participate in an impending "great
transformation," whether carried out "via elections or via revolution."[21]
In the thinly veiled codes of civil-military communications, the message
was unambiguous. Manrique and his followers were placing themselves at
the service of the military regime that would come to power after a coup
that all observers knew was imminent. Manrique's vision of an immediate
postcoup order was one of military government with widespread civilian
participation, not unlike that of the Revolución Libertadora that had
overthrown Perón in 1955, which had been staffed at all levels by anti-
Peronist civilians. He also clearly hoped, given his prominence within the
conservative movement, to play a major role in such a regime. The military's turn to direct institutional rule, however, dashed those hopes.
Shortly thereafter, while publicly affirming his support for the Proceso,
Manrique became one of the most persistent critics of the monopolization
of power by the military.

Manrique became the regime's most irritating critic among its supporters. He remained visible as a commentator in the pages of the *Correo de
la Semana,* his weekly newspaper and the media organ of his political
party. From this forum, he provided criticisms and suggestions on political
events, always with the stated goal of "contributing to the success of the
Proceso."[22] Even this sympathetically critical position proved too disrup-
tive to the military establishment. In November 1977, following a number
of unfavorable editorials about the regime's progress, the military authorities ordered the *Correo de la Semana* shut down and prohibited its circulation throughout the country.[23] Manrique remained steadfast in his support for the regime, but in contrast to his counterparts in the federalist
movement, his support was qualified. In subsequent years, he repeatedly
labeled himself "a critical friend of the Proceso" — a choice of words that
made clear his separation from the "friends of the Proceso" in the federal-
conservative movement.

The Military Government Initiates the Transition

Given its isolation from society, the regime's stability hinged on the internal unity of the military. In the early phases of the Proceso, that unity was forged by the regime's defensive objectives against armed insurgency and populism. The outward stability of the regime masked important internal tensions and divisions, but its leaders managed in the early years to overcome these by stressing their shared objectives in the struggle against armed insurgency. By late 1977, however, the insurgent threat had dissipated. Without this unifying ingredient, discord within the military hierarchy over the direction of the Proceso began to cause internal instability. The division of the national government among the three armed services made this instability felt at all levels of government.[24] In 1978, military unity was temporarily reforged by the threat of war with Chile over control of the Beagle Channel Islands, south of Tierra del Fuego. The agglutinating effect of this conflict, which was settled by a last-minute papal mediation, was short-lived. In late 1978, an internal memorandum prepared for President Videla acknowledged the troubles besetting the military government:

> The presidency has entered into a process of deterioration. . . . Most political forces — unions, political parties, the Church, the mass media, industry, and sectors of agriculture — are evolving from critical positions to outright opposition to the government. International pressures are also coinciding with this internal opposition. In sum, the military process is facing a situation of isolation and growing opposition; it is supported only by a financial sector that is beginning to evidence symptoms of corruption and small elitist groups on the Center-Right. . . . Justification on the basis of success in the struggle against subversion is losing its effectiveness among the population, while at the same time the Beagle Channel conflict has not brought cohesion on the internal front or generated support within the population for the armed forces.[25]

The economic, military, and political dimensions of military rule could no longer be framed in terms of the regime's original defensive program. It had lost its unifying power. Furthermore, it was becoming increasingly difficult, given the centrifugal pressures on the military, for the armed forces to rule alone. The Proceso would have to reach out to society. In 1979, the military government decided to launch an offensive program of political engineering to crystallize civilian support and ensure the Proceso's continuity.

The Military Calls for a "Dialogue" with Society

In September 1979, the Junta de Comandantes approved a document in which the armed forces raised the issue of a transition from direct military rule for the first time since the 1976 coup. Entitled *Bases políticas para el proceso de reorganización nacional,* this gave the first hints of an offensive program to restructure the Argentine political order, but in itself offered little of substance. Its first two sections, "Bases doctrinarias" and "Bases programáticas," portrayed the government's long-term objectives in terms of Western and Christian values, national unity, and other political bromides that had saturated military discourse over the previous three years. However, its third section, "Bases instrumentales para la acción política," announced the government's intention to steer a transition to a political order where parties would be "essential institutions of the political system."[26] In order to do this, the document called for the creation of a Movimiento de Opinión Nacional that would mobilize around the political objectives of the Proceso and promote them in the postauthoritarian order.

The government also announced its intention to initiate a "dialogue" with all sectors of society that would be the chief instrument of "consultation and information" between the state and society in the transition. It would, within the strict "limits to dissent" established by the *Bases,* consolidate civilian support for the regime and lead to the development of a legal and political framework for the post-Proceso order.[27]

The *Bases* represented a compromise between the service branches and internal factions in the military. This was reflected in the vagueness of the objectives listed in the document, which provided no specifics on timetables or concrete mechanisms for the transition from direct military rule. The only points to emerge with any clarity were the shared concern of the armed forces about the regime's growing isolation, and the consequent need to seek support from civilian society. However, very shortly after the publication of the *Bases,* two competing military visions of the new strategy's ultimate objectives emerged.

To hard-liners in the military, the call in the *Bases* for a "dialogue" with civil and political society was little more than a device to stabilize a regime weakened by growing internal divisions. General Leopoldo Galtieri, a prominent hard-liner who was then the second-ranking officer in the army, described the dialogue as a means to generate "a movement of national opinion that will support the Proceso to the end and help it accomplish its objectives."[28] No acceptance of a transition to civilian rule was implied in the hard-liners' position.

To the government's strategists, however, the call for a dialogue had further-reaching implications. It marked the start of what they saw as a carefully controlled transition to civilian rule, whose ultimate goal would be the restructuring of the competitive party system. The centerpiece of this strategy lay with the federal-conservative movement, which would serve as the basis for a new conservative party capable of mobilizing mass support and carrying on the legacy of the Proceso. To the government strategists, the survival and continuation of the Proceso, and the elimination of the populist politics of the past, were inextricably entwined with the success of this project of conservative party building. Few officials were as blunt about this objective as General Albano Harguindeguy, President Videla's minister of the interior, and architect of the government's plan, who repeatedly stated that his objective was no more and no less than "to create a centrist [conservative] political force."[29]

Harguindeguy's counterparts in the government generally approached the issue more delicately. They were, after all, treading on the conflictual terrain of regime succession, and this was a terrain where competing military projects clashed and personal rivalries festered. Nothing was more likely to make these tensions erupt than open discussion of the "inheritance of the Proceso," particularly if it broached the subject of civilian participation.

In 1979, the government's leaders thus found themselves in a predicament imposed by internal conflicts in the armed forces. They had committed themselves to the objective of eliminating the existing political class. Yet they were precluded by internal rivalries from creating an official military party or serving as accoucheurs at the birth of a pro-official party. If their political engineering was to succeed without sparking an adverse reaction from military hard-liners, they had to proceed gingerly. They could not be seen as actively creating a new political movement.

The initiative for creating a new civilian conservative buttress to the military regime thus had to come from outside the government. "Valid interlocutors" were needed who would be willing to shoulder the political load of party building and organization without challenging the military's hold on power. The Proceso's political architects realized that these interlocutors would have to come from the preexisting political leadership, and the federal-conservatives were the logical choice.

The provincial party leaders were not, however, an ideal choice. They were prone to fragmentation and political bickering. They were non-ideological. Their commitment to higher ideals began and ended with the protection of local political fiefs and regional economic interests. They could also be easily bought by the central government with offers of patronage-laden provincial government posts. These leaders were clearly not the stuff of which the postmilitary millennium was to be made.

But they were eager and available. Furthermore, they were not Peronists or Radicals, a fact that with a little well-articulated casuistry would permit the military government to sidestep the ban on dealings with the preexisting political class.

They were also compliant. Their aspirations to become a national political force were wholly dependent on the military regime's goodwill, and this would guarantee their subordination to its agenda. This was important, for what the regime had in mind for this new conservative force was not the existing conservative movement's program. If the conservative political leadership was to serve as the carrier of the Movimiento de Opinion Nacional, it would have to unite behind military's project. In the late 1970s, this was a price most conservative leaders were willing to pay.

The catch to the military government's plan was that it required a heavy dose of self-sustaining momentum on the civilian side. This was, after all, to be a "spontaneous" phenomenon, and the impetus for unification of the highly fragmented conservative movement had to come from within the movement itself. The success of the military government's project, particularly in terms of warding off countermoves and competing plans from within the armed forces, hinged on the ability of the conservatives to overcome decades of fragmentation.

The military government thus proceeded cautiously. It sent signals to political society that did not spark adverse reactions in the armed forces. It went to lengths to dispel the image of a concerted attempt to create a new political party, asserting instead that its goal was only to encourage the spontaneous formation of "currents of opinion" in society favorable to the regime. The government's delicate handling of this issue is reflected in the following statement, made by President Videla four months after the publication of the *Bases*:

> The Proceso does not seek the creation of a military or official political party. It must, however, encourage the search for currents of opinion in order to inculcate its objectives into them and thus achieve the desired inheritance. Such a current of opinion must be a buttress to the Proceso so that when it finds itself compelled — and I hope this never happens — to go for broke in an election, it does not fall victim precisely to the anti-Proceso for failing to generate a successor capable of carrying on with its objectives.[30]

In short, the government's plan was to steer this autonomous "current of opinion" through a number of evolutionary stages in a carefully choreographed transition: starting as buttress of the regime, moving on to full partnership in government, and maturing, at some distant point in the future, into full-fledged party status. Military control of the state would be vital to this strategy. It would provide the appropriate combinations of repression and rewards to unify the conservative movement and split the nonconservative majoritarian parties. State power would give conservatives the space to organize, the incentives to unify, and valuable experience in national government. It would also be vital for suppressing competing political activity by the UCR and the Peronist Party. The ban on nonconservative political organization would remain fully in force, and incentives would be provided for the conservative wings of the UCR and the Peronist party to join the federal-conservatives as junior partners in the new political alliance.[31]

The historic opportunity for the fragmented political class of Argentine conservatism had finally arrived. The perennial conservative call for "unification of the Center" now had its complement in the military regime's invocation of "an inheritance for the Proceso." The civilians would have to put the pieces together, but the glue for their long-sought unification would be provided by military control of the state.

The Regime's Supporters Respond

Federalist responses to the regime's overtures were swift and favorable. Conservatives understood that the government had initiated a process of political liberalization that, while maintaining coercive pressure on Radicalism and Peronism, would provide conservatives with unprecedented opportunities for political mobilization and institution building. The most enthusiastic response came from FUFEPO, which immediately took the lead in organizing the rest of the federal-conservative movement.

At their turn in the "dialogue" with the minister of the interior, the FUFEPO leaders adhered closely to the military government's script. Asserting that "the armed forces do not have to render accounts on their struggle against subversion," they gave their full support to the military's conduct of its dirty war against leftist opposition.[32] They also endorsed the institutionalization of military participation in a future civilian order. Finally, the federalist leaders announced their complete adherence to the military government's objective of creating a pro-regime Movimiento de Opinión Nacional and expressed their eagerness to organize it. As a demonstration of their loyalty to the military government's scheme, one of their first steps was to create a foundation to identify and train a new leadership cadre from outside the traditional political elite. This foundation was committed, in the words of one conservative activist, "to nothing more and nothing less than the training of the future intermediate-level leaders of the post-Proceso" era.[33] The regeneration of civilian political political society, the act of political engineering that filled the dreams of military planners, would now be attended to by FUFEPO's leaders as they thrust themselves into the task of building a conservative inheritance for the Proceso.

The Conservative Movement Divides

Not all the parties of Argentine conservatism responded to the government's initiative with the unqualified support of FUFEPO and its allies. The consensus that did exist among conservatives hinged primarily on a handful of issues. First, support for the Proceso's conduct of the dirty war; second, the usefulness of continued suppression of Peronist and Radical political organization; and finally, the need for the resources and benevolence of the militarily controlled state for the construction of a new conservative movement. Here, however, agreement ended. The implementation of "centrist" unification was not blessed with the same degree of consensus on other key issues.

Divisions within the conservative movement were driven by two familiar historical legacies: organizational fragmentation and regional economic cleavage. The first meant that any effort to achieve organizational unity had to overcome entrenched institutional interests, and to find a formula for sharing power among established leaders with their own provincial followings, organizations, and conflicting goals. The second source of division was even more ominous for the military leadership's plans. It pointed to a fundamental contradiction in the military regime's strategy: it had designated the federal-conservative movement to serve as carrier of a project that would perpetuate the legacy of an economic program designed by the Buenos Aires-based liberal technocracy. By 1979, this economic program was wreaking havoc on the economies of the interior provinces, where much of the existing party structure and electoral support for the new conservative movement was located. The federalist leadership found itself compelled to mobilize an already fractious movement behind an economic program that was generating growing opposition from its regional constituencies. This would prove a difficult task.

The most visible divisions on the organizational side hinged on the questions of conservative identity and strategy: the FUFEPO leadership equated the historic conservative goal of "unifying the Center" with the military's desire to build an "inheritance to the Proceso." It was thus more than willing to subsume the former into the latter and subordinate the civilian conservative agenda to that of the military. In this way, the national identity the federalist movement had historically lacked would be obtained through its symbiosis with the Proceso.

Other sectors of the federal conservative movement, however, sought a strategy of greater autonomy from the military. They saw the military ban on nonconservative political activity as an opportunity to reorganize their movement, but they were reluctant to recast it in the image of the Proceso. Francisco Manrique was the most prominent of these reluctant partners.

The success of the government strategy required that Francisco Manrique, the one conservative leader with a proven ability to mobilize votes at the national level, join his fellow federalists in the Movimiento de Opinión Nacional. No other conservative leader possessed his visibility in national affairs, or his ability to mobilize electoral support in the Buenos Aires region. If the MON was to generate the momentum required of it by its military sponsors, Manrique's participation was vital.

Manrique, however, was unwilling to subordinate his personal leadership, political agenda, and the institutional identity of his party to a militarily conceived conservative force led by his rivals in the federal-conservative movement. He also knew that FUFEPO's leaders would be unwilling surrender the capital they had gained from their closeness to the regime by granting Manrique's Partido Federal leadership of the new movement. Manrique thus expressed only qualified support for the government's plan. Rather than signing on, he presented himself as leader of an alternative conservative project — one that while "inheriting" the benefits of the military's control of the state, would be more than merely its offspring in a new civilian-led order. His response to the military's overtures was to stake out a position of friendly autonomy toward the regime. He proclaimed his support for the *Bases,* the military's conduct of the dirty war against leftist opposition, and military plans to form a National Security Council to monitor civilian governments.[34] However, he also used the "dialogue" as a forum for criticism of the military regime's policies.

Most troublesome for the government were Manrique's denunciations of its economic program. He bashed the economic team's liberal technocrats for their lack of "social sensitivity" and their indifference to the deterioration of national industry and the provincial economies.[35] Manrique's denunciations of the government's economic policies touched a chord in many in the federalist movement, and they were quickly echoed by other leaders. Silvestre Begnis, the former governor of Santa Fe province, who had co-signed the 1976 FUFEPO-MOLIPO declaration of support for the military coup, declined the minister of the interior's invitation to the dialogue. Instead, he wrote an open letter to the government crit-icizing the impact of its economic policies on the domestic economy and prohibited his followers from participating in the Movimiento de Opinión Nacional. When FUFEPO's leaders began organizing, they found that open sentiment against the regime's economic policies was gathering mo-mentum among the movement's rank and file. At an August 1980 conven-tion of member parties organized by the leadership to plan the MON's organization, proceedings were repeatedly sidetracked by criticism of the government's economic policies from provincial party delegates. In the face of this opposition, the convention's leaders could only, in the tactful words of one observer, "abstain from making pronouncements on con-temporary issues, and place themselves in a 'holding pattern' until the installation of new military authorities in 1981."[36]

A holding pattern was about all the conservative leadership could man-age. Manrique's reluctance to join the Movimiento de Opinión Nacional and growing federalist divisions over economic policy, crippled the civil-military conservative project. MON's adherents amounted to little more than a handful of provincial organizations. The military government looked anxiously to its conservative supporters to seize the initiative that it was precluded by hard-liners from pursuing directly. The conservative political leadership, however, were incapable of autonomous political or-ganization. If they were to serve as the basis for a new conservative move-ment, they would need far more assistance from the militarily controlled state than the government was able to provide.

The Military Government Modifies Its Strategy

In March 1981, the presidency passed in orderly succession from General Jorge Rafaél Videla to General Roberto Viola. The Viola government took immediate steps to facilitate convergence between the military and poten-tial civilian allies. Its first measures to restore the stability of the regime targeted sectors that had been damaged by its free-market policies. Shortly after taking office, the new president announced a major shift of economic policy: the laissez-faire economic policies of his predecessor would be replaced by policies favoring national industry and the domestic economy. The government also decentralized economic decision making and re-paired its relations with industry and agriculture by appointing represen-tatives of those sectors to head their respective ministries in the cabinet. In addition, the new president moved to demilitarize the executive branch of the national government. Of a total of thirteen cabinet posts, seven were offered to civilians.

Viola's assumption of the presidency also brought about a change in the government's strategy toward the old political establishment. The ultimate objective of fostering the emergence of a new conservative party was unchanged, but there would be a change in the relative position of the government's interlocutors. Whereas President Videla had sought to give the federal-conservatives the lead in organizing the Movimiento de Opinión Nacional and lure moderate Radicals and Peronists into the scheme, Viola decided to reverse that hierarchy. The second-best option for the military government was now to deal directly with the moderate elements of the majoritarian parties and provide them with the opportunity to lead the MON.

In many ways, the Viola government was repeating a pattern that had long been a part of Argentine conservatism's history. Having failed to overcome regional and organizational cleavages to lay the basis for an autonomous conservative party, the regime's political strategists turned to their second-best alternative. They would pin their hopes on the possibility that the ideological dualities of the mass-based parties could be manipulated, and that their conservative wings, properly nurtured, could carry their parties' ready-made mass base into the conservative fold.

The Viola government thus announced a new dialogue with civilian society. The government committed itself to elaborating a new statute for political parties, and the preexisting ban on dealing with the traditional party leadership would be jettisoned. Furthermore, the government's new minister of the interior, General Horacio Liendo, publicly declared that Peronism now constituted a "valid interlocutor," and that both its party leaders and representatives in the labor movement would be given an important role in future negotiations.[37]

The conservative leadership rallied behind the government of President Viola. That they did so at a moment when they were being displaced as keystone of the Argentine transition was ironic, yet it reflected a recognition of the reality of the situation. Given their own political weakness, as well as the hostility of hard-line elements in the military to a civilian-led transition, the Viola government represented their only hopes of staying alive politically. They thus accepted the government's decision to reach out to conservative sectors of radicalism and Peronism as a way of salvaging the Movimiento de Opinión Nacional. In addition, the Viola government's reversal of its predecessor's economic policies gave them a new opportunity to mobilize their constituencies in the interior behind the Proceso.

This task was greatly aided by the military government's new openness to civilian participation in the government. It offered the federalists a major opportunity to regain what had always been the basis of their

political power: control of provincial governments (laden with opportunities for local patronage and clientelism), and access to national power
and ambassadorial appointments, made possible by control of the state by
a friendly political force. Having failed to generate their own momentum
at the national level, they, too, returned to time-tried patterns of conservative political behavior.

Their loyalty was amply rewarded by the military government. Many
of General Viola's closest advisors were members of FUFEPO and its
political allies.[38] Conservatives also gained control of three governorships
and several mayoralties, including that of the industrial city of Rosario.[39]
If the traditional parties of Argentine conservatism were to play only a
supporting role in a new national conservative movement, these benefits
provided more than acceptable consolation.

The problem for the military government during this stage of the transition was not its civilian interlocutors, but the military, which undermined
its overtures to the civilian political establishment every step of the way.
The announcement of Viola's appointment to the presidency by the Junta
de Comandantes had been delayed for several months, betraying deep
conflicts within the military hierarchy over his appointment and casting
doubt on his authority vis-à-vis the armed forces. Furthermore, with Viola's transfer from the junta to the presidency, the hard-line General Leopoldo Galtieri became head of the junta. The military thus came under the
control of hard-line opponents of the president.

The military government accordingly found itself isolated from the
armed forces. Its efforts to gain credibility with interlocutors in civilian
political society were hampered by assertions from military hard-liners
that "real power" lay with the Junta de Comandantes, and that the president's own authority was subordinate to it. Two weeks following Viola's
assumption of the presidency, the Junta delivered a document to him
cryptically entitled "Orientations No. 2," which was never officially released, although its contents were leaked to the press (undoubtedly by the
military hard-liners themselves). In it, the president was instructed to de-
lay his opening toward civil and political society, to postpone key aspects
of the liberalization process promised by the *Bases políticas,* and to limit
his political initiatives to the narrow objectives articulated by military
hard-liners after the publication of the *Bases.*[40]

The Junta's opposition dramatically reduced the government's credibility in civil and political society. As a result, potential civilian interlocutors aside from the president's stalwart allies in the conservative leadership responded tepidly to the military government's overtures. Their
reticence, in the face of the forcefulness of the government's hard-line

opponents, dashed the government's hopes of seizing the initiative from the hard-liners.

Nonconservatives Strike Back: The Formation of the Multipartidaria

The fate of the Movimiento de Opinión Nacional was sealed by the emergence of the Multipartidaria, an alliance of nonconservative political parties created to press for an end to military rule. The Multipartidaria was founded on July 14, 1981, and was led primarily by the UCR, with the Peronist Party playing a supporting, but important role.[41] The establishment of the Multipartidaria was political society's explicit rejection of the regime's goals of restructuring the party system and doing away with preexisting political alignments. It also gave testimony to the military government's loss of control over the transition process. Now the Viola government was isolated on two fronts: from a military institution led by hard-liners, and from a political society that rejected the government's initiatives and demanded a timetable for return to civilian rule. Political initiative had completely slipped away from the military government.

The formation of the Multipartidaria also made the isolation of the conservative leadership complete. Their fate was linked to that of a military government cut off from both the armed forces and the most relevant actors in civilian political society. The situation was bitterly ironic. With Viola's ascent, they had achieved everything they had initially hoped for — a permeable military government and access to much-coveted provincial power bases. But they were now more vulnerable than ever to internal military conflicts, which, try as they might, they were unable to influence. As "friends of the Proceso," they were also isolated from a political movement that had seized the initiative and was united in its determination to bring the Proceso to amend.

From this point on, the parties of Argentine conservatism were to become helpless spectators of parallel events that held their political fate in the balance: the pushing and pulling between an increasingly desperate military government and the assertive Multipartidaria alliance, and the relentless demolition of the military government's credibility by hard-liners in the military.

The Hard-line Coup and Collapse of the Regime

In December 1981, Viola was ousted from office by hard-liners in the military and replaced by Galtieri. Four months later, Argentine forces invaded the British-held Falkland Islands, five hundred miles from Argentina's southern coast, in a desperate gamble to reunify the armed forces and the country behind the crumbling military government. Britain's victory sealed the Proceso's fate, and precipitated an ignoble withdrawal of the military from power.

The events that led from Viola's ouster in December 1981 to the April–June 1982 misadventure in the Falklands were driven by conflicts within the military that lay outside the influence of civilian and political society. On the eve of the announcement of Viola's removal from office, the daily *La Nación* observed that "civilian political actors, both those close to the Proceso and those distant from it, are following the course of events as mere spectators."[42] They would remain in this state until the regime's collapse. Throughout this period, civilian political actors, both within the conservative movement and outside it, concentrated on adapting to the unpredictable and rapidly changing flow of events.

Upon assuming power, General Galtieri proclaimed a return to the "sources of the Proceso." This meant a reassertion of military-institutional power and a reversal of the previous government's openings to civilian political society. To drive the point home, the new government announced a return to free-market orthodoxy. After a brief selection process, during which prominent members of the liberal technocratic elite paraded through the new president's office with competing economic projects, Galtieri chose Roberto Alemann to head the Ministry of the Economy and implement a program of harsh fiscal adjustment. The new minister announced that his chief goals in office would be to "privatize, deregulate, and deinflate."[43]

General Galtieri also announced the return to original designs for the Movimiento de Opinión Nacional. His was to be the most limited version of the scheme, which was now to be no more than a civilian support for the military regime. All discussions about the future of the Proceso would be tightly controlled by the military, and no timetables for a return to civilian rule would be provided. In addition, "valid civilian interlocutors" would be once again circumscribed to a narrow circle of regime supporters. Much to the relief of federalist leaders, these included the parties of FUFEPO and its shrinking coterie of allies. Federalists quickly shed whatever remnants of devotion they had held for their hapless former sponsor, General Viola. Shortly after his ejection from the presidency, they proclaimed their support for Galtieri by hosting an enormous and highly publicized "friends of the Proceso" barbecue in his honor in the province of La Pampa.

FUFEPO's leaders performed a delicate balancing act during this period. Horacio Guzmán, FUFEPO's president, was reconfirmed by Galtieri as governor of Jujuy province. He struggled to maintain his organization's official support for the Proceso and to stem a growing movement within its ranks that advocated autonomy from the regime. Galtieri's return to free-market orthodoxy had sparked strong opposition from the parties of the battered interior provinces, and the FUFEPO leadership faced serious problems in keeping its fractious coalition together. Its only hope for survival, in the face of internal opposition and isolation from the rest of political society, was to gain greater access to official power. Its efforts during the six months preceding the Argentine surrender to Britain at Port Stanley were thus aimed at largely fruitless attempts to gain a more prominent role in the military government's decision-making circles.[44]

In reality there was not enough time for the FUFEPO strategy to bear fruit. The flow of internal military conflict and events in the Falkland Islands overshadowed all else and pushed the conservative leadership into political irrelevancy. The months following Argentina's defeat were marked by a political lull, in which political actors in the military and civilian society absorbed the significance of events in a state of cautious inactivity. When the dust settled the political initiative lay with the Multipartidaria. Its leaders — the "traditional political class," whose eclipse had filled the plans of military and conservative leaders alike — would thenceforth set the terms for a transition to democratic rule.

The Call for Elections

In July 1982, General Reynaldo Bignone was appointed president to coordinate a transition to civilian government. Shortly after becoming president, Bignone announced that free elections would be held in 1983 to choose a president and inaugurate a new democratic regime. Bignone had been appointed president by the army with the explicit mandate to bring the military regime to a conclusion. Following the defeat in the Falklands, the military descended into an internal war of accusations and recriminations among the three service branches, each attempting to fix blame for the defeat on the others. The air force and the navy withdrew from the governing Junta, leaving the army alone to find an honorable end to the Proceso.

The president's main preoccupation under these circumstances was to engineer a speedy transition that minimized instability during the remaining months of military rule and protected the military from reprisals after it gave up political power. All other political objectives were subordinated to these two imperatives. The government's logical "interlocutors" during this period were therefore the leaders of the UCR and Peronism, the most important political parties in the Multipartidaria alliance.

"The virtual tactical alliance between the government of General Bignone and the democratic forces has in fact become the central axis of national politics," wrote *La Nación*.[45] The Multipartidaria leaders kept up their part of the deal by demobilizing their followers and bargaining with the government on the modalities of the military's withdrawal from power. Their negotiations remained limited to the specifics of that withdrawal — timetables, conditions for the upcoming elections, and the contents of new regulations governing the organization of political parties.[46] The Multipartidaria also resisted efforts by the government to seek guarantees for the military in the postauthoritarian order or to make fundamental changes in the political system. A return to the status quo ante of political competition remained the priority of the Multipartidaria's leaders. The beleaguered military government had little alternative but to comply.

For their part, the abandoned leaders of the federalist movement found themselves under siege from all sides. Their association with the military regime had discredited them in most sectors of society. They also faced revolts from their rank and file, who demanded that they be replaced by younger leaders "untarnished" by collaboration with the Proceso.[47] FUFEPO's leaders nevertheless attempted to influence events during the transition. Accusing President Bignone of moving "to the rhythm of pressures exerted by the Multipartidaria," they lobbied the military for changes in electoral rules and political structures that would improve their position in future electoral contests.

The regime, however, was too concerned over its own future to waste political capital bargaining on behalf of its civilian supporters. The conservative plight was reflected in an editorial by *La Nación* shortly before the military government issued a new decree on political party organization: "There is growing evidence that as many or more parties, federations, and alliances will be recognized as there were ten years ago. . . . It seems unlikely that Argentina's fragmented political reality will be altered by legislative art into a scheme such as the one imagined four years ago by the authors of the regime's plans for the new political order."[48] The newspaper's prediction proved correct, and three weeks later it stated its implications in more direct language: "The measure will be enacted without any favorable angles for the parties that considered the advent of the Proceso a necessity."[49]

By early 1983, there was little for the parties of Argentine conservatism to do but begin to organize for what would doubtless be a disheartening electoral campaign. Their future would now be decided by the blind interplay of electoral competition, and they were entering it more fragmented and discredited than ever. The political status quo seemed incontrovertibly on its way back. Seven years of harsh authoritarian rule and political engineering had accomplished nothing.

Conclusion

The 1983 Argentine transition to democracy was unique in many respects. It followed military defeat by a foreign power and was given impetus by the disintegration of the military's capacity to rule. It also brought to light human rights violations on an enormous scale, a fact that contributed even further to public repudiation of the armed forces' conduct in power. There was, however, another less noticed aspect of the Argentine transition that made it unique in Latin America: the degree to which the conservative political leadership was unable to influence the events leading to the instauration of a new civilian-led regime.

In most Latin American transitions from authoritarianism during the 1980s, civilian forces associated with the authoritarian regime were able to influence the process of negotiation leading to civilian rule. If too weak or discredited to do so autonomously, they were able to count on a military backer with sufficient remaining clout to ensure that the new rules and arrangements being forged would not exclude them from power in the postauthoritarian order. Nowhere in Latin America were conservative leaders as unable to influence the transition from the authoritarianism as the leaders of Argentine conservatism between 1982 and 1983. No conservative party formed part of the Multipartidaria that spoke for the civilian political leadership, and no members of the authoritarian regime, whether civilian or military, negotiated on their behalf during this period.

The conservative leadership's exclusion from the transition process gave testimony to the failure of the conservative civil-military project embodied in the Proceso de Reorganización Nacional. More important, it threw into dramatic relief a new reality of Argentine conservative politics: the bankruptcy of a conservative strategy that had historically seen the militarized state as a means to overcome its weakness in the party system. The armed forces were no longer the compliant partners of civilian conservatives that had overthrown the radical government of Hipólito Yrigoyen. Fifty years of constant involvement in politics had turned them into an autonomous and internally divided institution that sought to impose its own agenda on the Argentine political process. Seven years of rule during the Proceso had also revealed them to be ham-fisted and reckless as holders of power.

Federalist leaders had seen in the Proceso a historical opportunity to put an end once and for all to conservative electoral fragmentation. They thus flocked to the call by its military leaders to join them in their grand design for a nonpopulist political order. They may have been partners in this endeavor, but during the Proceso, the conservative-military relationship was always asymmetrical. Civilian conservatives were never given control of events. They were designated to implement a new conservative program but were not to set the agenda for it. In fact, the agenda they were advancing was in direct conflict with the interests of their regional constituencies. Conservatives could lead the new project as long as they remained faithful to the carefully scripted role prepared by their military allies. Political power would therefore come at the price of abdicated political autonomy.

The Movimiento de Opinión Nacional foundered on the same structural reefs that had impeded conservative party building in the past. The military regime had entrusted the design and implementation of economic policies to a liberal technocratic elite whose economic power base lay in the Buenos Aires region. It sought to give continuity to those policies through the agency of the federal-conservative movement. At one level, this division of labor made sense. The military could not turn to the liberal technocrats to organize the new political movement. The Proceso's inheritors had to mobilize mass support. The liberals had technical expertise, were well connected with economic power, and knew how to design economic programs. But they were technocrats. They lacked political organization. They lacked popular support and were inexperienced in the art of electoral mobilization. They lacked an ideological appeal capable of generating mass support. Federalist leaders, on the other hand, were organized into political parties. They possessed local party machineries and had the support of local electorates and experience in party politics. Although they were members of a political elite despised by many in the armed forces, these credentials qualified them for the tasks of political organization that military leaders, increasingly apprehensive over the staying power of their regime, wanted implemented. The two leadership currents of Argentine conservatism — federalists and liberals — were thus assigned separate tasks apropos of the military's goal of restructuring Argentine political life. The only problem with the plan was that the two leadership currents of the conservative movement were not linked to the same constituencies, guided by the same objectives, or driven by the same interests. In the end, it proved too daunting a task for federalists to serve as "inheritors" of a socioeconomic program that was wreaking economic havoc on their provinces.

Ultimately, however, the civil-military project of political engineering required unity of purpose within the military. It was, after all, military control of the state that was to provide the necessary combinations of coercive power and resources to nurture the new conservative movement's growth. The civil-military conservative project was obliterated by the crisis raging within the armed forces. Bureaucratic autonomy, competing political projects, personal and interservice rivalries — all had contributed to making the military an unpredictable political ally.

With the collapse of the Proceso Argentine conservatism was left isolated and exposed in the Argentine political system. No state benevolence would rig the institutional structure of a democratic order in the conservatives' favor to ease the uncertainty of democratic competition. No bans would be in place on Peronism or other popular parties. No state offices or resources would be made available to conservative leaders that they could not get through the popular vote. In 1983, it was clear to all observers that the "military option" for Argentine conservatism, either as a direct route to power or as an instrument of pressure on elected governments, would not be available in the foreseeable future. All avenues through the state to national power were exhausted. Conservatives faced a profound change in the structure of opportunities that had guided their political action for over fifty years. Faced with the imminence of a new democratic order, Argentine conservatism had no choice but to set its sights on building a presence in political society.

Chapter Four

Party Leaders and Democratic Transitions:

Argentine Conservatism in the 1983 Founding Elections

Party politics must be learned bit by bit, threading and unthreading, tying and untying.

La Nación, July 10, 1983

"Founding elections," write Guillermo O'Donnell and Philippe Schmitter, "are moments of great drama."[1] They commonly bring arduous and uncertain negotiations to a close, crystallize new political alignments that will shape politics for years to come, and inaugurate periods in which the democratic subordination of political forces that supported the prior regime is submitted to its greatest tests. The "founding elections" of 1983 in Argentina set the stage for the subsequent development of conservative party politics. They created a new set of expectations by conservative leaders about the viability of long-term strategies of institution building in political society. They also set the stage for the emergence of a new conservative electoral project in the pivotal Buenos Aires region. The results of the intraconservative struggle in those elections established the ideological agenda of the conservative movement, gave visibility to a specific party that would act as a magnet for new political activists, and resolved the struggle between conservative parties for the support of the upper-class electorate. With these ideological, leadership, and core-constituency issues settled, the foundations were established for conservative party building in the politically propitious environment inaugurated in 1983.

The 1983 elections thus marked a turning point for the internal dynamics of conservative party politics. The real stake for Argentine conservatives in those elections was, not the capture of political positions, but the shaping of a new balance of power within the conservative movement. At the institutional level, the elections were over which of the many competing organizational expressions of conservatism would become dominant. At the social level, the struggle would be about building support among the electorally unclaimed upper classes. In this sense, the struggle in 1983 was about the capture, not of mass support, but of core-constituency support. The dominant conservative party in the early years of democratic politics would be the party that successfully claimed the upper-class electorate as its core constituency.

Nowhere was this struggle more pronounced than in the Buenos Aires region, where, in contrast to most of the interior, no single party could claim the support of the conservative electorate. Yet this was where the bulk of Argentina's wealth and influence was located. The most powerful sectors of industry, finance, and agriculture, as well as the majority of mass-media resources, were in Buenos Aires. Furthermore, a third of the national population resided in this region, most of it in the greater urban area of the capital city of Buenos Aires. This made the intraconservative contest for control of Buenos Aires particularly important in 1983. The party that won Buenos Aires would dominate Argentine conservatism and become the axis for all subsequent efforts at national conservative party building.

The most significant outcome of this contest was the triumph of the fledgling Unión del Centro Democrático (UCEDE), led by its founder, the veteran liberal technocrat and party organizer Alvaro Alsogaray. In this chapter, UCEDE's founding and early organization are examined. Its origins in the authoritarian and technocratic struggles of previous decades are traced through a biographic look at its founder, Alsogaray, arguably the most important conservative leader in the fifty years since the overthrow of Juan Domingo Perón.

Alsogaray has certainly been Argentine conservatism's most consistent and ubiquitous leader during this period. His career provides telling insights into the praxis of Argentina's conservative elite. It also provides a revealing glimpse of the variety of power resources available to the conservative leader, and of the mobility between polity arenas that these resources provide in the fluid institutional contexts of Latin American politics.

Conservatives in the Wilderness

With the return to democratic competition, both currents of Argentine conservatism faced a situation of isolation and political ostracism. The federalists were in a difficult position. To the Argentine electorate, they were the "friends of the Proceso," and this identification would haunt them throughout the 1983 election. In their provinces, they were held responsible for economic problems that had not been of their making. Nationally, they were condemned for their political association with authoritarianism and could expect little gain from a political process dominated by a public reencounter with the values of democracy and constitutionalism.

For the liberals, the problem was more complex. Party politics had taken center-stage in an almost unprecedented way. Representation in the party system would be vital for political relevance in the postauthoritarian period. Yet no significant liberal party existed in Buenos Aires. Federalist leaders and supporters could regroup behind their provincial party organizations, but no such option existed for liberals in the Buenos Aires region. The turn to technocratic politics by the political elite after the 1940s had eroded conservative party politics in the region. Save for a handful of minuscule parties with negligible popular support, the party universe of liberalism was barren. The turn to party politics in Buenos Aires would thus not have an organizational legacy to support it. All aspects surrounding the activities of party politics — building organizations and party networks, developing ideological appeals, recruiting leadership cadres, building a mass following — would have to be started from scratch.

The situation for the liberals was aggravated by their intimate public association with the failed economic policies of the military regime. Several years of "liberal" economic policies during the Proceso had failed to bring their designers' promises of fiscal health and economic growth to fruition. Even discounting the economic damage done by the Falklands War, the country's economic performance during the Proceso was less than stellar. In 1981 (the year prior to the April 1982 Falklands invasion), inflation averaged 156 percent per annum, uncompensated for by GDP growth, which only averaged 1.6 percent between 1977 and 1981. Furthermore, industrial production declined steadily during this period, reaching a rate of decline of 4 percent in 1981. Most damning to the laissez-faire economists was the effect of these policies on foreign indebtedness and income distribution. While financial sectors reaped enormous profits from speculation and foreign exchange operations facilitated by an increase in the foreign debt from $8 billion 1975 to $36 billion in 1981, industrial wages fell by over 33 percent during the first five years of the Proceso. The share of salaried sectors in the national income fell from an average of 46 percent during the early 1970s to 32 percent between 1976 and 1980.[2] By the end of the Proceso, the country was saddled with an enormous debt burden and a more unequal society, but had little new capital investment to show for it.

Liberals protested that the authoritarian regime's leaders had betrayed rather than an implementated economic liberalism. Yet the public association between *liberalismo* and the massive economic problems facing the country was ironclad. In the debates of the electoral campaign, Martinez de Hoz was paramount among the villains in the Proceso's cast of characters, and much to the liberals' chagrin, the former economics minister's name and liberalismo were virtually interchangeable in the lexicon of electoral politics.

In the euphoria of Argentina's democratic awakening, the economic agenda embraced by the public and its political leaders was social democracy, not laissez-faire economics. The military regime had brought seven years of almost uninterrupted hard economic times for Argentina's middle and lower classes, and expectations were high that democracy would reverse that trend. Few in the public and the leadership paid heed to the structural economic crisis that was then gathering momentum and would soon engulf Argentina and the rest of Latin America. The oft-repeated campaign slogan of the Radical candidate Raúl Alfonsín, "With democracy we eat, we live, and we educate," captured the prevailing public association of democracy with welfarism and redistribution. The corollary of that association was obvious: authoritarianism and social injustice were the handmaidens of economic liberalism. As a result, free-market supporters found themselves completely out of step with the discourse, debates, and expectations of Argentina's democratizing society. Burdened with these legacies they turned to the task of organizing for the 1983 elections.

The Birth of the Unión del Centro Democrático

On June 21, 1982, one week after Argentina's troops surrendered to British forces on the Falkland Islands, Alvaro Alsogaray assembled five hundred followers at the posh Plaza Hotel in Buenos Aires to proclaim the founding of a party that would serve as the "political expression of modern liberal thought" in the postauthoritarian order. The Proceso was dead, he told his supporters, and there was no point in seeking the realization of its objectives under the current political regime. "Nothing can be expected regarding the fundamental reforms that it once promised," he announced. "The Proceso no longer has the authority to carry them out."[3]

The quest for the Proceso's "promise," which Alsogaray and his followers interpreted to be the liberal restructuring of the Argentine economy, would now have to shift to the electoral arena. It would be an uphill struggle, but Alsogaray was in an advantageous position to carry it out. He had strong name recognition, was well connected to wealth and influence, and had a devoted cadre of followers. He had also been repeatedly passed over by the military as candidate for minister of the economy during the Proceso. Thus, fortuitously, he was one of the few historic liberal leaders not tarnished by association with the military regime. This, along with his visibility in the op-ed pages of the major conservative dailies as a critic of the Proceso's economic policies, could be parlayed into a claim to lead a new liberal electoral movement that was not continuous with the disastrous experience of military rule.

Alsogaray's call was heeded by an impressive group of followers. Many had been his followers in past political battles, but these were complemented by new cadres of intellectuals, junior technocrats, businessmen, and young activists without prior experience in conservative party politics. The congressional and local tickets eventually presented by the party for the 1983 elections reflected this diversity. The two senatorial candidates were Carlos A. Sanchez Sañudo, a retired admiral and prominent laissez-faire conservative ideologue, and Alfredo Borré, one of Alsogaray's loyal followers in past party and technocratic struggles. The second candidate on the ticket for the Chamber of Deputies was Juan José Manny, another of Alsogaray's longtime followers. But there were new faces as well. The third candidate on the congressional ticket was Armando Ribas, a young Cuban-born economist who had served in mid-level technocratic posts during the Proceso, and was now gaining prominence in the major conservative dailies as a critic of its economic policies and an exponent of political liberalism. The fourth candidate was Manuel Mora y Araujo, a prominent sociologist and pollster who many years before had cut his political teeth in the tempestuous struggles of Communist Party politics. Mora y Araujo's sophisticated analyses of the changing social bases of Argentine electoral politics were published regularly in the major newspapers and academic journals. Also prominent among Alsogaray's recruits was a thirty-three-year-old woman named Adelina Dalesio de Viola, who gained early press attention for her uncharacteristically (for liberals) charismatic qualities and earthy political style.[4]

The party founded by Alsogaray was first named Unión Republicana. A legal challenge from a previously unknown party of that name forced Alsogaray and his followers to search for a new name. After much deliberation, the Unión del Centro Democrático (Union of the Democratic Center), a name that avoided ideological controversy, was chosen. The difficulty experienced in coming up with a name for the party reflected the quandary then faced by liberals. As Alsogaray himself noted at the time,

The natural thing would have been to call the new party 'Liberal" or "Social-Liberal," but the word *liberal* is strongly tarnished. . . . In Argentina, at this moment, the economic policy-making experiences of the military governments since March 24, 1976, which the general public and, above, all the politicized sectors and the mass media identify as "liberal," obviously constitute a factor of disrepute for that denomination. For these reasons, we have serious doubts about the convenience of using the term *liberal* in the party name.[5]

Alsogaray's call for a new political party formalized his break with the military regime. It was also driven by a stinging indictment of the Proceso. In this sense, he was in keeping with the public rejection of the military regime that was then mounting in all sectors of society. But Alsogaray's criticisms were more nuanced than those of his contemporaries, both within the conservative movement and in other sectors of political society. His was not a break with the military, whose task of neutralizing the "subversive uprising" had been successfully accomplished, he argued, and deserved recognition. The military had also put an end to the "politico-economic chaos" that the prior Peronist government had unleashed on Argentine society.[6] The military regime had incurred "grave errors and failures," but these lay primarily "in the economic realm,"[7] and responsibility for this, given the military's assignment of economic policy to civilians, had to be more widely distributed:

Responsibility for these errors and failures does not only belong to the military. In the economic domain they are unambiguously attributable to a small group of technocrats and politicians that indebted the country to incredible levels, gave impulse to the highest inflation in the world, and ushered in the current wave of recession and unemployment. This group had the most extraordinary opportunity on March 24, 1976, to heal the economy and put an end to the statism, interventionism, and "developmentalism" that over more than thirty years had corroded the very foundations of the Republic. But it made no fundamental efforts to eliminate that pernicious system. It only altered some of its forms, maintaining the essence of the previous *dirigismo*. And worst of all is that it did so under the guise of liberalism, incurring a deplorable intellectual fraud that the country will pay for dearly for a very long time.[8]

The economic failure of the Proceso and the delegitimation of economic liberalism had been caused by a failure of leadership. To Alsogaray, however, it was not a failure of military leadership. In 1976, the political leadership of Argentine liberalism had resided in the technocratic elite, and this elite had been invested with tremendous power. Economic policy lay outside the competence of the military institution, and upon taking power, the armed forces had entrusted economic policy to this cadre of political leaders. Given this division of political responsibility, it was the job of the liberal elite to lead the armed forces, not to be led or sidetracked by them from the pursuit of its goals. The Proceso's demise, according to Alsogaray, had resulted from a failure of civilian leadership:

> If I had been minister during that period, you should have no doubt that the armed forces would have marched in another direction. Martinez de Hoz willingly financed their whims, and the armed forces — or better said, the officers who got involved in politics, which is not the armed forces — gave free rein to their fantasies. That's how he raised the foreign debt to $20 billion. . . . If he had taken another position — for example, the position I might have taken — maybe the military would not have accepted it. But the truth is that it was never proposed. So I prefer to place the responsibility on him. Because in all cases, when a man puts the liberal thesis on the line, he must be prepared to resign. If you propose a complete program, and the military junta does not accept it, well, sir, resign. But do not sacrifice the idea.[9]

The reversal of this abdication of leadership was what Alsogaray saw as the most urgent task for liberals in the new democratic order. Now, however, the venues of persuasion and proselytization would have to shift: from the authoritarian labyrinths of elite politics and the militarized state to the fluid and unpredictable arenas of political society.

Master of Technocratic Politics, Founder of Political Parties: A Political Biography of Alvaro Alsogaray

Few in the liberal leadership were as suited to lead the task of party building in the new democratic order as Alvaro Alsogaray. This would not be the first time that he had taken the struggle among technocrats into the arena of party politics. By liberal standards, he was quite a veteran at that game. His political career had been one of constant flux — of maneuvering political agendas through mazes of civil-military coalitions, managing the bureaucratic intricacies of executive-branch politics, building support in circles of economic influence, and plunging into the organizational imperatives of the electoral proselytization. His strategies shifted constantly from one arena to another in response to the vicissitudes of the political struggle and the rapidly changing opportunities of Argentine politics.

Furthermore, in contrast to his rivals in the technocratic elite, who had avoided tarnishing their employment credentials with unnecessary involvement in party politics, he had been a relentless organizer of political parties. The quintessential Latin American conservative leader, Alsogaray had straddled all polity arenas throughout his career. There were few resources in the Argentine political system that he had not mobilized at one time or another in pursuit of his agenda of economic liberalism.

The value of examining Alvaro Alsogaray's political career thus transcends mere biography. It provides a portrait of political leadership in the rapidly changing institutional context of Argentine politics. Charles Anderson has suggested that in the institutional tentativeness and instability of Latin American politics, "no particular techniques of mobilizing political power, no specific political resources, are deemed more appropriate than others."[10] In this context, versatility in the mobilization of "power capabilities," rather than specialization in one currency of power, is key to the political influence and longevity of leaders.

Anderson's observations apply particularly well to the Latin American conservative leader, who, by virtue of the social power of his or her constituencies, will be a political protagonist across regime types. Regardless of the shifting nature of Argentina's institutions, coalitions, and political arenas, a remarkably consistent and small cadre of civilian conservative leaders controlled key levers of state power in the post-1955 period. To be a conservative leader in Argentina after the 1940s required ability to inspire confidence in a numerically small but powerful and diverse constituency. It required connections to the world of business and economic influence. It required knowledge of, and influence within, the military institution. But at key moments of regime change, it also required proficiency in electoral organization and ideological proselytization. To stay "on top of" politics in Argentina's rapidly changing institutional context, a conservative politician had to be versatile in the use of political resources and capable of manipulating the powerful social and military constituencies that made such versatility possible.

Throughout his career, Alsogaray was driven by the goal of controlling economic policy and charting Argentina on a course toward a free-market economy. Like Melville's Captain Ahab, he was obsessively single-minded in that goal. However, the path to Alsogaray's fixed purpose was not, as in Ahab's case, "laid with iron rails." Alsogaray's chosen paths would always be multiple, and the institutional vessels carrying him toward his purpose would constantly change. Whether as technocrat, civil-military coalition builder, or political party activist, Alvaro Alsogaray would be the most ubiquitous member of Argentina's conservative leadership cadre.

Alsogaray was born in 1913, in the province of Santa Fe, to an illustrious military family whose service extended back to the early days of independence.[11] Following the family tradition, Alvaro and his two brothers, Federico and Julio, began their careers in the armed forces. Federico would reach the rank of brigadier in the air force. Julio would rise to the rank of lieutenant general in the army, and would become its commander in chief in 1966, under the government of General Juan Carlos Onganía.

Alvaro entered the Colegio Militar in 1929. From the beginning, he proved a precocious cadet. He excelled in the entrance examinations, and, in spite of not meeting the minimum age requirements, was admitted with a full scholarship at the age of sixteen. He earned the school's highest grade-point average during his first three years, and for this accomplishment he was made the academy's flag carrier — the highest honor that could be bestowed on a cadet — for three years in a row. This meant not only that he held the honor longer than any previous cadet, but also that he received it after his first year at the academy — also an unprecedented achievement.[12]

Alsogaray pursued his military career in the army's aeronautics branch. He was certified as an army flier, and along the way studied aeronautical engineering at the army's Superior Technical School. He finally received a degree in aeronautical and mechanical engineering from the University of Córdoba, a credential that would endow him with the title of *ingeniero* throughout his long career as a civilian political leader. He retired from the army in 1946 with the rank of captain.

Shortly thereafter he was appointed by the Peronist government as president of the newly created Merchant Air Fleet, the precursor to the national airline company, Aerolíneas Argentinas. This was his first technocratic experience in government, and it was short-lived. By now his ideological orientations were becoming clearly defined. His political upbringing and class background had always made him instinctively suspicious of populist experiments, and these suspicions were fully confirmed by the Peronist government's proclivities to populist authoritarianism.

His opposition to Peronism was reinforced by his baptism into the faith of economic liberalism. In the late 1940s, he struggled through an English copy of Friedrich Hayek's *The Road to Serfdom,* a book whose circulation was then banned in Argentina. Hayek's ideas, he later noted, "had a profound impact on me. I had seen that Peronism here was leading us exactly down the road that Hayek had warned against, and I became convinced of the need to put a free-market system in place in Argentina."[13] He also became mesmerized by the postwar German reconstruction experience, and became an enthusiastic follower and local exponent of the ideas of Ludwig Erhard, the architect of the German economic "miracle," initiating a correspondence with Erhard that would last over twenty years. Alsogaray would give a name to the socioeconomic utopia he sought to implant in Argentina. It would be an *economía social de mercado* (social market economy), following the nomenclature introduced by Erhard to describe the capitalist restructuring of the postwar German economy.[14]

Alsogaray's first high-profile battle against statism took place after the September 1955 overthrow of the Peronist regime. Alsogaray was an active participant in the military-led Revolución Libertadora that ended the first Peronist experiment. He was called upon to serve in the Revolución Libertadora during its brief initial phase as undersecretary of commerce under General Eduardo Lonardi. Lonardi's tolerance of nacionalista advisors at senior levels of his government, and his reluctance to fully suppress the Peronist Party and unions, led to his removal by liberal currents in the military. General Eugenio Aramburu replaced Lonardi as president, and a more unambiguously anti-Peronist and liberal phase of the Revolución Libertadora was inaugurated.[15] Alsogaray was promoted to the Ministry of Industry by President Aramburu, but he lasted less than eight months there.

His immediate adversaries in the Revolución Libertadora were fellow technocrats in the ministries of Finance, Agriculture, Labor, and Commerce. Fearing major social revolts, they resisted radical dismantling of the economic policies and institutions established by the Peronist regime. But his greater rival, one whose ideas he would engage in battle for the rest of his public life, was Raúl Prebisch, the most influential exponent of Latin American developmentalist thought. Prebisch's advice had been requested by the leaders of the Revolución Libertadora for the formulation of a post-Peronist development strategy. In late October 1955, Prebisch presented an economic plan to the government that recommended wide-ranging reforms aiming at the gradual reversal of the economic institutions put in place by Peronism. The program gave primacy to measures leading to the reintroduction of market mechanisms and the redirection of wealth from the constituencies of Peronism to social sectors battered by the Peronist regime. These included the privatization of a number of public enterprises, the progressive elimination of price controls, the gradual elimination of exchange controls, the restructuring of economic policy-making institutions, the relative improvement of the agricultural export sector over domestic industry, and the pursuit of foreign credit and investment.[16] They represented a substantial turnabout from the economic populism of Peronism, and were widely seen, by opponents and supporters alike, as part and parcel of the Revolución Libertadora's liberal transformation of Argentine society. But for Alsogaray, the young disciple of Friedrich Hayek and Ludwig Erhard, they fell far short of what was necessary. To him they represented the replacement of one form of planning by another — the mere trading of populism for developmentalism. The root evil of all these models — state planning and intervention — would be left in place. Alsogaray became a steadfast opponent of the Prebisch Plan within the cabinet and provoked an open conflict with the plan's supporters over the continuation of price and exchange controls.

> The four ministers under the intellectual influence of Prebisch were defenders of the ideas of Keynesianism. They were, at heart, dirigistas and interventionists. Because of this, they failed to understand what Peronism really was about. They thought that the political manifestations of Peronism were the perverse part of the system, and they thought that changing the men, banning the Peronist March, banning Peronist symbols and names — that is, repressing the mere forms — would be enough. The rest could not be all that bad, since, after all, it enjoyed the support of the population. We had price controls, wage controls, exchange controls. There was also the famous "circular 191," by which everything was controlled except haute couture and fine men's tailoring (I don't know why exceptions were made in those cases). In practice, therefore, they carried out Peronism without Perón.[17]

The battle between Alsogaray and his technocratic adversaries was taken to the Junta, and the military leaders sided with the pro-Prebisch majority in the cabinet. Rather than face the resignation of large numbers of economic policy makers, the Junta opted for the departure of Alsogaray and his one cabinet supporter, Dr. Alizón García, the minister of finance.

To Alsogaray, the defeat was as much ideological as political. At one level, he had failed to mobilize a critical mass of supporters within the cabinet to counter his adversaries. More important, however, his loss had resulted from the growing ideological power of developmentalist and interventionist ideologies, not only in Argentine society, but in the circles of politically and economically influential elites that had coalesced in the revolution against Peronism. His resignation had not even caused a stir in those circles, as the Junta had known it would not. His silent departure had, therefore, been made possible by the absence of a network of advocates of free-market reform within the political and economic elite. His brief experience in power made Alsogaray realize that without such a network, the doctrines of economic liberalism would never become public policy: "We reached the conclusion that our ideas would never be put into practice in Argentina if we did not become advocates for them in the political arena. This meant entering party politics."[18]

Toward the end of 1956, Alsogaray and his followers founded the first of three political parties he would establish in the course of his public life. It was named the Partido Cívico Independiente, and its goals, as described by Alsogaray, were straightforward: "In socioeconomic matters, along with their juridical and political correlations, it advocated the abolition of the National Socialist regime inherited from Perón, as well as of the inflationary and dirigista systems that were being put in place to replace it. In their place the party proposed implanting a free-market system, and, more specifically, an economía social de mercado."[19]

Alsogaray also founded his own think tank, the Instituto de la Economía Social de Mercado, to buttress his party's ideological work, develop contacts with like-minded organizations and thinkers overseas, and fine-tune his overtures to the business and financial communities. The period preceding the 1958 elections was filled with frantic evangelical work on behalf of the free-market cause. The Partido Cívico Independiente published a weekly newspaper, *Tribuna Cívica,* that served as the main vehicle for this activity. It was filled with long editorials and articles — virtually all written by Alsogaray — that provided the liberal view on subjects ranging from economic policy to education, oil production, and international affairs. The newspaper's articles were strident in their anticommunism and antipopulism. It also filled its pages with long reprints of Hayek's thought, including, in one issue, a verbatim transcript of talks he delivered while in Argentina as a guest of the Instituto de la Economía Social de Mercado.[20]

As the election approached, the party's newspaper aimed its attacks at the developmentalist platforms of the two Radical factions vying for power. Confronting an entire party spectrum committed to state interventionism and economic planning, the PCI was much like a lone wolf howling for the liberal cause. Furthermore, it was apocalyptic in its predictions of the political future under the likely victors. From its newspaper's pages, Alsogaray warned of dire consequences following the elections, stating that, in the face of continued inflation, economic instability, and Peronist labor agitation, "neither of the two Radical factions will be able to govern."[21] "The next two years are lost," he continued, "and then, when confusion mounts and there is nobody able to clear it, the institutional life of the country will degenerate into a veritable chaos."[22]

It was this reality that Alsogaray offered his supporters as the most important justification for voting for the PCI. In the face of an imminent victory by one of the Radical factions, support for his minuscule PCI was justified by the need to demonstrate support for an influential "nucleus" of leaders capable of stepping in to restore order following the Radical deluge.[23] Alsogaray was well aware that there was no possibility of his party's attaining power outright through the electoral process. His conception of the value of a political party appears, however, to have been more fluid than that of a simple mobilizer of majorities. It was also a generator of influence and visibility. The PCI might mobilize a handful of votes, but these votes, particularly if they were well connected, would not be insignificant as a resource for gaining access to power in the crisis-ridden period that would follow the elections.

On the eve of the election, as the military government stumbled to its conclusion amid economic problems and labor unrest, Alsogaray delivered his postmortem on the Revolución Libertadora in the pages of *Tribuna Cívica*. Arturo Frondizi, the candidate of the Unión Cívica Radical Intransigente (UCRI), was the likely victor in the upcoming presidential elections. He was suspected by the military of leftist and Peronist leanings. These suspicions were given credence by his nationalist and antiimperialist past and the heterogeneous antiliberal coalition that supported him against Ricardo Balbín, the Radical anti-Peronist candidate preferred by the military. The military's fears were later confirmed by revelations of a secret electoral pact Frondizi had made with Perón, promising the legalization of the Peronist Partido Justicialista in exchange for Perón's instructing his followers to vote for Frondizi in the election.[24]

Little had been accomplished in finding a solution to the Peronist problem. Conservatives contemplated their future, and they found few causes for optimism as the Revolución Libertadora came to a close. Alsogaray's diagnosis of the Revolución Libertadora's disappointing results honed in on its economic program. Political failure was, and always would be, little more than the reflection of a deeper failure in the socioeconomic domain. In this case, the Revolución's economic strategy had failed both to crystallize a new social coalition behind an alternative economic strategy and to break the power of the Peronist union movement. Alsogaray refused, however, to place the burden of guilt on the armed forces. They were entitled, as he put it, "to contemplate with satisfaction their mission accomplished."[25] The blame lay elsewhere. In an indictment that would be echoed in another postmortem he made twenty-five years later when the Proceso came to its own ignoble conclusion, he made clear how responsibility should be divided between soldiers and civilians:

> The revolutionary leaders called upon economists, politicians, and independent men whom they presumed most capable to carry out the various responsibilities. . . . On February 28, 1956, Dr. Prebisch and

four ministers prepared a document that signaled the point of departure for the socioeconomic failure of the revolution. The scheme outlined in that document — wage and price freezes, retroactivities, threats, and exhortations — implied continuing along the dirigista lines developed by Perón. . . . The revolutionary leaders had to shoulder the failures caused by the dirigista policies that were recommended by their civilian advisors. They had done what their technocratic and democratic advisors had recommended and were harvesting the failure caused by those recommendations. It has been difficult for public opinion to detect this subtle division of responsibilities. But it is the price the revolution's leaders must pay for the error they committed.[26]

The Partido Cívico Independiente performed dismally in 1958. Nationally, it only garnered 0.6 percent of the vote in the presidential election. Most of these votes were in the capital city of Buenos Aires and in Buenos Aires province. In the congressional elections in those districts, the PCI scored slightly higher, but failed to gather enough votes to send a single deputy to congress.

Less than one year into Frondizi's administration, true to Alsogaray's apocalyptic predictions, the president was awash in political and economic problems. He faced repeated coup conspiracies and ultimatums from the military establishment, as well as destabilization efforts from the Peronist movement, which had mobilized into open opposition. In late 1958, Frondizi's vice president resigned under a cloud of unconfirmed allegations about involvement with pro-coup sectors.[27] Pressures and counterpressures against the president also turned his cabinet into a veritable revolving door of entering and departing ministers. Furthermore, inflation raged at a rate of over 100 percent annually, and the government found itself unable to contain either a growing budget deficit or a run on the peso that had depleted the Central Bank's foreign reserves. On June 22, 1959, one week after a failed coup attempt, President Frondizi shocked supporters and opponents alike by appointing Alsogaray, his most vociferous ideological opponent, minister of the economy.

The reasons for Alsogaray's appointment have been a heated and unresolved topic of debate to this day. Both Frondizi and Alsogaray have denied that it was made in response to a direct demand from the military, and no clear evidence has emerged to challenge those denials. However, Alsogaray did have extensive contacts within the military and was very well regarded by some of its more influential sectors, including Frondizi's secretary of the army, General Solanas Pacheco.[28] Alsogaray's brother Julio, then a colonel, was also a rising star in the military bureaucracy. Whether requested by the military or not, the appointment would certainly have neutralized pro-coup sectors in the military. Furthermore, Alsogaray's connections to the economic elite, and his impeccable public credentials as an advocate of fiscal discipline, were certain to restore confidence in a business community whose nervousness had sparked a major run on the currency and had made it impossible for the government to control inflation. As Frondizi would write twenty-five years after these events, "in order to prevent a coup d'état, which was only avoided on the eve of its eruption, I appointed the ingeniero Alsogaray to the cabinet. . . . Alsogaray in those days was still influential among the middle classes and among certain sectors of the armed forces, which made his appointment an effective way of warding off the coup. . . . Alsogaray was a factor for political stability."[29]

Alsogaray's version of this event has varied over the years. In statements and publications, he was often argued that Frondizi's decision was based on an ideological shift in part driven by exchanges he had had with Alsogaray on economic issues.[30] More recently, however, his version has coincided fully with Frondizi's:

> In reality he appointed me because he thought that I could stabilize the political climate. The military had more confidence in me. Even though I never had formal contact with them, I had been pursuing a very intense campaign of public illumination, and the military believed in that. Thus Frondizi's political calculus, and also that of Frigerio [Frondizi's developmentalist advisor], was, "Let's appoint Alsogaray to stop the political tidal wave."[31]

Alsogaray's appointment had an immediate pacifying effect on the military and the business community. With these two fronts of instability neutralized, Frondizi was able to return a modicum of normalcy to his government.

These moves gave Frondizi's government a new lease on life, but Alsogaray, using his leverage on the government to the fullest, exacted major concessions. From a president whose political platform had centered on an economic strategy of developmentalism, Alsogaray demanded complete control over economic policy and decision-making institutions. He demanded not only the Ministry of the Economy but the Ministry of Labor as well, and these demands were met by Frondizi. In a 1985 monograph, one of Alsogaray's long-time collaborators and supporters described the conditions imposed on the president:

—That the incorporation of the ingeniero Alsogaray into the cabinet of Dr. Frondizi was not to implement economic policies determined by the president, but solely and exclusively those decided upon by the new minister of the economy.

— That the totality of the economic and financial management of the country had to be in the exclusive hands of the ingeniero Alsogaray, as well as the management of labor affairs. In order to do this, the minister had simultaneously to hold the double responsibility of minister of the economy and minister of labor.

— That the totality of the secretariats of state of both ministries and directorships of the official banks (Central Bank, the Banco de la Nación, the Industrial and Mortgage banks), as well as the key civil service positions in those ministries, were to be appointed by the ingeniero Alsogaray or were to be those that enjoyed his complete support.

— All of these conditions were accepted by Dr. Frondizi, [who dedicated] himself thereafter to other duties in the national government.[32]

Alsogaray held his position in the Frondizi government for twenty-two months. His tenure had a strong calming effect on the business community. Inflation declined from a monthly rate of 9.8 percent to 3 percent during his first month in office, and by 1960 averaged less than 1 percent a month. The Argentine peso also stabilized at 83 pesos to the dollar, an improvement from 103 pesos to the dollar when Alsogaray had assumed office. These developments permitted Frondizi to stabilize his political front as well. By April 1961, he had built enough support within the military high command to thwart a coup attempt by his army chief of staff and to remove him from the political scene. His party, the UCRI, also won a number of by-elections in the provinces.[33] Emboldened by these advances, he no longer saw the need to put up with his imperious antidevelopmentalist minister of the economy. In a bid to regain control over economic policy making, he removed Alsogaray from his post. To assuage military and business fears, he appointed another "liberal" technocrat, Roberto Alemann, to the position, but did not invest him with the powers enjoyed previously by Alsogaray. Second-level positions were filled with the president's supporters. Rogelio Frigerio, the president's closest developmentalist advisor, and a major bête noire to the military, was given an unofficial but prominent advisory role in economic policy making.[34]

Less than a year later, Frondizi was overthrown by a military coup. Shortly before the coup, in a last-ditch effort to save his government, he once again offered Alsogaray the Ministry of the Economy. The ship was sinking, however, and other opportunities loomed for the ingeniero in a military-controlled post-Frondizi government. This time the president's offer was declined.

It would not be long before Alsogaray occupied the ministry once again. The military officers who overthrew Frondizi replaced him with his vice president, José María Guido. One crisis-ridden month after Guido's assumption of office, Alsogaray was again offered the position of minister of the economy. This time he accepted, beginning what would prove to be his most unpopular term in office. To ease the government's fiscal crisis, he paid government employees' salaries (which were two months overdue) partly with government-issued bonds. These bonds, which after his departure from the ministry plummeted to one-third of their face value, remained notorious in the public mind as "los bonos de Alsogaray." This would haunt him throughout his career. His eventual withdrawal from the ministry less than eight months later was not, however, caused by popular pressure or opposition from his developmentalist foes. It was brought about by the opposition of the business community to his economic reform plan. The industrial sector was being buffeted by the effects of economic recession and the effects of Alsogaray's stabilization plan. Alsogaray sought to redress this by requesting the imposition of a 5 percent tax on agricultural exports (which had benefited from a 60 percent devaluation of the Argentine peso) to be used for the benefit of industry. Evidently, he had overestimated the willingness of his supporters in the agricultural sector to share the burdens of free-market stabilization. In this case, he was no longer the economic elite's buttress against the transgressions of an ideologically suspect democratic government. This was a government under tight military control, and the incentive for business to "endure the winter" of economic stabilization, as his slogan in Frondizi's government had exhorted, was much reduced. In December of 1962, representatives of industry, agriculture, and finance requested the minister of war's support for Alsogaray's removal from office. He resigned shortly thereafter.

During his passage through state power, Alsogaray's organization in political society, the Partido Cívico Independiente, withered. Prior to Alsogaray's appointment as minister, the PCI had initiated an active campaign of opposition to the government. Upon assuming the ministry under Frondizi, however, Alsogaray felt it improper for his party to engage in political activity. "With me in the government, and with my entire team accompanying me in that task, it was not appropriate for there to be two official parties."[35] With much of its leadership in government, the PCI therefore abstained from participating in the elections of 1960 and 1961. Its organization, fund-raising, and proselytization came to a standstill during this period. The effects of this hiatus on its electoral capabilities were felt even after Alsogaray's departure from Frondizi's government, and the PCI decided to abstain from the legislative elections scheduled for

March 1962 too. At the end of that year, its legal status as a party was revoked by the National Electoral Commission because of its failure to meet minimum-vote requirements in the previous electoral periods.[36]

Alsogaray again erupted into public view with the June 1966 coup that overthrew the Radical president Arturo Illía. His brother Julio, now a general, was an active participant in the coup and played a key role in the actual operations that removed President Illía from the Casa Rosada. The coup, named the Revolución Argentina by its architects, was supported by a variety of forces and ideological currents in the military and civil society, and from the outset it was marked by a struggle between these forces for political hegemony. Julio and his brother Alvaro were the most conspicuous leaders of the liberal currents in the Revolución Argentina. Their influence was manifested early. They took the leading role in writing the revolution's *Actas Fundacionales,* which proclaimed its goals to be an eventual return to republican democracy and the installation of a noncorporatist, free-market economy. In the struggles that would mark the Revolución Argentina's troubled years, they would repeatedly point to the liberal bases of the *Actas* to denounce the betrayal of the revolution's original goals by their adversaries in the government.

In the initial battles for hegemony, the liberals suffered a number of setbacks. Nationalist and paternalist currents had their way in the shaping of economic policy, and a "socially conscious Catholic entrepreneur," Jorge Salimei, was appointed minister of the economy.[37] Alvaro was shunted off to the prestigious but safely distant post of ambassador to Washington, from which, in concert with his brother, he attempted to influence the course of the Revolución Argentina.

In 1967, the Revolución Argentina took a liberal turn. President Onganía replaced Economics Minister Salimei with Adalbert Krieger Vasena, a prominent technocrat with extensive contacts and experience in the large and internationalized branches of business. At this time, Julio Alsogaray was also made army chief of staff. Krieger Vasena's selection was made after intense competition with such ever-present technocratic candidates as Alvaro Alsogaray, José A. Martinez de Hoz, and Roberto Alemann. According to Guillermo O'Donnell, he had the support of "a virtual plebiscite of the upper bourgeoisie and the media."[38] These were still the days of developmentalism in Argentina, and Alvaro Alsogaray's doctrinaire free-market stand was out of step with a business community anxious for an active state role in the development of investment opportunities. Their desire converged with the pro-industrialist outlook of paternalist currents in the armed forces. Krieger Vasena was thus an ideal compromise candidate. His impeccable establishment credentials and support in the upper bourgeoisie made it impossible for liberals in the Revolución Argentina to veto his appointment. In contrast to Alsogaray, however, he was seen as pragmatic in economic affairs—a prominent member of the "liberal" technocratic elite, but not rigidly wedded to the tenets of orthodox laissez-faire thought.[39]

Conflict between the Alsogarays and the Revolución Argentina's leadership increased progressively during the following years. Krieger Vasena's economic policies achieved considerable success in reducing inflation rates and stimulating economic growth, but these were achieved by very different policies than those favored by the disciple of Hayek. Instead of monetary restrictions and cuts in public spending, the Krieger Vasena plan relied on such cost containment mechanisms as wage and price controls to restrain inflation. Its investment strategy also involved an important transfer of wealth from the agricultural sector to industry, primarily in the form of a withholding tax on agricultural exports, which offset a 1967 currency devaluation, and gave the state important new revenues for the promotion of industry.

Conflict also grew as the regime's paternalist faction, bolstered by the government's successful economic policies, sought to consolidate its position. Julio Alsogaray, who had been struggling to expand liberal control over the military institution, was removed as army chief of staff by President Onganía in August 1968. His ouster caused a major political stir and was seized upon by the liberals and their allies in the media as evidence of the government's intention to institutionalize a corporatist-authoritarian regime. The liberals had lost the internal struggle, and Alvaro Alsogaray resigned his ambassadorship to return to the op-ed pages of conservative dailies as a critic of the regime's policies. In the course of his resignation, he wrote a letter to the president in which he denounced the government's betrayal of the Revolución's founding principles:

> Over the past twelve years of government service and public speaking, I have been expounding a system of ideas that have become closely identified with me. These ideas inspired the revolutionary documents. . . . Many believe, therefore, that these ideas are now being implemented fully. I must point out emphatically that this is not the case, that these are not the socioeconomic policies that I have defended, and that we are in the presence of a different theory. . . . The crux of this divergence resides in the fact that we are once again heading on the road to dirigismo instead of trusting frankly and decisively in the roads of freedom.[40]

Alvaro Alsogaray's next foray into politics was in the arena of party politics. In 1972, he founded a new political party, Nueva Fuerza, to compete in the 1973 presidential elections. Nueva Fuerza sought to unite several existing conservative parties under its political label while maintaining a clearly defined free-market agenda. But it departed from prior conservative party-building attempts in one important way. Alsogaray succeeded in mobilizing major corporate financial contributions for the campaign, and this support placed its imprint on Nueva Fuerza.[41] The campaign employed U.S.-style advertising techniques never before seen in Argentine electoral politics. It also replaced the traditional liberal appeal with a markedly pro-business image, presenting Nueva Fuerza as a new vehicle for the values of entrepreneurship and growth.

Alsogaray paid a price for this corporate support in visibility and autonomy. His financial backers took control of the party's campaign strategy and pushed him into the invisible back stages of the party's organization. His name did not figure in the party's documents, even though their unsigned articles and editorials were marked by the same unmistakable style and tone as his writings in *Tribuna Cívica* a few years before. He did not even figure in the official organizational chart published by the party in 1972.[42] Evidently, Alsogaray was seen by his financial backers as too dogmatic in his ideology, and too tainted by the struggles of the recent past, to mobilize widespread support in the business community or among the public at large. Bowing to the power of their financial contribution, Alsogaray reluctantly stepped aside:

> I did not present myself as a presidential candidate. The party's organizers failed here, because they and their political wizards believed that my image before the public was bad. They then sought an image designed by computer, but it turned out to be far worse than mine. You can't design candidates by computer. I was fully aware of this, but the technical advisors that were linked to our financial supporters believed they knew better. . . . But the corporate support we received was unprecedented [for a liberal party]. That is why I could not argue when I wanted to argue. Once they had decided to make such a generous contribution, well, I was not going to stand in the way.[43]

The presidential candidate chosen by the party was Julio Chamizo, a dapper-looking, mustachioed businessman, who was portrayed by the party's image-makers as the epitome of "self-made" business success. His background was packaged in the party's publicity as a bootstrap-propelled rise from poverty to wealth. It stressed his status as the son of Spanish immigrants, his rise from being a fifteen-year old messenger for a commercial firm to full partnership seven years later, the founding of his own agricultural export-import firm at twenty-five, the founding of a beef export company seven years later, which was co-owned with, and eventually sold to, his employees.[44] It was an Argentine Horatio Alger story, extolling the power of entrepreneurial individualism to shatter class barriers and counter the lack of upward mobility under corporatist collectivism.

Unfortunately for Nueva Fuerza and its business backers, the message failed to penetrate among the Argentine electorate. Peronism was on its way back, and no amount of slick advertising techniques or refurbished images could make a free-market party attractive to significant sectors of the population. Nueva Fuerza garnered an embarrassing 1.97 percent of the popular vote in the elections of March 1973.[45] To make the humiliation complete, a coalition of federalist-conservative parties led by Francisco Manrique mobilized a conservative record-breaking 15 percent, indicating that the Nueva Fuerza "pro-business liberals" were a small minority even within a conservative movement that had shown unexpected vigor.

Alsogaray stayed out of the public fray during the chaotic Peronist interlude of 1973–76. In the final days of Isabel Peron's rule, he was more ambivalent about the desirability of a coup than he had been in 1966. Three days before the military struck, he publicly warned against haste in overthrowing the Peronist government. In a statement he would refer to repeatedly after the fall of the Proceso as evidence of his democratic credentials, he argued in favor of giving constitutional procedures more time in accomplishing the same objective.[46]

Alsogaray was passed over in the military's selection process for minister of the economy. While publicly supporting the regime's political goals and the war against "subversion"[47] he returned to his familiar role as critic of the government's economic policies in the op-ed pages of La Prensa and La Nación. In subsequent years, he attempted to gain the attention of military leaders through the delivery of occasional "memoranda," and in late 1981, he submitted an elaborate alternative economic plan to the newly installed Galtieri. Galtieri, however, passed over him in favor of his long-time competitor Roberto Alemann.

In early 1982, Alsogaray warned against starting a war with Great Britain. Swimming against the feverish tide of popular support for the war after the Argentine invasion, he publicly pressed the military leaders for a negotiated end to the conflict. After the war, his attacks on the supposedly antiliberal thrust of the Proceso's policies reached a feverish pitch. This struggle would spill over into the electoral campaign of 1983, when Alsogaray, as leader of the fledgling Unión del Centro Democrático, took his crusade for economic liberalism into its new political phase.

The 1983 Elections

Argentine conservatism went to the polls divided in 1983. Negotiations for a national conservative alliance had failed, and the traditional divisions that pitted liberals against the federalists and interior against Buenos Aires prevailed once again against conservative unity. To this was added a heavy dose of organizational fragmentation, which further diluted conservative cohesion. The federalists were divided. FUFEPO, Manrique's Partido Federal, and other federalist parties reached agreement on "programmatic issues" for the campaign, but their union was shattered by leadership and organizational rivalries — notably, the refusal of FUFEPO's most important leaders to subordinate themselves to an alliance led by Manrique, their key rival during the Proceso. Manrique ended up leading the main federalist ticket, which linked his Buenos Aires-based Partido Federal with several provincial parties. This only happened, however, after the most influential sectors of FUFEPO had withdrawn from the national alliance and returned to the backwaters of provincial politics. In Buenos Aires, Manrique's Partido Federal would mount the most serious challenge to the liberals for hegemony over the conservative electorate. An alliance of two other regional parties, the Partido Demócrata Progresista and the Partido Socialista Democrático, would also run candidates in the region.

Alsogaray's Unión del Centro Democrático presented itself as the standard-bearer of liberalism in the presidential elections. The party succeeded in attaining legal status as a national party, and it competed in local elections under its own party label in provinces outside Buenos Aires. Most of its energies and organization were, however, focused on local and congressional races in the city of Buenos Aires and its surrounding areas in Buenos Aires province. The two-party dynamic of the presidential election gave little hope of more than a negligible showing by conservative parties. Here the UCR would play its traditional role as a second-best anti-Peronist electoral vehicle. Furthermore, as the campaign of the Radical candidate Raúl Alfonsín gathered momentum, offering the first realistic hope of defeating Peronism at the polls, conservative party leaders knew that a major voter exodus to the UCR in the presidential election would be unavoidable. Alsogaray attempted to stem that exodus shortly before the October election by pledging the UCEDE to vote for the Radical candidate in the electoral college, but this appeal had little effect on the presidential campaign.[48] The electoral strength of the conservative parties would be manifested in the congressional races, and the UCEDE's campaign reflected this priority.

Early in the campaign, Alsogaray and the UCEDE demonstrated a drawing power in the region that surprised both adversaries and supporters. In April 1983, he organized a rally 4,000 strong at the Boxing Federation in the city of Buenos Aires. He improved on that performance in June 1983 by filling the Luna Park stadium with 15,000 cheering supporters in a show of force for those in the conservative movement "who doubt our capacities for mobilization."[49] In contrast to the standard fare of conservative rallies, this one was complete with a marching band and youth "columns" in the "popular" sections of the stadium that waved placards and cheered in rhythmic political chants. The party's decision to charge admission fees was one sign, however, that this was not a "populist" rally. So was the social composition of the attending public, which was described by *La Nación* in the following terms: "A majority of the people there were of middle age and beyond, of an apparently high social extraction, judging by their attire, and of a composure and seriousness seldom seen in popular demonstrations of this type."[50]

In contrast to his opponents in the conservative movement, who had come to the campaign with messages of moderation, social solidarity, and ideological pragmatism, Alsogaray's message seemed oddly out of step with the prevailingly upbeat discourse of the democratic transition. His political statements were doomsday-prone, warning of chaos and the return of leftist or "national socialist" military dictatorships in the event of a Radical or Peronist victory.[51]

He was equally unyielding in his positions on the departing military regime. In this area he succeeded in alienating both his counterparts in the conservative movement and important segments of a public increasingly mobilized around the issue of human rights. He was unrestrained in his attacks on the military regime's civilian participants, many of whom were prominent in both liberal and federalist party circles. He was also unwilling to compromise on the issue of responsibility for wide-scale human rights abuses during the military regime's dirty war against leftist opposition, an issue on which other conservative leaders were more reluctant to express their views openly. To Alsogaray the military's actions were to be presumed above reproach. They constituted legitimate "acts of war" and could not be judged by legal norms established for times of peace, lying outside the purview of civilian judgment and prosecution. Those in the growing human rights movement advocating a different approach to the issue were dismissed by Alsogaray as practitioners of the ancient Argentine art of demagoguery.[52]

His generosity to the armed forces did not, of course, extend to the thousands of students, workers, and activists who were "disappeared" and killed without due process by the military government. In contrast to the dirty war's military participants, the voiceless disappeared labored under the presumption of guilt: "Without proof to the contrary," Alsogaray announced in his definitive statement on the topic, "we must consider all disappeared persons as falling under the category of 'killed in combat.' "[53]

In economic matters, Alsogaray was also unyielding and dogmatic. While the UCR candidate proclaimed that democratic politics would bring a new age of social democracy, and the federalists proclaimed their commitment to social solidarity, Alsogaray warned darkly of the coming cataclysm of collectivist politics. While federalists, Radicals, and Peronists spoke of the possibilities of growth and social welfare in the new democratic age, Alsogaray stressed the limits and dangers of democratic politics under a deficit-prone state and in an inflationary economy.[54]

There was a method to Alsogaray's seeming electoral madness. At a time when most of political society attempted to keep up with the public's generalized embrace of democracy and social justice, Alsogaray targeted the skeptics, those social sectors and individual voters who had found much to support in the military regime's original antipopulist goals. Alsogaray was carving out a niche among those sectors not traditionally attracted to the appeals of social distributionism and popular unity. He sought to build a coalition of those historically excluded by "populist" politics, the voters "without an owner" in the traditional political leadership. The social sectors that had mobilized behind the Proceso could be reorganized for the democratic struggle, not by a repudiation of its goals, but by their reaffirmation in a new electoral project. The Proceso itself might be repudiated, but its goals would be given continuity by the UCEDE's presence in political society.

In their bid to project a moderate and "centrist" image to the electorate, the federalists were adjusting their appeal to the prevailing political mood of the transition. They hoped to repeat their 1973 performance by attracting parts of the UCR's electorate (and to a lesser extent the Peronist electorate). They had their eyes on building a mass base among the middle and lower strata. The flaw in this strategy at this key moment of party formation was neglect of their potential core constituencies in the upper classes. Furthermore, their appeals made them virtually indistinguishable from their Radical and Peronist opponents. Voters had few incentives to mobilize behind them if similar goals could be attained with greater certainty through one of the majoritarian parties. In the elections of 1983, no conservative party could hope to be lifted out of oblivion by pragmatically motivated voters. These would be drawn to the more certain victors —

who, incidentally, were also more credible as custodians of democratic values than the former "friends of the Proceso."

Alsogaray's strategy was therefore more in line with the conservative imperatives of the 1983 founding elections. The "moderate" electorate was lost to Argentine conservatism. At stake was the internal reorganization of the conservative electorate, not the broader struggle for mass support. The conservative party with influence in national politics after this election would be the one that emerged victorious in the internal struggle — the one that successfully put down roots among the unclaimed upper classes and ideological true believers in the electorate. Alsogaray's dogmatic message, his stress on economic issues, and his skepticism about Argentina's future under democratic rule thus carved out a niche in the ideological debate and offered a clear alternative to the agendas of the majoritarian parties. This would not generate mass support, but it would mobilize a committed core of followers in the most influential segments of society, giving the party a solid foundation to build upon during the democratic period.

The 1983 Election Results and Social Alignments

The 1983 election was a watershed in Argentine politics, and in the narrower world of conservative party politics as well. For the first time since the emergence of Peronism in 1945, the Peronist Party was defeated in fair and open presidential elections. The Radical candidate, Raúl Alfonsín, emerged triumphant over his Peronist opponent, Italo Luder, by a margin of 51 to 40 percent. What decades of electoral proscription and authoritarian political engineering had failed to accomplish, the blind interplay of electoral competition accomplished in October 1983.

The 1983 elections signaled democracy's conservative skeptics that the Peronist "problem" was indeed resolvable, and that there were non-Peronist alternatives under democratic rule. The Radical presidential candidate, Alfonsín, accomplished this feat by assembling a heterogeneous social coalition, much of it at Peronism's direct expense. In addition to making significant inroads into Peronism's traditional support among the proletariat and the lower classes, he mobilized solid support among intellectual and Center-Left sectors of the electorate that in the past had gravitated toward Peronism. Nevertheless, the key to Alfonsín's victory lay in the massive swing behind his candidacy of voters who in the 1973 election had supported conservative parties. Table 4.1 shows the shift that took place between these two elections.

As can be seen from table 4.1, the shift of Peronist and leftist voters was

Table 4.1
Argentine Presidential Elections Results, March
1973 and October 1983 (%)

Party	1973	1983
Conservative[a]	20	4
UCR	21	51
PJ	49	40
Left[b]	8	3

Source: Departamento de Estadísticas, Ministerio del Interior, Buenos Aires.

[a]1973: Alianza Federalista Popular, Alianza Nueva Fuerza, Alianza Republicana Federal, Partido Socialista Democrático. 1983: UCEDE, Alianza Federal, Alianza Socialista Democrática–Demócrata Progresista.

[b]1973: Frente de Izquierda Popular, Alianza Popular Revolucionaria, Partido Socialista de los Trabajadores. 1983: Partido Intransigente, Frente de Izquierda Popular, Partido Obrero, Movimiento al Socialismo, Partido Demócrata Cristiano, Partido Socialista.

overwhelmingly in favor of the UCR. These shifts were not enough, however, to give that party a victory. From the numbers listed, if all votes subtracted from Peronism and the Left were added to the UCR, its total would only reach 35 percent, five percentage points short of the Peronist total, and sixteen short of its 51 percent total. Radicalism's comfortable margin of victory came from the exodus of votes from the conservative camp. Alfonsín, the candidate of Radicalism's left wing, had campaigned as a socially progressive democrat on the one hand and as an anti-Peronist on the other. This duality of political objectives provided a broad umbrella able to shelter a socially and ideologically disparate electoral coalition. To the conservative electorate, the big issue of the 1983 presidential election was the Peronist–anti-Peronist dichotomy. Alfonsín's potential to provide a democratic alternative to Peronism thus overrode conservative concerns over his unambiguously Center-Left ideological orientation. As a result, the UCR for once fulfilled its promise of serving as a vehicle for the pragmatic anti-Peronist vote.

This dynamic made the presidential election essentially a two-party contest: 94 percent of all votes cast went to the Radical and Peronist parties. The rest were fragmented among a veritable constellation of microscopic parties. Of these, the Center-Left Intransigent Party made the best showing, 2.3 percent. Frondizi's Movimiento de Integración y Desarrollo mobilized its smattering of hard-core supporters for a showing of 1 percent. For conservatives, the driving force of the anti-Peronist issue made this unambiguously a contest between the two majoritarian parties. The most telling evidence of this was the voter drought experienced by conservative presidential candidates. No single conservative party mobilized more than .5 percent of the national presidential vote.[55]

Actual party support was better reflected in the congressional elections, whose results were not skewed by the two-party dynamic of the presidential election. These elections provide a more accurate picture of the outcome of the intraconservative struggle. At the national level, they were still heavily lopsided in favor of Peronism and the UCR: 86.6 percent of all votes cast for representatives to the Congress were shared between those two parties. Conservatives mobilized a mere 3.8 percent nationally.[56] At the provincial level, however, the story was somewhat different. In several provinces, in spite of the general discredit suffered by the conservative leadership, local conservative parties retained a respectable share of the congressional vote, and in a handful of instances they captured provincial governorships.[57] In most interior provinces, local results reconfirmed preexisting conservative power relationships, and established conservative parties hung on to well-entrenched, if reduced, electoral power bases.

In the pivotal region of Buenos Aires, the elections inaugurated a new order for conservatism. The total vote share gathered by conservative parties in the city of Buenos Aires was 10.7 percent. Of this, 8.7 went to the UCEDE. Only 2 percent went to the federalist ticket led by Francisco Manrique. The congressional elections results for the city of Buenos Aires are shown in table 4.2.

As a result of these elections, the UCEDE placed two deputies in the national congress, Alvaro Alsogaray and the second candidate on the

Table 4.2
Results of Congressional Elections in the
City of Buenos Aires, October 1983

Party	%
UCEDE	8.7
Federal	2.0
UCR	49.5
PJ	23.6
PI	5.9
Christian Democratic	3.8
Other	6.6

Source: Departamento de Estadísticas, Ministerio del Interior, Buenos Aires.

Table 4.3

Social Status Indicators and Party Vote, City of Buenos Aires,
Congressional Election, October 1983 (correlation coefficients)

Party	University education	Occupation: employer/partner	Poverty
UCEDE	.838*	.532*	−.346*
Federal	.850*	.431*	−.382*
UCR	−.304*	−.003	−.236*
PJ	−.682*	−.591*	.602*
PI	−.691*	−.214*	−.01

Note: Social Status indicators are based on 1980 Argentine census figures
and the "poverty index" of the 1980 census.

*Significant at the .01 level (one-tailed). N = 209

UCEDE slate, Juan José Manny. No federalist representatives were sent to congress from the Buenos Aires region.[58]

More significant than the total vote count, however, was its composition. Statistics on the social composition of the vote received by political parties in the congressional elections of 1983 reveal that the struggle between federalists and the UCEDE for core-constituency support was handily won by the UCEDE. Using three measures of social stratification — the educational level of populations living in the electoral districts, occupation, and a poverty index developed by the Argentine census — tables 4.3, 4.4, and 4.5 show the statistical correlations between social status variables and party vote:[59]

As table 4.3 shows, the correlations between socioeconomic status and party vote were very similar for the UCEDE and the Partido Federal, indicating that their voter coalitions were of similar social composition. No other parties consistently had as positive a relationship to high-status voter populations as these two. The struggle for upper-class support was thus more important for the success of these parties than for other parties competing in the election.

If we look at the relative success of each of these parties in that struggle, however, we see that the UCEDE proved far more attractive to the upper-class electorate than its federalist rival. Figure 4.1 shows the average vote percentage gained by all parties in electoral districts of different socioeconomic levels.

Figure 4.1 shows the socially top-heavy nature of the UCEDE's electoral support. The lopsidedness of its coalition in favor of the upper social strata exceeded that of the Federal Party. It also exhibited a far greater

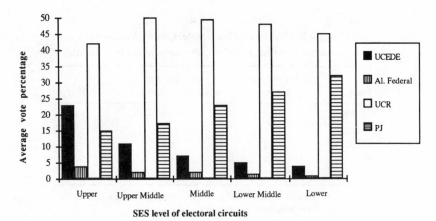

Fig. 4.1. Socioeconomic status and party support, City of Buenos Aires, 1983 congressional election. "SES level" (in other tables and figures sometimes referred to as "status") is a composite of three socioeconomic status indicators used by the Argentine census: % of population with a university education, % of population whose occupation is listed as "employer or partner," and % of the population classified as living in poverty. "SES level" is the average of the three indicators in each of the city's 209 electoral circuits. The poverty indicator was inverted to reflect the percentage of the population *not* living in poverty. The 209 electoral circuits were then grouped into five levels of stratification. "Upper" represents the top 10th percentile, "Upper middle" represents the 75th to 90th percentiles, "Middle" represents the 25th to 75th percentiles, "Lower middle" represents the 10th to 25th percentiles, and "Lower" represents the bottom 10th percentile.

internal bias toward upper-class areas than the Peronists' own internal bias toward lower-class areas. The UCR exhibited a relative evenness in the social distribution of its appeal to the electorate. It was most favored by its historic core constituencies in the middle classes, but proved far more effective than any other party in equalizing its support across class lines.

If we look at the social dynamics of ticket-splitting by conservative voters, we see both a strong tendency for upper-class conservative voters to split their votes between congressional and presidential tickets, and a marked contribution of upper-class ticket-splitting to the vote totals of the Radical presidential candidate. The damage done by ticket-splitting to the UCEDE's national campaign is striking. The data in table 4.4 suggest that at all socioeconomic levels, the overwhelming number of those who voted for the local UCEDE ticket did not do so for the presidential ticket. Among upper-class voters, the presidential percentage total trailed the congressional total by 18 points: 78 percent of all upper-class voters who voted for the UCEDE congressional ticket did not vote for the UCEDE presidential ticket. Ticket-splitting was proportionately even greater among lower-status populations. However, given the small total numbers in these categories, their impact in absolute terms was less than for upper-class populations.

The correlation matrix in table 4.5 gives an indication of the link between UCEDE voter ticket-splitting and the positive gap between the UCR's presidential and congressional totals. The table displays a striking coefficient of -.957 for the correlation between the UCEDE's presidential ticket losses and the UCR's presidential ticket gains in the 209 electoral circuits of the city of Buenos Aires. Furthermore, the data suggest a strong relationship between social status and gains and losses from ticket-splitting for each party. The higher the social status value, the greater the gains for the UCR presidential ticket, and, conversely, the greater the losses for the UCEDE's presidential ticket. Large numbers of voters in affluent districts who supported the UCEDE appear to have voted with their hearts in congressional races, but gave their pragmatic support to

Table 4.4
Social Status and Ticket-Splitting among UCEDE Voters, 1983 Election, City of Buenos Aires

SES level of electoral circuits	Presidential % total minus congressional % total	Percentage of UCEDE congressional ticket supporters not supporting presidential ticket
Upper	−18.0	78.0
Upper middle	−9.6	87.0
Middle	−5.7	81.0
Lower middle	−4.4	88.0
Lower	−3.6	90.0

Table 4.5
Ticket-Splitting, Social Status, and Party Gains and Losses, 1983 Election, City of Buenos Aires (correlation matrix)

	Status	UCEDE P(−)C	UCR P(−)C	PJ P(−)C
Status	1.000			
UCEDE P(−)C	−.711	1.000		
UCR P(−)C	.762	−.957	1.000	
PJ P(−)C	−.203	.255	−.254	1.000

Note: P(−)C = presidential total minus congressional total.
All values significant at the .01 level (one-tailed). N = 209

Raúl Alfonsín in the presidential election. The impact of ticket-splitting on the results of the presidential election was greatest in affluent districts of the city, and it operated strongly to the benefit of the UCR.

Conclusion

The 1983 elections marked a major turning point for Argentine conservatism. The defeat of Peronism in the national elections signaled the start of a brand-new political context. Democratic elections would no longer be automatically associated with a Peronist-led tyranny of the masses. The UCR victory, made possible largely by the pragmatic swing of conservative voters behind the Center-Left candidacy of Raúl Alfonsín, had shown that the Peronist menace could, at least temporarily, be held at bay through the democratic process. In spite of the dismal electoral results obtained by conservative parties, this new reality gave democracy some breathing space. The erosive effects of conservative fear and alienation were at least temporarily stayed.

The elections also went a long way toward resolving the internal struggle for control of the conservative movement in the Buenos Aires region. The intraconservative struggle there had been limited to the city and greater urban area of Buenos Aires. But this would subsequently have repercussions throughout the rest of the province. Furthermore, the metropolitan area's importance as a center of national economic, political, and cultural power gave the outcome of that contest national political consequences. The UCEDE was not merely a party that had won 8.7 percent of the vote in citywide elections. It was a party that had mobilized considerable support among people with money and influence in the Buenos Aires region — people invested with positions of leadership in the variety of social, economic, and intellectual activities that would shape the society's debates in the impending democratic period. The UCEDE thus entered democratic political society as a small party, but the regional prominence and social weight of its constituencies would make it an inevitable player in national politics.

With the UCEDE's victory in this internal struggle, Buenos Aires now had the makings of a dominant conservative party, and this meant that no national conservative project could be conceived without the UCEDE. The evolution of national conservative politics would thus be intimately tied to the UCEDE's own evolution. Furthermore, the ideological orientation of Buenos Aires conservatism under the UCEDE's leadership would be unambiguous. It would be liberal.

Chapter Five

Conservative Party Building:
The UCEDE in Buenos Aires, 1983–1989

I am the representative of the Argentine middle class.
ADELINA DALESIO DE VIOLA

Conservative Mobilization in Latin America's "Lost Decade"

In the 1980s, Latin America was swept by two major tides. On the one hand, democratization changed the legal and institutional structures of political life. On the other, Latin America experienced the deepest and most generalized economic crisis since the Great Depression, a crisis driven by the collapse of the Latin American developmentalist state. The convergence of these two factors in the 1980s shaped the dominant characteristics of politics in the region. It is in this light that the emergence of the new conservative electoral activism in Latin America can best be understood. Democratization imposed new institutional requirements, as well as new organizational possibilities, on the political action of conservative leadership. The crisis of the developmentalist state provided the social conditions for that political action to flourish.

The leadership of Latin American conservatism underwent major transformations during the 1980s. The transformations were both generational and ideological. In the founding elections of the democratic transitions, conservative party politics was dominated largely by its "traditional" political leaders. In the indirect Brazilian elections of 1985, Paulo Maluf, a long-time conservative politician and close ally of the military regime, was the standard-bearer of Brazilian conservatism. In Peru, Fernando Belaúnde Terry, a former president and long-time leader of Acción Popular, led his party to victory in the 1980 elections. In El Salvador, the Partido de Conciliación Nacional (PCN), the old electoral instrument of civil-military governments, was the primary expression of conservatism in the early 1980s. In Argentina, the UCEDE revolved around the authoritative figure of Alvaro Alsogaray.

The more open environment of the democratic consolidation period, however, unleashed new conservative leadership struggles. Party politics was no longer the domain of a select group of leaders. It became a new arena for the mobilization of activists, professionals, and business elites previously removed from electoral politics. This internal struggle transformed Latin American conservatism. New agendas and ideological currents were introduced, new leaders emerged, and new collective appeals were launched to Latin America's electorates. In a few short years after the transitions, a new set of actors were ascendant in Latin American conservatism. In El Salvador, the Alianza Republicana Nacionalista (ARENA) displaced the PCN as the dominant conservative party, and ARENA was itself subjected to transformation as the mobilization of business elites opened the way for Alfredo Cristiani and other new leaders to emerge.[1] In Peru, Mario Vargas Llosa's Movimiento Libertad became ascendant in the conservative movement, and transformed its agenda and political action. Fernando Collor de Mello emerged as the dominant conservative candidate in the 1989 Brazilian presidential elections and went on to capture presidential office. In Argentina, Alvaro Alsogaray found himself under constant siege from new leaders who had joined the fray of conservative party politics in the mid 1980s.

Ideological conflict drove many of the struggles within Latin American conservatism. At the heart of this conflict was the embrace by the new conservative activists of *liberalismo,* or liberalism, the ideology of the limited state. Their agenda was the imposition of liberalismo as the dominant ideology of Latin American conservatism. In so doing they clashed with long-standing sectors of the conservative movement wedded to ideological currents that had traditionally dominated conservative party politics. These included statist and paternalistic currents, as in the case of Fernando Belaunde's Acción Popular in Peru and the federalist parties in Argentina, or Catholic currents of conservative ideology, as in the cases of the traditional leadership of the Partido Acción Nacional in Mexico and Peru's Partido Popular Cristiano.

The 1980s also saw important developments in the social coalitions of conservative party politics. These developments occurred both at the mass-base and core-constituency levels. At the mass-base level, long-term changes in Latin America's social structure accelerated during the state-centered economic crises of the 1970s and 1980s. These developments opened up new opportunities for conservative party leaders, as increasingly heterogeneous urban populations, buffeted by hyperinflation and declining state services, became available for new forms of mass mobilization. The unorganized poor, self-employed workers, service economy workers, professionals, and middle-class voters became the primary social targets of conservative leaders seeking to forge anticorporatist and antistate coalitions. As the social changes wrought by the decline of the developmentalist state eroded class-based bonds of political solidarity, these leaders found a more receptive environment for the vertical, individualizing appeals of conservative electoral movements.

At the core-constituency level, conservative party development was often propelled by a marked change in the political action of business. In a number of countries, conservative leaders succeeded in mobilizing organized business behind their antistate agendas. In such countries as Peru, Mexico, and El Salvador, the economic crisis produced a rupture in corporatist relations between the state and the bourgeoisie. In each of these countries, attempted government nationalizations of the banking system sparked mobilization by business behind conservative parties. These mobilizations marked a major change in the historically aloof posture of business organizations toward conservative parties, and gave strong impetus to the coalition-building efforts of conservative leaders.[2]

The new conservatism that emerged in the mid to late 1980s was the result of these manifold struggles. The formation of a new conservative political class, the pluralization of conservative party structures, internal struggles that led to the emergence of economic liberalism as the dominant ideology of the conservative movement, and the shifting social dynamics propelled by the ongoing crisis of the developmentalist state marked the early years of the democratic period.

Between 1983 and 1989, the UCEDE forged a multiclass electoral coalition in Buenos Aires and became an important player in the Argentine consolidation period. Its significance, however, goes beyond its impact on Argentine politics. As part of a development taking place throughout much of Latin America, the UCEDE provides a case study of the emergence of a conservative electoral coalition in the recent crisis-ridden period of democratic politics in Latin America.

Politics in Hard Times: The Political and Economic Context of the Postauthoritarian Period

After the October 1983 elections, Alvaro Alsogaray was full of optimism. At first glance, this might seem surprising. The votes he had gathered in the presidential elections barely registered a chemical trace in the total national vote count. The military was in shambles, and liberalismo was paramount in the new democratic society's gallery of ideological rogues. The national government was firmly under the control of Center-Left politicians from the UCR, who were openly hostile to the economic proposals of liberalismo and disdainful of its historic leaders. There would be no room in the key policy-making institutions of the Radical-controlled state for Alsogaray, Roberto Alemann, or the legions of mid-level liberal economists who had served in previous governments. Furthermore, there would be no military pressure to compel the government to include them in its ranks. To gain political influence, *liberales* would have to organize in their weakest arena: party politics.

These realities did little, however, to cloud the rosy scenario Alsogaray saw unfolding before him. Peronism had been electorally defeated. This was the one fruit of democratic politics that the incredulous conservatives savored over and over. With the Peronists no longer invulnerable at the polls, democratic politics took on a whole new meaning. The loyalties of the Argentine electorate had shown themselves susceptible to change. If conservatives were to be denied access to state power, democracy now at least offered space for new political organization. Shortly after the elections, Alsogaray, now a member of the Chamber of Deputies, expressed his optimism on the editorial pages of *La Nación*: "The remarkable result of the elections of October 30 resolved two fundamental problems: it put an end to Peronism as a totalitarian mass movement (in the future it may or may not organize itself as a political party), and it established new political bases for us to resolve the present crisis and initiate the recovery of the country."[3]

Alsogaray's political optimism was bolstered by severe economic constraints on the democratic government of Raul Alfonsín. The radical government's hopes for economic expansion were clouded by major problems inherited from the military regime, and these severely limited the options available to policy makers committed to Keynesian and social democratic agendas. The first of these constraints was a massive foreign debt. In 1984, the Alfonsín government's first year in office, the foreign debt reached U.S. $48.8 billion. As a result of mounting repayment obligations and declining new loans, Argentina was now experiencing negative net transfers with the international financial community, nearly U.S. $1 billion in 1983, and $3.3 billion in 1984.[4] The Argentine economy was also coming off years of average negative GDP growth and rising inflation. In 1981, GDP shrank by 6.2 percent, followed in 1982 by a decline of 4.6 percent. Improvements in GDP growth rates for 1983 and 1984 were offset by escalating inflation, which reached 433 percent in 1983 and rose to almost

Table 5.1
Indicators of Argentina's Debt Burden (U.S. $ millions)

	Foreign debt	New loans	Principal repaid	Interest repaid	Net transfer[b]
1970[a]	5,171	907	772	338	−203
1975[a]	6,581	920	1,422	723	−1,225
1980	27,157	4,708	1,853	1,337	1,518
1981	35,657	8,346	1,950	2,045	4,352
1982	43,634	7,054	1,294	2,435	3,325
1983	45,925	2,833	1,364	2,417	−948
1984	48,856	802	812	3,277	−3,268
1985	49,715	3,790	1,018	4,389	−1,617
1986	49,715	2,602	2,043	3,707	−3,147
1987	56,813	3,116	695	3,775	−1,354
1988[c]	60,200	2,600	1,759	2,757	−1,916

Source: Reproduced from William C. Smith, "Democracy, Distributional Conflicts, and Macroeconomic Policymaking in Argentina, 1983–89," *Journal of Interamerican Studies and World Affairs* 32 (Summer 1990): 5.
[a]Excludes short-term debt.
[b]Difference between new loans and payments on old loans.
[c]Estimate.

Table 5.2
Inflation and GDP Growth in Argentina, 1980–1985

Year	GDP growth	Inflation
1980	0.7	87.6
1981	−6.2	131.3
1982	−4.6	209.7
1983	2.8	433.7
1984	2.6	688.0
1985	−4.5	385.0

Source: Robert R. Kaufman, *The Politics of Debt in Brazil, Argentina and Mexico: Economic Stabilization in the 1980's* (Berkeley: University of California Institute of International Studies, 1988), 7.

700 percent in 1984.[5] The engine of this inflationary trend was the public sector deficit, which climbed steadily to a peak of over 16 percent of GDP in 1983. Tables 5.1 and 5.2 give an indication of the economic challenges facing the new democratic government.

External debt obligations, inflation control, and fiscal restraint in a stagnant economy — these were the imperatives facing a Radical government that had pledged itself to a program of equitable growth and demo-

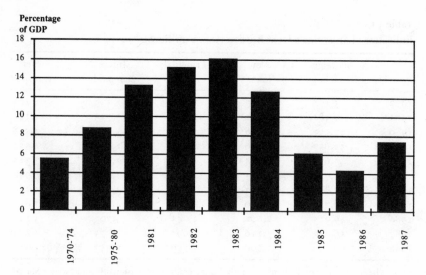

Fig. 5.1. Argentina's nonfinancial public sector deficit, 1970–87. Figures from World Bank, *Argentina: Reforms for Price Stability and Growth* (Washington D.C.: World Bank, 1990), 32.

cratic liberties. Never before had a democratic government in Argentina been called upon to rule in as adverse an economic environment as the Radical government that took power in December 1983. Alsogaray and his followers knew that the government's maneuvering room in economic matters was extremely limited. The severity of the economic crisis, and the narrow range of options it imposed, meant that the liberals would find a more receptive audience for their policy prescriptions than had existed in the past. If undemocratic constraints on the economic policy-making freedom of constitutional governments had faded from the political scene, the structural realities of the economic crisis would play a similar role in making liberal economic prescriptions heard in the debates of the post-authoritarian period.

In the initial years of the democratic consolidation, however, the political initiative lay with the Radical government. President Alfonsín quickly asserted his government's leadership in a number of areas. He established civilian supremacy over the armed forces early in the game by appointing a civilian defense minister and retiring all but three of the fifty-three generals who had served in the pre–Falklands War administrations.[6] He also reduced defense expenditures significantly.[7] In the area of human rights, he ordered the trial of the Proceso's military leaders for human rights violations and the conduct of the Falklands War. He also ordered an independent inquiry into the thousands of reported disappearances that took place during the period of military rule. The result of that inquiry was a 1984 report by the National Commission on the Disappearance of Persons (CONADEP) that uncovered systematic and extensive torture and executions by the armed forces during the period of military rule and documented nearly 9,000 cases of disappearance while in military custody.[8]

In economic matters, the Alfonsín government took a decidedly unorthodox stand. It followed an expansionist economic policy and defied the international financial community by suspending payments on the principal of the foreign debt and systematically delaying interest payments.[9] These policies, which were carried out by Alfonsín's economics minister and long-time UCR collaborator Bernardo Grinspun, were relatively short-lived. By the end of 1984, Argentina was compelled to resume payments to creditor banks and to reach an agreement with the IMF. The government also grappled with inflation, which averaged 24 percent monthly in the first quarter of 1985. With the economy nearing collapse, the government's first economic policy-making phase, labeled "the Keynesian Illusion," by one scholar, came to a close.[10] Overt fiscal expansionism and monetary pump-priming was discarded by President Alfonsín. Economic "heterodoxy," a state-managed approach to economic stabilization, was adopted as a new alternative to the free-market orthodoxy demanded by a growing chorus of domestic and international critics.

The government's new team, headed by Economy Minister Juan Vital Sourrouille, launched its heterodox stabilization plan in June 1985. It involved a combination of measures, including wage and price controls, deficit reduction, and a monetary reform package that created a new currency with a fixed parity in relation to the dollar.[11] Known as the Plan Austral, it scored major initial successes. The monthly inflation rate dropped from 30.5 percent in June to 6.2 percent in July, and 2 percent in September.

The program generated widespread support with the public and the business community. Furthermore, the government's popularity soared to new heights. The administration's approval ratings rose from 35 to 57 percent after the launching of the plan, and Alfonsín's personal popularity ratings increased from 64 to 74 percent.[12] These ratings were subsequently reflected in the congressional election results of 1985, in which the UCR held on to its congressional majority and won 43 percent of the vote, against a 34 percent showing for the Peronist Party. This groundswell of support, unprecedented for an economic stabilization plan, gave eloquent testimony to the newfound salience of inflation as a public concern in the democratic politics of the 1980s. Once an "acceptable" side effect of growth, inflation was now seen by both rich and poor as one of the primary impediments to economic well-being.

The Radical government's successes would, however, prove ephemeral. Little had been done to deal with the structural dimensions of the economic crisis, most notably, the deficit-prone state of public sector finances and the drain on the economy caused by the large and inefficient public enterprise sector. In early 1986, the economy registered signs of reactivation, and the economic team loosened austerity controls to permit the expansion to continue. While helping to generate a growth rate of over 5 percent in 1986, these measures, coupled with the postponement of needed structural reforms, placed new strains on the economy. As figure 5.1 shows, although it declined from 6 percent of GDP in 1985 to 4.3 percent in 1986, the nonfinancial public sector deficit shot back up to 7.4 percent in 1987. In that year, renewed demand pressures and public financial disequilibria caused repressed inflation to burst into the open. Monthly inflation rates rose from a low of 3.8 percent in April to 15.6 percent in September, the month when the third congressional elections of the democratic period were held. In spite of repeated new stabilization packages, the Radical government would never regain control of the economic situation. The specter of permanent hyperinflation and economic decline haunted the Radical government for the rest of its days, and its bold political initiatives fizzled away one by one.

With the inauguration of the Radical government's permanent economic crisis in 1987, the heterogeneous coalition that had mobilized behind it began to dissolve. The 1987 congressional elections, which to the UCR's misfortune, were held during the peak of an inflationary surge, dealt the party a severe blow. In what was interpreted by observers at the time as a *voto castigo* (punishment vote), the Radicals lost control of the Chamber of Deputies to the Peronists: 41.5 percent of the national con-

Table 5.3
GDP Growth in Argentina, 1986–1989

Year	% growth
1986	5.4
1987	−0.2
1988	−3.1
1989	−2.2

Source: *Argentina: Reforms for Price Stability and Growth* (Washington, D.C.: World Bank, 1990), 69.

Percentage of GDP

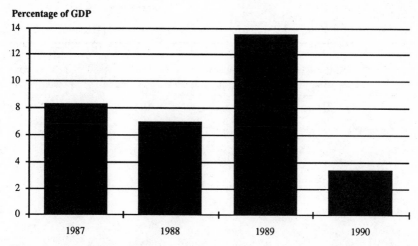

Fig. 5.2. Argentina's public sector deficit, 1987–90. Includes nonfinancial public sector deficit as well as quasi-fiscal deficit of the Central Bank. Figures from World Bank, *Argentina: Reforms for Price Stability and Growth* (Washington D.C.: World Bank, 1990), 69.

Percentage

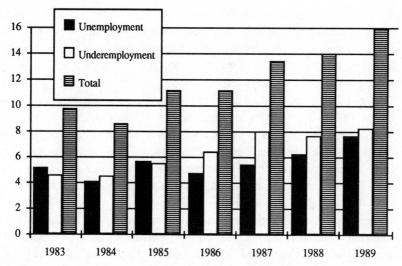

Fig. 5.3. Unemployment and underemployment in the federal capital and the Greater Buenos Aires urban area, 1983–89. Figures from Secretaría de Planificación, Instituto Nacional de Estadísticas y Censos (INDEC), *Boletín Estadístico Mensual,* various numbers. Annual figures are for the month of April.

Table 5.4

Real Wages, Inflation, and Purchasing Power in Argentina, 1983–1989

	Real wages Dec. 1983 = 100	Av. monthly inflation	Purchasing power Dec. 1983 = 100	Annual variation of purchasing power (%)
1983	93.4	15.0	104.5	23.5
1984	112.4	18.8	123.3	18.0
1985	90.3	14.1	101.6	−17.4
1986	92.2	5.1	109.0	7.4
1987	86.7	8.8	100.4	−7.9
1988	82.5	14.1	92.8	−7.6
1989:				
Jan.	86.2	9.3	95.8	4.2
Feb.	81.6	13.2	93.0	3.1
Mar.	75.3	24.9	80.2	−2.7
Apr.	75.3	54.3	63.7	−27.8
May	83.1	98.2	63.8	−20.9
Jun.	—	150.4	44.4	−48.2

Source: William C. Smith, "Democracy, Distributional Conflicts and Macroeconomic Policymaking, 1983–1989,"*Journal of Interamerican Studies and World Affairs* 32 (Summer 1990): 22.

gressional vote went to the Peronist Party, in its first victory since the return of democratic politics, compared to 37.4 percent for the UCR. In addition, the Peronists took all but two of the provincial governorships, including the supreme prize of gubernatorial positions, the governorship of the province of Buenos Aires.

The UCEDE also gained significantly in the 1987 congressional elections, when its share of the vote in the city of Buenos Aires rose from 10.4 percent in 1985 to 18.2 percent. With these elections, the UCEDE resoundingly displaced the Center-Left Partido Intransigente as the third party in the region. The number of votes it mobilized in Buenos Aires also made it the third party nationwide, although a huge difference still separated it from the UCR and the Peronist Partido Justicialista.[13] The UCEDE also made inroads into the province of Buenos Aires, increasing its total vote there from 4 percent in 1985 to 6.3 percent in 1987 and capturing two new seats in the Chamber of Deputies. The lion's share of this gain was located in the greater urban area of Buenos Aires, particularly the more affluent northern districts of Vicente López and San Isidro, where the UCEDE averaged 18.4 percent of the vote.[14]

The 1987 electoral upheaval indicated that, far from having attained a new coalitional equilibrium after 1983, the Argentine electorate was marked by a considerable degree of fluidity. The decisive UCR victories of 1983 and 1985 had marked, not a definitive realignment, but a temporary shift in voter preferences, which proved ephemeral once conditions changed. Furthermore, while the main beneficiary of the shifts was the Peronist Party, this did not mean that electoral changes, particularly in the most important urban area of the country, had reverted to the pre-1983 status quo. A significant share of the urban electorate had transferred its support to the UCEDE, a new party on the political scene.

Obviously, the immediacy of the economic crisis played an important role in these shifts. But deeper and longer-term changes also contributed to the electoral volatility of the 1980s. Argentine society had undergone considerable change in previous decades. With the regularization of elections, these changes were beginning to be manifested in shifting voter loyalties. Changes in the Argentine productive structure before and during the years of the Proceso, and the progressive decline of the developmentalist state, were beginning to play havoc with the social bases of long-standing political coalitions. The changes that had taken place had a particularly marked effect on urban areas, where nearly 87 percent of the Argentine population lives. Tables 5.5–5.9 give an indication of the changes undergone by Argentina's urban social structure.

A trend these tables show is the declining importance of industry in the absorption of labor and in its relative share of economically active populations. Table 5.5 shows that the proportion of salaried workers represented by industrial workers declined from 23 percent in 1954 to 13 percent in 1985. The relative expansion of the tertiary sectors of the economy is vividly displayed in the figures in table 5.6, which shows the sectoral distribution of new additions to the urban workforce. Whereas between 1947 and 1960, industry absorbed 41 percent of new workers, between 1970 and 1980 that proportion had dropped to 7 percent. More strik-

Table 5.5
Industrial Workers, All Salaried Sectors, and Economically Active Population in Argentina, 1954–1985

	1954	1974	1985
(a) Industrial workers	1,009,000	1,114,000	993,000
(b) Salaried sector	4,650,000	6,900,000	7,500,000
(c) Economically active population	6,700,000	9,500,000	10,500,000
(a) as % of (b)	23%	16%	13%
(a) as % of (c)	16%	12%	9%

Source: Héctor Palomino, *Cambios ocupacionales y sociales en Argentina, 1947–1985* (Buenos Aires: Centro de Investigaciones Sociales Sobre el Estado y la Administración, 1987), 110.

Table 5.6

Sectoral Distribution of New Additions to the Urban Salaried
Workforce in Argentina, 1947–1980 (%)

Sector	1947–60	1960–70	1970–80
Industry	41	4	7
Construction	11	20	7
Transportation	15	—	—
Commerce	5	20	33
Finance	5	8	17
Services	23	48	36
Total	100	100	100

Source: Héctor Palomino, Cambios ocupacionales y sociales en Argentina, 1947–1985 (Buenos Aires: Centro de Investigaciones Sociales Sobre el Estado y la Administración, 1987), 70.

Table 5.7

Occupational Distribution of the Economically Active Population, Argentina, 1960–1980 (%)

	1960		1970		1980	
	National	City of Buenos Aires	National	City of Buenos Aires	National	City of Buenos Aires
Employees/workers	72	76	74	75	72	72
Self-employed	12	11	17	15	19	18
Employers	13	13	6	8	6	9
Nonwage family workers	3	0.3	3	1	3	1
Total economically active population	100	100.3*	100	99*	100	100

Source: National figures from Censo Nacional de Población y Vivienda, 1980 (Buenos Aires: Secretaría de Planificación, Instituto Nacional de Estadísticas y Censos, 1980). City of Buenos Aires figures from Censo Nacional de Población y Vivienda (Buenos Aires: Secretaría de Planificación, Instituto Nacional de Estadísticas y Censos, 1960, 1970, and 1980).

*Percentages do not add up exactly to 100 because of rounded estimates for individual categories.

ingly, the proportion of new workers absorbed by commerce, finance, and services increased from 33 percent in the 1947–60 period to 86 percent in the 1970–80 period. This is reflected in the unionization figures presented in table 5.8, which show a general decline in industrial union membership, while service economy unions stayed relatively constant or, as in the case of banking unions, underwent considerable growth.

Table 5.7 shows that growing numbers of Argentines were also being pushed into self-employment, making it the occupational category undergoing the greatest growth after 1960. Whereas in 1960, 11 percent of the economically active population of the city of Buenos Aires were self-employed, in 1980 that proportion had risen to 18 percent, a growth rate of 64 percent over the twenty-year period. In addition, as can be seen in table 5.9, urban poverty levels increased significantly between 1974 and 1983. These developments marked the evolution of Argentine society in the decades preceding the return to democratic rule. José Nun has described Argentina's changing social structure as characterized by "heterogeneity and fragmentation on the rise."[15] This had important implications for electoral politics in the 1980s. The class-based collective identities forged at the workplace and by the unions in an industrial society were subjected to the strains of an increasingly atomized and individualizing occupational structure. As working conditions changed, so too would the patterns of political socialization.

New bases for populist mobilization were emerging from the gradual shifts in Argentina's social structures. After 1983, populism's potential lay largely outside the organized working class. It could be found increasingly among the atomized small entrepreneurs, self-employed workers, pauperized white-collar employees, university students, and service economy workers who were dismayed by a crumbling economy and alienated from the militant but impotent union movement. The bulk of these sectors belonged to the traditional middle-class constituencies of the UCR, but even the bonds of solidarity that had firmly linked the unorganized urban poor

Table 5.8
Membership Changes in the Ten Largest Argentine Labor Unions between 1973 and 1974

Unions	Membership in 1973	Membership in 1984	Variation %
Metalworkers	270,000	287,000	+6.3
Construction workers	260,000	110,000	−27.5
Civil servants	180,000	133,000	−26.1
Railroad workers	168,000	142,000	−15.5
Mechanics and automobile workers	121,000	54,000	−55.4
Textile workers	110,000	74,000	−32.7
Bank employees	84,000	186,000	+121.4
State employees	70,000	80,000	+14.3
Municipal employees (City of Buenos Aires)	70,000	65,000	−7.1
Meat packers	65,000	70,000	+7.7

Source: Edward Epstein, "Labor Populism and Hegemonic Crisis in Argentina," in *Labor Autonomy and the State in Latin America*, ed. Edward Epstein (Boston: Unwin-Hymen, 1989).

Table 5.9
Selected Indicators of Poverty, Greater Buenos Aires
Urban Area, 1974–1983

Year	% of homes below poverty line	General poverty index
1974	3.2	1.8
1975	6.7	3.0
1976	21.9	6.9
1980	7.9	3.4
1982	23.6	6.4
1983	14.2	6.8

Source: Luis Alberto Beccaria, "Sobre la pobreza en Argentina: Un análisis de la situación en el Gran Buenos Aires," Documentos de Trabajo INDEC, No. 9 (Buenos Aires: Instituto Nacional de Estadísticas y Censos, 1989), 13, 19.

Note: The poverty indicator "% of homes below poverty line" is an income-based indicator, subject to fluctuation due to the monetary instability of the Argentine economy. "General poverty index" is a combined index that links income with the "basic unsatisfied needs" index used by the Census Bureau for measuring economic conditions in Argentine homes.

to the working-class core constituencies of Peronism had been loosened by economic decline. Even in this Peronist stronghold, openness to new forms of political mobilization was a new — if initially unrecognized — fact of democratic politics in the 1980s.[16]

The Democratization of Conservative Party Politics

In the early years of the democratic period, the UCEDE gained visibility as a laissez-faire critic of the Radical government and an active participant in the democratic political process. The UCEDE saw its small contingent of congressional representatives grow from two in 1983 to seven in 1987. New political leaders were also rising up through the party's ranks and becoming visible in parliamentary debates. Federico Clérici, a Buenos Aires businessman and avowed anticlerical liberal, became a prominent public advocate of political liberalism in the Congress. Francisco de Durañona y Vedia, a Buenos Aires patrician and part-time historian, quickly acquired a reputation as a skilled and serious parliamentarian. María Julia Alsogaray, Alvaro Alsogaray's daughter, was elected to congress in 1985 and developed a major power base of her own in the party. She actively expanded the party's organizational networks throughout the city, and became an important party fund-raiser. She also became an important interlocutor between the UCEDE and other forces in political society. In 1987, she forged a parliamentary alliance between the UCEDE and conservative parties in the interior that made conservatism the third political force in the national congress. This third-party status gave Alvaro Alsogaray the second vice presidency of the Chamber of Deputies. The UCEDE gained considerable visibility from this appointment in congressional deliberations, and the Argentine public grew accustomed to the once unlikely sight of Argentine liberalismo's leader presiding over sessions of the Chamber of Deputies.

In the mid 1980s, however, conservative political activity began to exceed the bounds of Alvaro Alsogaray's actions and pronouncements. Liberalismo itself was now becoming dominated by new conservative intellectuals, who pushed its intellectual and ideological boundaries far beyond the ingeniero's vision. The backgrounds of the intellectuals who took on the task of liberal proselytization varied. They included longtime public figures like Mariano Grondona, one of the country's most influential mass media personalities, and arguably the conservative movement's leading theorist over the previous two decades of civil-military coalition building. In the early 1980s, Grondona embraced liberalism and published two books on the political and ethical dimensions of liberal thought.[17] He also used his visibility in the media as co-host of Argentine television's most popular news interview program, *Tiempo Nuevo*, host of a daily radio program, and a columnist for *La Nación* to propagate his new liberal worldview.

The new intellectuals also included technocrats who had served in the previous military regime and now plunged themselves into the fray of ideological debate and party politics. Among them were Armando Ribas, an economist who wrote columns for the op-ed pages of *La Nación* and business-oriented publications, and Jorge Bustamante, who in 1988 published a best-selling book denouncing the intricate array of privileges and monopolistic practices of Argentine corporatism.[18] They also included academic intellectuals such as Manuel Mora y Araujo, the emigré from the Left who now dedicated himself to the tasks of party building and liberal ideological proselytization. All these intellectuals were influenced by the international spread of liberal ideologies. They had read Friedrich Hayek's *The Road to Serfdom* at key points in their intellectual development and were active participants in forums for the propagation of liberalism in Latin America and the world.

The UCEDE also became a magnet for a variety of actors in a civil society newly politicized by the advent of democratic politics. Its expansion transformed its internal politics. Intellectuals, businessmen, student militants, youth leaders, and unorganized activists flooded the party and injected new blood into Argentine conservatism's political leadership. They also endowed this leadership with ties to movements in civil society that had been absent in previous decades. For example, the party's original charter included no provisions for the organization of a UCEDE youth movement, although youth movements are a deeply rooted tradition in Argentine political parties. By the mid 1980s, the UCEDE had one of Argentina's most dynamic party youth movements, and youth leaders became coveted allies in the party's internal power struggles. In addition, Argentine conservative parties had traditionally disdained partisan activism in the national university system. When the major parties mobilized intensively on campuses at the start of the democratic transition, neither the UCEDE nor any of the other small conservative parties had sought to build a presence in university politics. By the mid 1980s, however, the UCEDE was linked to the country's fastest-growing university student movement. The banners of the "Liberal Ecological Movement," "Liberal Women," "United Liberal Taxi-Drivers," "Liberal Youth Movement," and "Unión Para la Apertura Universitaria" were among those that bedecked the once staid world of Argentine conservative politics.

The UCEDE's growth sparked challenges to its closed and personalistic decision-making structure. This set in motion a series of chaotic power struggles that democratized the party internally, pluralized its leadership structure, and opened it to further inflows of new activists. A dialectic thus emerged between the UCEDE and its politicized followers that pushed the party toward more open and democratic forms of political action. "The party has gotten away from Alsogaray!" was a remark often heard in party circles during that period. While not entirely true, the statement does reflect the fact that by the mid 1980s, the party's expansion and transformations had acquired a momentum of their own, given impulse by actors who were autonomous of the will and actions of the party leadership.

The impact of this inflow of new militants on the party's internal power structure is reflected in the chaotic evolution of the party in the city of Buenos Aires. In 1983, the Convención Metropolitana, the party's deliberative body, had 120 members, all handpicked by Alsogaray to serve for four-year terms. Pressure from an internal coalition of forces compelled the party leadership to hold unscheduled elections in 1985 to add 60 new members directly elected by the party membership. The leadership also agreed to institute a schedule for replacing all handpicked Convención members with officials directly elected by the membership.[19] This was followed by further changes in the party rules in 1986, which instituted the direct election of candidates for public office, rather than their designation by the Convención. In all, as a result of internal struggles, the party's charter and electoral rules were changed six times between 1983 and 1989, reflecting the continuous tug-of-war that growth unleashed between the party's now-multiple centers of power.

The strongest organized challenge to Alvaro Alsogaray's leadership came from Unión Liberal, an internal faction organized by new conservative intellectuals that attracted an impressive group of youthful ex-technocrats, business executives, and professionals. These elites had joined the party in the hopes of gaining influence over conservative party politics, but found their paths blocked by Alsogaray's domineering presence and his handpicked coterie of old-guard liberales. Internal democratization thus became a major rallying point for the founders of Unión Liberal.

They began their work early. In 1983, as the party was in its earliest stage of organization, Manuel Mora y Araujo took on the editorship of *Tribuna Cívica,* which, carrying on the name of the official party organ of Alsogaray's old Partido Cívico Independiente, also became the official newspaper of the UCEDE. From its pages, Mora y Araujo and his collaborators disseminated their messages of political liberalism, internal democracy, and liberal economic reform. In issue after issue, the newspaper published articles by party intellectuals on all dimensions of liberal thought. It published statements of liberal "principles" to be learned by party members, and analyzed contemporary political issues in light of liberal principles. The newspaper also pursued its agenda for internal democratization. It celebrated the founding of a party youth movement, gave space to youthful militants to voice their views, and advised them on strategies of mobilization. It reported actively on the budding advances of the conservative university student movement, called upon UCEDE members to become active in the party's internal life, and freely published internal debates over its lack of internal democracy.

In mid 1985 old-guard members of the party attempted their first clampdown. They wrested *Tribuna Cívica* away from Mora y Araujo and his collaborators and gave editorial control to the Alsogaray-dominated National Committee of the UCEDE. By this time, however, Unión Liberal had organized itself fully as an internal party faction. It took the lead in challenging Alsogaray's power and made the party's democratization a central plank of its internal electoral campaign. While Alsogaray denounced the party's growing internal competition as a sign of fractiousness and internal disintegration, Unión Liberal's leaders celebrated it as evidence of pluralization. In 1985, shortly before internal elections that would add the sixty new members to the Convención Metropolitana, Unión Liberal tactfully made the case for diversity and pluralization to a membership strongly loyal to Alsogaray:

> The UCEDE is an ideologically coherent party. The leadership of Alvaro Alsogaray is also undisputed. . . . The brilliance with which he has expressed and continues to express his ideas, which are our ideas and those of all party members, assure him a natural leadership role that nobody challenges. Thanks to him and his long years of effort, the UCEDE came into being.
>
> Now the task before the UCEDE is to reach power. Are we in condition to accomplish this? We sincerely believe that with the present party structure that goal will not be possible. We must create conditions for new leaders to emerge at all levels. . . . The party must have many faces. It must have a solution for every problem. It must bring human warmth to the resolution of each crisis. It must think of all people. Members or not. Laborers or employers. Professors or students. . . . It must address such fundamental problems as university life, the family, State control over the mass media, health, education, human rights.[20]

Unión Liberal pursued its struggle against the party leadership throughout the 1985–87 period. It promoted the multiplication of internal factions and currents, steered university student leaders into the party, and forged and unforged alliances with different leaders and factions. In spite of its efforts, however, a majority of the party membership's predominantly well-to-do membership remained loyal to Alsogaray.[21] Neither Unión Liberal nor the other smaller factions succeeded in displacing Alsogaray as the leader of the party's dominant coalition. After a particularly bitter internal struggle over the nomination of party candidates for congressional and municipal elections in 1987, Unión Liberal went down to its final defeat. It was dissolved shortly thereafter.

The most important legacy of the 1987 defeat of the Unión Liberal challenge was a marked shift in the anti-Alsogaray forces' political strategy. The internal balance of power had proven unchangeable through appeals to the largely affluent pro-Alsogaray party membership. The reformers therefore shifted their sights beyond the party and embarked upon a strategy of electoral popularization. If the existing membership had proven impervious to their appeals, they would change the party's internal distribution of power by mobilizing new constituencies and expanding its membership. The internal determinants of the wave of party-led popularization that would emerge after 1987 were noted at that time by the conservative daily *La Prensa,* whose editorial pages often served as a forum for participants in the party's internal struggles:

> The ingeniero's victory has forced a reassessment by the UCEDE groups that brought an unprecedented level of internal competition to the party over the past two years. They will have to incorporate a substantial number of new members into the UCEDE if they hope to counter the power that today unquestionably resides in its founder. They will, in addition, have to broaden their work, transcending the boundaries of the 19th and 20th electoral districts, Pilar and Socorro [the city's most affluent districts], where Alsogaray monopolizes the loyalty of members of all ages.[22]

Alsogaray's hold over the UCEDE's membership thus gave birth to an opposition-led strategy of electoral popularization after 1987. The party's appeals to the public, its discourse, and the content of its antistate messages would change considerably after this period. They would be simplified and plebianized. They would shift from abstract realms of liberal thought and economic policy prescription to the grind and problems of everyday life. Since the start of democratic politics, conservative intellectuals had repeatedly called for such a strategy to make the party a viable electoral contender. However, it emerged as a driving mission for important segments of the party's leadership when the imperatives of internal struggle coincided with those of the broader electoral contest. The popularization of the UCEDE's message to the electorate would now emerge as a key element in the internal struggle for control of the party.

Politicizing the Concrete: The Popularization of Liberalismo

The UCEDE leaders who sought to push the popular potential of liberalismo to new limits had a recent precedent to draw upon. The first popular test of liberalismo had occurred just years before, in the rough-and-tumble of student politics in the national university system. In 1982, a group of student activists linked to small conservative parties founded the Unión para la Apertura Universitaria (UPAU), a student movement that competed in universitywide elections. In five years, UPAU grew from this small clique of activists to the country's second-largest student movement and competed with the UCR's student movement for control of the university system's most important schools.

The significance of UPAU's emergence lies in the relationship between university politics and national politics. Argentina's centralized public

Table 5.10
Growth of UPAU in the University of Buenos Aires,
1983–1988

Year	Votes	% of total votes
1983	461	1.1%
1984	3,320	7.31%
1985	7,986	15.61%
1986	13,253	21.00%
1987	35,706	31.63%
1988	20,562	28.63%

Source: María Victoria Murillo, "Influencia del neo-
liberalismo en la cultura política de los estudiantes de la Uni-
versidad de Buenos Aires" (manuscript, 1989), 60.

university system is governed by an arrangement that gives an equal share
in administrative decision making to students, alumni, and faculty. In
addition, the student body of each school elects the leaders of student
councils, which channel student demands to university authorities and
organize activities for the student body. These arrangements are the focus
of a permanent electoral campaign year-round on university campuses,
which is closely linked to party politics and generates a great deal of
national attention. Political parties devote copious financial and human
resources to these campaigns. The news media devote considerable reporting and editorial space to student politics, and newspapers give front-
page attention to the outcomes of student elections. University politics is
also an important training and recruiting ground for the national political
parties in the search for future political leaders.[23]

This national attention is not merited the actual stakes in university
elections. Student councils are largely ineffective, and their impact is limited to the most basic issues affecting campus life: public telephones, student cafeterias, school newspapers, and so on. Student participation in
university decision-making councils can decide the election of university
officials and influence university policy making, but this influence seldom
transcends the boundaries of university life. The investment of time and
resources by so many sectors can only be justified by the bellwether relationship of university politics to national politics. Carlos Maslatón,
the founder of UPAU, and godfather of the new conservative style and
method of university politics, has stated the matter succinctly: "University
politics is pure form. It has no content. It is competition for the sake of
competition. If it were not for the impact it has on national politics,
university politics would have no meaning."[24]

The "meaning" of UPAU's success in the universities was soon perceived by dissident leaders of the UCEDE: it provided the first electoral test of the popularized liberal message. Capitalizing on widespread student discontent with an overburdened state university system, UPAU's leaders altered the terms of the debate that had traditionally governed university politics. They focused, not on the broad political issues that had marked student electoral campaigns, but on the grind and shortages students faced in their everyday lives at the university. UPAU's leaders stressed such prosaic issues as course offerings in university curricula, student cafeteria food menus, and other issues related to the administrative and practical aspects of university life.

To critics and conservative admirers alike, UPAU had helped to "depoliticize" the world of student elections.[25] Yet UPAU's emphasis on the practical and routine aspects of university life had little to do with depoliticization. It was Argentine conservatism's first successful attempt to politicize the fiscal crisis of the Argentine state. In the specific context of state university politics, UPAU's electoral appeal centered on those concrete and tangible aspects of the state's economic crisis that most visibly affected the lives of thousands of university students, and raised them as issues for political mobilization. From the abstract world of economic ideas and political philosophy that governed the discourse of Argentine conservatism, UPAU's student leaders descended to the concrete world of textbook shortages, crumbling physical facilities, and classroom overcrowding, which they made legitimate objects of politicization. The politicization of the concrete, which would later be expanded by the UCEDE to the national political arena, received its first test in the corridors of Argentina's university system. It confirmed that the grinding effects of the Argentine state's economic crisis on the daily life of average citizens could become powerful stimulants of electoral mobilization.

The precedent set by UPAU's student militants in the university system found its way into the UCEDE's electoral strategy and discourse. Party intellectuals had long called for the party to embark on a strategy of popularization. The intellectual revival of liberalismo, they recognized, had been vital to consolidating the support of militants and core constituencies. Alternative strategies of persuasion were, however, required to make inroads into the large urban lower and middle strata. As Manuel Mora y Araujo once noted:

The upper classes are liberal because they tend to be more cultured — I would say, more educated. Political and ideological proposals with great philosophical consistency (and this is the case for both liberalism and

Marxism) appeal to sectors with high levels of education. For them to spread to lower social sectors *political mediators* are needed, something liberalismo, to this date, has not possessed. . . . These sectors, as they do not read too many books . . . will accept these ideas to the degree that they feel they address their problems, their concerns. This will take place not through autonomous reasoning, but through a process of social communication.[26]

The UCEDE politician who emerged as the party's undisputed "social communicator" was a young city councilwoman from the city of Buenos Aires, Adelina Dalesio de Viola. One of the party's early founders, she joined Unión Liberal in its ill-fated 1987 challenge of Alsogaray. She had taken a particularly prominent role in that struggle, openly, and often stridently, deriding Alsogaray's supposed unpopularity with the general electorate and denouncing his authoritarian control of internal party politics. By then she had gained considerable public notoriety, which she cultivated deliberately, as the "populist" and "unrefined" adversary of the UCEDE's elitist old guard—"la negra de la UCEDE," as she once called herself.[27] Her colloquial style of speech, exuberance, and commonsense language contrasted sharply with the aloof, pedantic, and "oligarchic" demeanor of liberalismo's historic leadership. Her message to the party centered consistently on the need to broaden its base, to transcend its status as "a club of ideas." As part of this, she encouraged the adoption of popular styles of mobilization, fostered the entry and growth of the youth and university movements in the party, sponsored seminars for "liberal women," and played a key role in the translation of the party's cerebral message into language and themes aimed at reaching the middle and lower classes. The dissident defeat in the 1987 internal elections was generally perceived by party militants as a repudiation by the party membership of Adelina's aggressive attacks on the party's historic authority figure, as well as by apprehension at her decidedly unrefined and populist style on the political stump.

Adelina de Viola's unpopularity with the party leadership, and with much of its socially and temperamentally conservative membership as well, was countered by her popularity with the media and the public at large. She was courted relentlessly by the press and used her position as leader of the small UCEDE block in the city council as a platform for disseminating her message of concern about the problems of the city's large middle class. Polls published throughout the southern winter and spring of 1988, when the Argentine congress debated a bill calling for direct elections of the mayor of the city of Buenos Aires, showed her as the overwhelming favorite over potential UCR and Peronist candidates.[28]

Viola's popularity with the electorate permitted her to retain an important quota of internal power in the UCEDE in spite of repeated defeats in internal struggles. In the party's 1988 internal elections, she was catapulted to power through a short-lived tactical alliance with the Alsogaray faction, and she subsequently gained complete control of the UCEDE's congressional campaign for the city of Buenos Aires. Thereafter, the party's campaign was characterized by two features: its personalization around the charismatic figure of "Adelina," and its open bid for the middle- and lower-class vote.

The groundwork for the UCEDE's popularization campaign in the 1989 elections was carefully laid by its allies in the mass media. Max Weber once noted that in modern democracies, "the political publicist, and above all the journalist, is nowadays the most important representative of the demagogic species."[29] His observation is particularly relevant to the role played in the popularization of the liberal message by Argentina's most influential television and radio journalist, Bernardo Neustadt. Throughout the 1980s, Neustadt played a crucial role in giving the UCEDE's message a platform for dissemination to mass audiences. Neustadt co-hosted *Tiempo Nuevo,* Argentina's most-watched television program, and bombarded his viewers on Tuesday evenings with complaints about the state's inefficiency and perniciousness. In those weekly broadcasts, and in his daily morning radio program, he invoked a mythical figure, Doña Rosa, to incarnate the average lower-middle-class housewife bewildered and harassed by inefficient state services, inaccessible telephones, rising crime rates, decreasing family incomes, and skyrocketing inflation.[30] His television show gave ample air space to UCEDE leaders and free-market advocates. It became Argentine conservatism's main media platform against the Radical government in its troubled final years, and during the 1988–89 electoral campaign, it served as the UCEDE's most important media vehicle.

The liberal message also found other channels of dissemination. A book entitled *El Estado y yo, por Juan García (taxista),* published by an institute closely linked to the UCEDE, had a fictitional cabdriver as its main protagonist. The book, which was on *La Nación*'s list of top ten best-sellers for 1988, was filled with statistics on the state's inefficiency and harmfulness toward average citizens, conveyed to the reader in anecdotes and commonsense terms by Juan García, the street-smart taxi driver. On the book's back cover, its publisher described its objectives in the following terms:

Hundreds of calculations, equations, and computer-hours have served to confirm the cost that the people must bear due to the inefficiency of the state. . . . But the people, sole owners and at the same time chief victims of the state, do not understand the language of economists and their computers. To communicate with the sovereign, we must democratize our language, passing from the abstract to the concrete, from the number to the person, from the concept to the experience. . . . *El estado y yo* seeks to make the numbers "economists know" reach the people through the experiences we citizens must endure daily.[31]

Adelina de Viola's own campaign of walks and speeches throughout the city's poorer neighborhoods, which included opening UCEDE offices and spreading the values of popular capitalism in the city's most squalid slum settlements, were filled with references and statistics from *El Estado y yo*, carefully organized and woven into her speeches by a team of UPAU activists. To these statistics she added her own populist flair. In speeches throughout the city's middle- and lower-class neighborhoods, Adelina blasted the Radical municipal government's neglect of local problems. Hospitals without beds, children dying for lack of medication, inadequate and poorly provided basic services by an uncaring and capricious state . . . these were the themes that fueled her fiery, indignant, and tear-filled speeches. In lower- and lower-middle-class neighborhoods, Adelina vituperated against the municipal government's proposed budget for repairing Santa Fe Avenue, which runs through the posh Barrio Norte of Buenos Aires. The UCR's budget called for "window dressing for the rich neighborhoods," she asserted, while consigning "our beloved southern neighborhoods" to total oblivion.[32] Adelina, a rising young leader of the party of the aristocratic Alsogarays, thus addressed the people, not as a generous and concerned member of the upper classes, but as one of them. "Our" neighborhoods were being ignored by the radical power elite. The tears that inevitably flowed down her cheeks and glistened in the footlights with her ostentatiously donned jewelry (middle-class ostentation, not the discreet ostentation of the oligarchy), communicated pride in her popular origins, and rebellious indignation over their careless neglect by "populism."

In the congressional elections for the city of Buenos Aires in 1989, the UCEDE received 22 percent of the vote, an increase of 35 percent over 1987. Given the expectations generated by Adelina de Viola's campaign, however (polls had shown the UCEDE in first place just prior to the election), its third-place showing was a disappointment. Two factors dampened the conservative performance in the elections, one affecting the party's ability to expand its mass base, the other cutting into its upper-class support. The first of these was the fact that the congressional elections coincided with presidential elections. The UCEDE ballot in the city of Buenos Aires was headed by its presidential candidate, Alvaro Alsogaray, an unpopular candidate among the social sectors targeted by Adelina de Viola's campaign, Alsogaray's name at the head of the citywide ballot created problems for voters attracted to Adelina's *liberalismo popular* but inclined to vote for either the Peronist or the UCR candidate for president.

With an unpopular candidate heading the UCEDE's slate, Adelina de Viola's quest for support from middle- and lower-class voters was largely dependent on ticket-splitting, which was promoted vigorously and openly by Viola in her many television appearances and walks throughout the city. In one instance, to the anger of the UCEDE hierarchy, she even resorted to the gimmick of handing out plastic scissors to voters in lower-income neighborhoods. However, the practical difficulties involved in ticket-splitting in Argentina were a disincentive for voters sympathetic to the UCEDE's local candidate.[33] Furthermore, ticket-splitting tends to be an upper-class phenomenon. The UCEDE's congressional campaign was explicitly aimed at attracting votes from low-income voters, precisely those voters most averse to braving the physical impediments to ticket-splitting provided by Argentine electoral rules. Notwithstanding these difficulties, the UCEDE's local tickets in Buenos Aires exceeded the presidential ticket's vote total by nearly 50 percent, reflecting a strong disparity between public support for Adelina's new liberalismo popular and the elite brand associated with the party's presidential candidate.

Adelina de Viola's campaign was also hampered by core-constituency problems. Electoral results revealed clear disenchantment among the party's traditionally conservative constituencies with the UCEDE's experiment with popularization. Perhaps the best indication of this can be found in a surprisingly successful challenge from a federalist candidate in the city of Buenos Aires. The Confederación Federalista Independiente (CFI), a coalition of provincial conservative parties that endorsed the UCR presidential candidate, ran its own candidate for congress in the city of Buenos Aires. The CFI's candidate, Santiago de Estrada, descended from an illustrious conservative family. At the time of the 1989 elections, he was serving as Argentine ambassador to the Vatican (as his father had before him). De Estrada openly challenged the UCEDE for the support of the traditionally conservative electorate, invoking Catholic social doctrine (in contrast to the "individualism" and "secularism" of the UCEDE's liberalism), and presenting a refined, dignified demeanor that contrasted sharply with Viola's populist flairs. His campaign was aided by Adelina de Viola's own excesses in her bid to appeal to the urban lower classes. In one notorious incident, she berated Foreign Minister Dante Caputo, head of the UCR's congressional ticket in the city of Buenos Aires, in a widely televised debate. Viola's attacks focused on such issues as the foreign minister's lavish dinner bills and travel expenses, which she compared to the average worker's monthly income. She was irreverent toward her adversary and peppered her comments with street-wise colloquialisms. Her behavior in the debate was widely criticized in conservative circles. Perhaps the most harmful of these criticisms came from the ideological paragon of the conservative establishment, *La Nación*. Shortly before the elections, the newspaper decried Viola's "bad taste" in an editorial: "The debate was frustrated to a considerable degree by an insistence on attacks more proper to family arguments or street disputes. . . . To seek popularity is one thing. To fall into populism as a political method is another."[34]

Adelina de Viola's populist strategy came at a cost in core-constituency support for the UCEDE. The rival CFI's decidedly nonpopulist candidate's strongest support was registered in the high-status neighborhoods where the UCEDE had ruled virtually unchallenged since the 1983 elections. Adding injury to insult, he was also elected to congress, depriving the UCEDE of a valuable seat in its own home turf of Buenos Aires.[35] Tensions between building a mass base and holding on to core-constituency support thus emerged to constrain the UCEDE's party-building efforts. These would not, however, be the only core-constituency-related problem plaguing the party. The UCEDE was also frustrated by the reluctance of the Argentine business community to embrace conservative party building as a method of advancing its interests in the political realm.

Business: The UCEDE's Elusive Constituency

The support of organized business is critical to a conservative party with aspirations to national power. When galvanized, the financial, political, and ideological resources of a politically mobilized business community can give a major edge in the competitive struggle for mass support. During the "lost decade" crises of the 1980s, conservative parties in a number of Latin American countries benefited from an unprecedented mobilization of business groups in electoral politics. The surge of conservative party politics was closely tied to the political activation of business. In Argentina, however, the political struggles generated by economic crisis did not result in a similar activation of business. The UCEDE's growth was hampered by business's historical reluctance to become openly identified with conservative party politics. This would become the party's most serious core-constituency problem during the party-building period of the 1980s.

As a segment of the electorate, the well-to-do of Buenos Aires voted primarily for the UCEDE. Individual businessmen and women joined the party, became involved in its activities, and contributed financially. In its corporatist incarnations, however, the Argentine business class remained aloof from the UCEDE's persistent appeals for support and engaged in separate streams of political action. The difficult relationship between the UCEDE and business was driven by two factors: tension between the party's ideology of economic liberalism and the economic interests of the Argentine bourgeoisie, and a tradition of political action by Argentine business that eschews party commitments.

Argentine business development has historically taken place under the tutelage of the state. Throughout the post-World War II period, the industrial and commercial sectors were intricately dependent upon state subsidies and protection and had profitable connections with state enterprises. This economic dependence has not always, however, been reflected in the political discourse of and ideologies espoused by the business community. In the distributional struggles of the post-Peronist period, industry often made common cause with the country's powerful agricultural exporters against populist adversaries. As a result, Argentina has on paper had one of the most economically liberal business communities in Latin America. This did not, however, make business elites particularly responsive to the UCEDE's appeals for support of its free-market agendas during the 1980s. It was one thing for business to accept the ideological leadership of Argentina's big agricultural exporters in distributional struggles with labor. It was quite another thing in the 1980s to support electoral platforms that threatened to dismantle the intricate array of state-business subsidies and relationships that made up what Mario Vicens and Pablo Gerchunoff have characterized as Argentina's system of "assisted capitalism." As these authors note, in 1987, government subsidies to private industry totaled over U.S. $3 billion, a sum that represented 4 percent of gross domestic product. These subsidies exceeded the U.S. $2.7 billion spent that year to service Argentina's foreign debt.[36] If public sector subsidies to the commercial and financial sectors during that period are also taken into account, the total state subsidy to the Argentine private sector in 1987 rose to 5 percent of GDP.[37] This equaled 60 percent of the 1987 public sector deficit, which at that time was a driving force behind Argentina's skyrocketing inflation.

The UCEDE was careful not to overemphasize business-state dependence in its political literature and propaganda. But its doctrinaire positions on free-market economics nevertheless tempered business support, and attacks by individual UCEDE leaders on "subsidized capitalists" and the "rent-seeking bourgeoisie" did not help to enlist business to the liberal cause. In my own interviews with business leaders, I frequently heard complaints about the "liberal ideologues" of the UCEDE's "lack of understanding" of the real world of business. There seemed to be a widely held perception in the business community of the liberales as a political stratum detached from the world of business and unaware of its practical dimensions. This was acknowledged by Ricardo Zinn, a prominent industrialist who served as the UCEDE's fund-raiser for the 1989 campaign. Zinn, who characterized his own mission as "building bridges" between the UCEDE and the business community, described frequent meetings in which he had assured business leaders that the free-market posture of the UCEDE was a long-term "ideal," to be accomplished step by step, without disrupting the viability of business activities.[38]

Aside from the wariness of economic liberalism of industrial and commercial interests, there was an additional problem for the UCEDE: a tradition of political action by all Argentine business sectors that eschews party commitments. "Stay close to power; influence what you can through direct contact with the executive power; avoid unnecessary partisan affiliations," said an influential businessman in characterizing the Argentine bourgeoisie's conception of politics.[39] This outlook translated into a preference for corporatist organization and direct firm-state contacts rather than the more uncertain long-term option of party building in pursuit of business objectives.

These patterns of business political action are not unique to Argentina. Throughout Latin America, the development of national business classes has taken place under the tutelage and protection of the state. This historic structural reality has given rise to similar patterns of political behavior by other Latin American business elites and has been a major impediment to conservative party development. In the 1980s, however, conservative party growth in several countries was spurred by an unprecedented mobilization of organized business into electoral politics. In Mexico and El Salvador in the early 1980s, and in Peru in 1987, economic crises and reformist state policies led to a profound deterioration in state-bourgeois relations. In each of these countries, this deterioration led to government initiatives to nationalize the privately owned sectors of the banking system. Bank nationalizations sparked important countermobilizations by the business community, which found vehicles for its opposition in existing conservative parties and electoral movements. Mexican business mobilization gave major impetus to the emergence of free-market "neo-Panista" currents in the Partido Acción Nacional (PAN), and catalyzed the party's coalition-building efforts on behalf of its agendas of democratization and antistatism.[40] In El Salvador, business mobilization dynamized the Alianza Republicana Nacionalista (ARENA), led to the partial displacement of its paramilitary founders by newly mobilized business elites and professionals, and eventually contributed to the rise of Alfredo Cristiani to the presidency.[41] In Peru, business activism gave major impetus to the antistatist mobilization efforts of Mario Vargas Llosa's Movimiento Libertad. A statement by a prominent Peruvian businessman, which contrasts sharply with the statement of his Argentine counterpart quoted above, captures the newfound bourgeois vocation for party politics in several of these countries: "This experience has taught us that Peruvian businessmen must participate in politics. This will be vital if we are to prevent misguided politicians from destroying in a few short moments what we have constructed over several generations through sacrifice and effort."[42]

The Argentine experience contrasts sharply with these cases. In spite of the mutual suspicions of social democratic Radicals and the business community, the government of Raúl Alfonsín nurtured its relations with business. Access to the state, through either organized industrial chambers or direct firm-state contacts in the case of the most important firms, was largely uninterrupted throughout the Plan Austral period and during the later crisis-ridden years of the Alfonsín administration. There was no clear state-business rupture comparable to what occurred in Mexico, Peru, and El Salvador. As a result, Argentine business elites had few sustained incentives to mobilize behind party politics in the years preceding the 1989 national elections. This deprived the UCEDE in its critical formation period of a resource available to its counterparts in some other countries: the financial and political power of business mobilization in electoral politics.

The start of the new democratic period in 1983 had seemed propitious for conservative leaders courting business support. Relations between the military government and its erstwhile business supporters had come under serious strain. The isolation of General Videla's economic team under the first military government had been followed by unpredictable swings in economic policy. Military rule had not delivered on the promise of predictable policy making and access to decision makers that had made it attractive to the business community in earlier years. By 1981, all the major business associations had publicly distanced themselves from the military government. After the Falklands War defeat, they unanimously supported a return to civilian rule.

Support for democracy does not, however, automatically translate into involvement in party politics. In Argentina, democratic rule offered business elites the promise of reforged relations with the state. The UCR government quickly lived up to this promise by institutionalizing business participation in policy making. Its most important overtures were to industry, whose participation it involved in an industry-labor "Economic and Social Council" that negotiated wage and price controls and consulted with the government on a range of issues related to the Plan Austral's implementation.[43] The Unión Industrial Argentina and a handful of smaller federations participated in the council and gave their full support to the government. To sweeten the deal, government also announced moderate privatization and foreign investment initiatives that went down well with business elites. Furthermore, its verbal commitments to fiscal discipline did not threaten the web of subsidies and government disbursements that were crucial to the industrial sector's well-being. This initiated a pattern of industry-government cooperation that deepened in subsequent years. The business-state alliance would eventually displace government-labor consultations over economic policy as the country's economic crisis deepened toward the end of the 1980's.[44]

Initially, the government's strategy toward the private sector sought to exclude agricultural interests. In a clear break with the previous military regime, the UCR government took a markedly pro-industrial stand. Its pronouncements were filled with references to "industrial modernization" and criticisms of the military regime's bias in favor of the financial and agricultural-export sectors. These positions were backed up by the exclusion of agricultural interests from government-business consultative arrangements. Agricultural exporters and their interest associations were not invited to join the government's corporatist negotiation arrangements during the early years of the Alfonsín administration. This exclusion sparked the first business-state crisis under Alfonsín.

Shortly after the enactment of the Plan Austral the country's most important association of agricultural interests, the Sociedad Rural Argentina (SRA), and other agricultural producers' federations moved into open opposition against the government's economic policies. They had long resented their exclusion from economic policy making. However, the economic pinch caused by an overvalued currency and food price controls, which the Plan Austral's architects saw as central to their inflation-containment efforts, turned resentment into open conflict. Throughout 1986, agricultural groups launched a series of demonstrations, producer strikes, and lockouts. They also mounted a major mass-media campaign denouncing the economic program's impact on agriculture.

Agriculture's political activation created new opportunities for the UCEDE, whose ideological platform converged most closely with the interests and traditional free-market positions of agricultural exporters. The UCEDE publicly and enthusiastically supported the agricultural producers' mobilization, and party leaders intensified their overtures to agricultural elites.[45] However, before such ties could be developed, the UCR government reached out to the agricultural sector and took dramatic steps to incorporate it into the policy-making process. It formed a new council for state-agricultural economic consultation, and, to ease the sector's economic plight, reduced export taxes on agricultural products. More significant, in March 1987, the president removed the incumbent secretary of agriculture from the national cabinet and replaced him with Ernesto Figueres, who had close ties to agriculture and was widely regarded as a spokesman for the sector's interests. The crisis between the government and agriculture quickly subsided. The influential Sociedad Rural Argentina, which only months earlier had led the sector's antigovernment mobilizations, now announced its support and expressed pleasure at the presence of a "real interlocutor" on the government's economic policy-making team.[46] In spite of continued tensions between the government and agriculture, the latter's foothold in the economic policy-making institutions of the state eroded any interest it might have had, "as an organized sector," in a party-based strategy of opposition to the government.[47]

The UCEDE nonetheless continued its efforts to attract business support. Approaches to all sectors of business for financial contributions were made, and support from businessmen and individual business concerns was received. This support was dependent, however, on the ideological commitment of individuals rather than on a shared sense in the business community of the importance of conservative party politics to the pursuit or protection of their class interests.[48] The continuity of state-business ties deprived the UCEDE of the resources and momentum that active business commitment to party politics can provide. This reality remained a pivotal core-constituency impediment to its emergence as a contender in Argentine electoral politics.

The Social Bases of Conservative Party Politics: Statistical Analyses

The social bases of electoral politics underwent considerable change during the 1983–89 presidency of Raúl Alfonsín, particularly in the city of Buenos Aires, Argentina's most important metropolitan region. By examining the evolving nature of the urban electorate's support for the UCEDE and comparing it with that of the party's main rivals, this section provides a view of how the social bases of a new conservative coalition were forged. It also provides a more general profile of how urban electoral politics evolved during this volatile period of economic crisis and political democratization.

The UCEDE in the Elections of 1985 and 1987: Internal Consolidation and Multiclass Coalition Building

In September 1985, when the first elections for the renovation of congressional, provincial, and municipal authorities were held, the political initiative in Argentine politics was held by the radical government of Raúl Alfonsín. The Plan Austral had been launched less than three months before, and its rapid success in bringing down inflation and returning economic stability was translated in a resounding radical success at the polls. This gave opposing parties little room to expand their own electoral support. The 1985 elections thus served primarily to ratify the electoral alignment that had emerged during the 1983 elections. No major changes took place in the distribution of social support for the major political parties, either at the national level or within the metropolitan region of Buenos Aires. As table 5.11 shows, support for the UCR, although it declined from 49.5 percent in 1983 to 42.9 percent in 1985, still gave it an overwhelming margin over all other parties. Peronism registered a slight increase in electoral support, rising from 23.5 percent to 25.2 percent. Faster growth was registered by the smaller parties, notably the UCEDE, the Center-Left Intransigent Party, and the Partido Federal. The UCEDE gained a respectable increase, from 8.7 percent in 1983 to 10.4 percent in 1985. The Intransigent and Federal parties registered greater growth, from 5.9 percent to 7.9 percent for the former, and from 1.9 to 5.8 percent for the latter.

For the UCEDE, the 1985 elections were primarily a time of consolidation. In absolute terms, its greatest growth was where it was already strongest: in the electoral circuits located in the top 10th socioeconomic percentile. Its average vote percentage in those circuits rose from 23 percent to 28 percent (see figure 5.4). The UCEDE's support also grew relatively evenly across social sectors. In relative terms, its fastest growth was in the poorest electoral circuits, but this was growth on an extremely small initial base. The small yet even growth registered by the UCEDE indicated that while consolidating as a small party and strengthening its support among its upper-class core constituencies, it was making no inroads into

Table 5.11

Congressional Election Results, City and Province of Buenos Aires, 1983–1989

	1983		1985		1987		1989	
	City	Province	City	Province	City	Province	City	Province
UCEDE	8.71	1.12	10.37	3.99	18.18	6.28	22.06	9.90
UCR	49.47	49.38	42.90	41.46	39.06	37.55	28.45	26.5
PJ	23.57	40.31	25.21	36.78	23.93	45.08	31.53	48.4
P.I.[a]	5.87	3.77	7.88	10.00	4.34	3.28	–	–

Sources: 1983–87, Departamento de Estadísticas, Dirección Nacional Electoral, Ministerio del Interior (Argentina); 1989, Rosendo Fraga, Argentina en las Urnas (Buenos Aires: Editorial Sudamericana, 1990), 53, 63.
[a]Intransigent Party (Center-Left).

Table 5.12

Social Status Indicators and Party Vote, Congressional Elections of 1985 and 1987, City of Buenos Aires (correlation coefficients)

	UCEDE		P. Federal		UCR		PJ		PI	
	1985	1987	1985	1987	1985	1987	1985	1987	1985	1987
University education	.827*	.829*	.195*	–	−.204*	−.193*	−.782*	−.778*	−.737*	−.680*
Employers	.518*	.530*	.197*	–	.076	.019	−.619*	−.589*	−.337*	−.275*
Poverty	−.340*	−.397*	−.353*	–	−.221*	−.187*	.609*	.584*	.078	.048
Self-employed	−.343*	−.306*	.156*	–	.468*	.427*	.032	.046	.398*	.381*
Employee/worker	−.089	−.135*	−.138*	–	−.296*	−.239*	.307*	.307*	−.131	−.132

* Significant at the .01 level (one-tailed). N = 209.

sectors outside those constituencies. The construction of a mass base would be the task of later elections.

The 1985 elections did, however, signal the end of the Partido Federal's challenge to the UCEDE for conservative electoral dominance. The federalist vote total in the city of Buenos Aires increased significantly, but this growth in absolute terms was accompanied by a marked change in the social composition of the Partido Federal's electoral support. The party's performance contrasted with that of the UCEDE, whose across-the-board increases in voter support did not affect the relative intensity of its appeal among the upper classes. The figures in table 5.12, contrasted with those in table 4.3, show that 1985 correlations between UCEDE vote totals and indicators of high socioeconomic status remained largely unchanged from

1983.[49] However, they declined significantly for the Partido Federal. In 1983 the correlation between the federalist vote and electoral circuits with high proportions of university-educated voters was .850 (see table 4.3). This correlation coefficient was slightly higher than the UCEDE's coefficient of .838. In 1985, it had declined to .195 for the Partido Federal. Similarly, the coefficient for the "employer" category in 1983 was .431 for the Partido Federal. As table 5.12 shows, that coefficient also declined, to .197, in the 1985 elections.

The result of this election was a confirmation of the UCEDE's ascendancy in the conservative battle for core-constituency support. The Partido Federal withdrew from the struggle for the conservative electorate shortly thereafter, forming an alliance with the UCR (whose social coalition it now resembled more closely). In the 1987 elections, its candidates ran as part of the UCR slate in the congressional and municipal elections. The federalist challenge to dominance of the region's conservative party politics was, for the moment, over.

As we have seen, the 1987 elections were a double blow to the Radical government. Nationally, the UCR went down to defeat before the Peronist Party. National congressional elections gave the UCR 37.4 percent of the vote, against 41.5 percent for the Peronists. In addition, the latter swept all but two provincial governorships, including the pivotal governorship of the province of Buenos Aires. The repudiation of the Radicals by the electorate also initiated the decomposition of the urban social coalition that had sustained the Radical Party since the return to democratic politics.

Peronism was the main beneficiary of this decline, both at the national level and in the province of Buenos Aires, where it reversed the comfortable plurality held by the UCR in 1983 and 1985. In that province, the Peronists received a 45.1 to 37.6 percent margin over the radicals.[50] Throughout the country, therefore, discontent with Radical inability to stem the economic crisis was translated into a surge of support for the political alternative offered by Peronism.

In the city of Buenos Aires, however, it was a different story. In the capital city the new "manufactured will" that emerged as a protest against hard economic times was that provided by the UCEDE, whose labors of political organization and ideological proselytization now paid their first electoral dividends. As the figures in table 5.11 show, the local beneficiary of the mounting economic crisis was not Peronism. In contrast to its performance throughout the rest of the country, the Peronist Party actually underwent a slight decline in Buenos Aires. It was the UCEDE whose vote total jumped—to 18.2 percent from its 1985 total of 10.4 percent. Furthermore, the UCEDE was the only party in the city of Buenos Aires to

Table 5.13
Gains by Selected Parties in the City of Buenos Aires, 1987
Congressional Election (%)

SES level of electoral circuits	UCEDE	UCR	PJ	P.I.
Upper	8.9	−4.0	−1.2	−2.0
Upper middle	8.4	−4.1	−1.2	−3.3
Middle	7.5	−4.1	−1.3	−3.7
Lower middle	6.6	−3.8	−0.9	−3.7
Lower	5.8	−3.6	−1.6	−3.5

Note: "SES level" (in other tables and figures sometimes referred to as "status") is a composite of three socioeconomic status indicators used by the Argentine census: % of population with a university education, % of population whose occupation is listed as "employer or partner," and % of the population classified as living in poverty. "SES level" is the average of the three indicators in each of the city's 209 electoral circuits. The poverty indicator was inverted to reflect the percentage of the population *not* living in poverty. The 209 electoral circuits were then grouped into five levels of stratification. "Upper" represents the top 10th percentile, "Upper middle" represents the 75th to 90th percentiles, "Middle" represents the 25th to 75th percentiles, "Lower middle" represents the 10th to 25th percentiles, and "Lower" represents the bottom 10th percentile.

register electoral growth in those elections. Table 5.13 shows that this growth took place across all social strata.

The figures in table 5.13 indicate that while the UCEDE appears to have grown mostly at the expense of the UCR, its growth at each socioeconomic level exceeded the UCR's loss. The UCEDE was therefore also gaining votes from other parts of the political spectrum. It was the city's key beneficiary of the redistribution of social support brought about by the decline of the Peronist and Intransigent vote, and by the absorption of the Partido Federal by the UCR in those elections.

But there was an even more significant story in terms of the young conservative party's development. For the first time since the start of the democratic consolidation, the UCEDE experienced far greater growth rates in the lower-class sectors of the electorate than in its core constituencies among the upper social strata. In absolute terms, it still gained more percentage points in upper-class districts than in lower-class districts. But its growth rates were more than three times higher in the lower-class districts than they were in its upper-class strongholds. Table 5.14 compares the UCEDE growth rates in different SES-level electoral circuits for 1987 and contrasts them with the more even cross-class growth rates experienced by the party in 1985.

The UCEDE's ascent during this period can also be contrasted with the decline of the UCR, as well as with the fluctuating fortunes of the Peronist Party between 1983 and 1987, shown in figures 5.4, 5.5, and 5.6.

A more finely tuned view of the social dynamics of urban party politics can be obtained from the data on the 1985 and 1987 congressional elections presented in table 5.12, which compares statistical correlations between the vote for each of the main parties in the city of Buenos Aires and key social and occupational variables provided by the Argentine census.

The most unambiguous finding presented in table 5.12 is a continued strong association between high social status and a vote for the UCEDE. The correlation coefficient for university education and support for the UCEDE remained virtually unchanged from 1985 level. The same can be said for the correlation between the "employer" category and the UCEDE vote. The UCEDE also continued to show a negative association with high-poverty populations, which continued to be strongly associated with support for Peronism, and little discernible statistical association with "employee/worker" category populations, which also tilted toward Peronism.

Table 5.14
UCEDE Growth Rates, 1985 and 1987

SES level of circuits	Growth in 1985 elections	Growth in 1987 elections
Upper	21.3%	32.6%
Upper middle	26.4%	60.4%
Middle	17.1%	95.1%
Lower middle	18.0%	110.2%
Lower	33.0%	107.0%

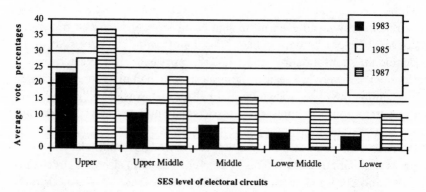

Fig. 5.4. Socioeconomic status and UCEDE voter support, City of Buenos Aires, congressional elections.

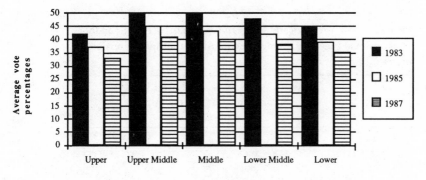

Fig. 5.5. Socioeconomic status and UCR voter support, City of Buenos Aires, congressional elections.

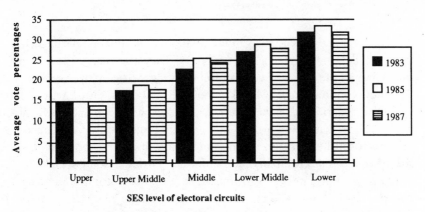

Fig. 5.6. Socioeconomic status and PJ voter support, City of Buenos Aires, congressional elections.

The UCEDE may well have given birth to a new mass base in Buenos Aires, but it was in no way a party of the underprivileged. It was merely gaining the makings of a mass conservative electoral coalition: multiclass, but maintaining a special affinity with the more privileged sectors of the electorate.

The UCEDE and the Self-Employed

The UCEDE appeared to fare poorly among the self-employed in these elections. As the figures in table 5.12 suggest, self-employed voters were strongly in the UCR's camp in both 1985 and 1987. Their vote was also positively associated with the much smaller Center-Left Intransigent Party.

Table 5.15

Socioeconomic Variables and UCEDE Growth between 1985 and 1987,
Congressional Elections, City of Buenos Aires (multiple regression
analysis)

	Parameter estimate	Standardized regression coefficient	t-value
Intercept	1.49		
University education	−.04	−.73	12.9*
Employers	.007	.048	0.8
Poverty	.005	.098	1.9
Self-employment	.022	.164	2.9*
Employee/worker	.006	−.064	1.0

Note: R-squared coefficient is .652. Standard error is .216.
*Significant at the .01 level (one-tailed). N= 209.

If we look at the UCEDE's *growth* in different occupational categories, however, the statistics tell a different story. They also shed some light on the dynamics of conservative coalition building. Self-employed voters on the whole continued to stay loyal to the UCR. However, the growth of the UCEDE's coalition, as is the case with most growing conservative coalitions, was predicated on incremental gains in large social sectors outside its core constituencies, not on the sudden and massive capture of those social sectors. The crumbling pieces of other parties' eroding social coalitions are what generally provide the bricks and mortar for new multiclass conservative coalitions. The results of the multiple regression analysis presented in table 5.15 suggest that the greatest relative impact on the UCEDE's growth between 1985 and 1987 came from the UCR's traditional supporters among the self-employed.

The standardized regression coefficient of .164 suggests that the highest positive relative impact on UCEDE growth, came from the self-employment variable. The regression coefficient of .022 for self-employment was also the only positive statistically significant coefficient. Given the surge in inflation in the months prior to the elections, these results should not be surprising. The self-employed, unprotected by the automatic indexation mechanisms provided for salaried workers, are the economic sector most vulnerable to the ravages of inflation. The results of the regression analysis suggest that the UCEDE's antistate and anti-inflation appeals were indeed penetrating into those sectors, giving them the most positive association with the UCEDE's new growth.

The Fruits of Popularization: The 1989 Congressional Elections

The 1989 elections strengthened the UCEDE's status as a multiclass conservative party. Several indicators provide evidence of this. The first of these is the actual social composition of the UCEDE's voter coalition. Figures 5.7 and 5.8 provide glimpse of that composition and its evolution since the 1983 elections.[51]

The charts in figures 5.7 and 5.8 show the effects of the party leader-

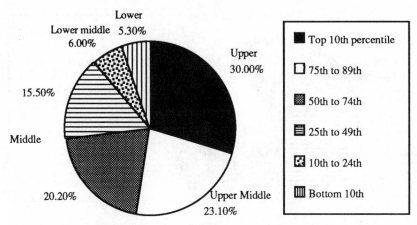

Fig. 5.7. Social composition of UCEDE voter coalition, City of Buenos Aires, congressional election, 1983. Based on SES levels of electoral circuits from which votes were drawn.

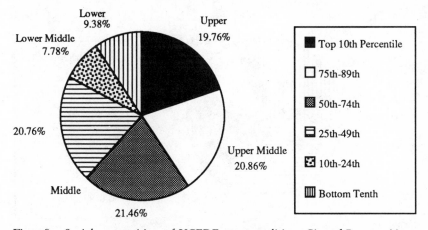

Fig. 5.8. Social composition of UCEDE voter coalition, City of Buenos Aires, congressional election, 1989. Based on SES levels of electoral circuits from which votes were drawn.

ship's populist strategies. In 1983, the UCEDE mobilized over 171,000 votes in the city of Buenos Aires. In 1989, that total rose to approximately 450,000 votes. Data provided in the charts on intensity of voter support show that this growth took place at all socioeconomic levels. However, as figures 5.9 and 5.10 indicate, the locus of the party's internal growth shifted away from its core constituencies in the upper classes. In 1983, the largest share of the UCEDE's electorate, 30 percent, came from electoral

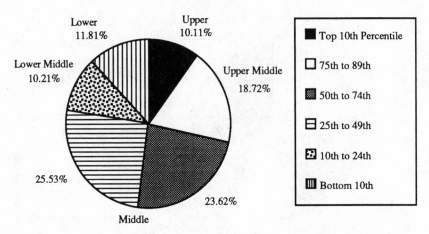

Fig. 5.9. Social composition of UCR voter coalition, City of Buenos Aires, congressional election, 1989. Based on SES levels of electoral circuits from which votes were drawn.

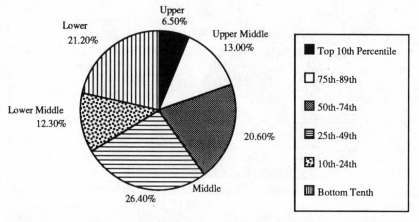

Fig. 5.10. Social composition of PJ voter coalition, City of Buenos Aires, congressional election, 1989. Based on SES level of electoral circuits from which votes were drawn.

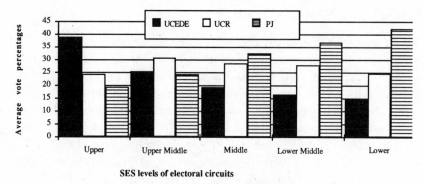

Fig. 5.11. Socioeconomic status and party support, City of Buenos Aires, congressional election, 1989.

circuits located in the top 10th SES percentile. In 1989, voters in those circuits comprised only 19.8 percent of the party's electorate. Now the largest share of UCEDE voters came from middle-class districts: 42.2 percent of the total. Furthermore, as a comparison of figures 5.7 and 5.8 will show, the largest relative growth took place in electoral circuits below the 50th SES percentile.

Comparing the UCEDE's voter coalition in 1989 with those of the UCR and the Peronist Party gives an indication of the differences in the parties' relationship to the electorate. All three parties drew heavily on the electoral districts located in the "middle" stratum. Not surprisingly, the UCR coalition was most heavily dependent on the middle class, with almost half (49.15 percent) of its voters coming from circuits grouped in the 25th–75th SES percentiles. The PJ's reliance on this stratum was similar to that of the UCR: 47 percent of its voters came from middle-SES-level circuits. The Peronist bias in the middle-class districts was, however, weighted toward the lower half (25th to 49th SES percentiles), in contrast to the relatively even distribution of middle-class voters for the UCR and the UCEDE.

The nature of electoral competition among these three parties placed a sizable burden on the UCR, which found its middle-class constituencies providing an important numerical base of support for both the UCEDE and the Peronist Party. Furthermore, the field in the top and bottom 10th percentiles was largely dominated by the UCEDE and the Peronists, who, in addition to drawing sizable portions of their vote from those sectors of the electorate, also continued to command their most intense voter loyalty.

UCEDE Growth and the Urban Poor

Where did the UCEDE's new electoral support come from in 1989? Table 5.16 shows that statistical correlations between the UCEDE's vote and selected occupational and socioeconomic variables did not undergo dramatic variation from previous elections. Its association with high social status remained highly positive, and its association with low social status remained negative. The sources of the UCEDE's new growth did, however, shift. The results of a multiple regression analysis presented in table 5.17 show that in 1989 the strongest statistical association with the UCEDE's growth was registered in the "poverty" category.

The standardized regression coefficient of .369 for "poverty" suggests that new support from the urban poor had the greatest relative impact on the UCEDE's growth in the 1989 elections. The t-value of 7.3 for "poverty," second only to that for "university education," indicates the

Table 5.16
Socioeconomic Indicators and Party Vote, City of Buenos Aires, 1989
Congressional Election (correlation coefficients)

	UCEDE	UCR	PJ	CFI
University education	.791*	−.090	−.741*	.652*
Employers	.551*	.085	−.610*	.503*
Poverty	−.393*	−.254*	.592*	−.513*
Self-employed	−.277*	.415*	.012	.009
Employee/worker	−.180*	−.273*	.353*	−.266*

*Significant at the .01 level (one-tailed). N = 209.

Table 5.17
Socioeconomic Variables and UCEDE Growth between 1987 and 1989,
Congressional Elections, City of Buenos Aires (multiple regression analysis)

	Parameter estimate	Standardized regression coefficient	t-value
Intercept	.621		
University education	−.013	−.619	11.2*
Employers	.004	.067	1.1
Poverty	.006	.369	7.3*
Self-employment	.004	.077	1.4
Employee/worker	−.005	−.142	2.2*

Note: R-squared coefficient is .652. Standard error is .081.
*Significant at the .01 level (one-tailed). N = 209.

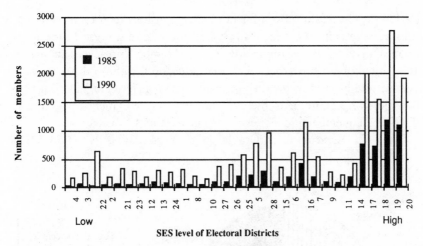

Fig. 5.12. Socioeconomic status and growth of UCEDE membership, City of Buenos Aires, 1985–90. Data are for the 28 electoral districts of the city of Buenos Aires.

strength of the statistical significance of the relationship between poverty and UCEDE growth. These results suggest that the strategy of popularization led by Adelina de Viola had a definite impact among the city's poor. With a new discourse and a concerted strategy of electoral organization, the UCEDE demonstrated in 1989 that the messages of liberalismo could indeed penetrate the most underprivileged strata of Argentina's urban population.

The Social Bases of Party Membership

Another indication of popularization can be found in the changing membership dynamics of conservative party politics. Here we can get a glimpse of the effect of organization (as opposed to such factors as mass-media influence) in contributing to the party's growth.[52] In 1985, the UCEDE was a party whose membership was overwhelmingly from upper-class neighborhoods. Its presence in the poorest districts of the city was negligible. By 1990, however, this situation had evolved. The party still had its largest share of members living in the top 10th percentile SES neighborhoods, but its presence in lower-class neighborhoods increased significantly. The data presented in figure 5.12 compare the number of UCEDE members in 1985 and 1990 in each of the twenty-eight electoral districts of the city, indicating that it managed to increase its membership substantially in the non-upper-class districts.[53] While membership roughly doubled in the city's four most affluent districts (pushing its total number up substantially from the large 1985 base), the rate of growth in the four poorest districts was significantly higher. Membership levels increased an average of six times between 1985 and 1990 in those districts. The highest rate of growth for the entire city was registered in Villa Lugano (District No. 22), home to the city's largest slum settlements, which saw the UCEDE membership increase over sixteen times its 1985 level.

The UCEDE made considerable progress expanding its membership

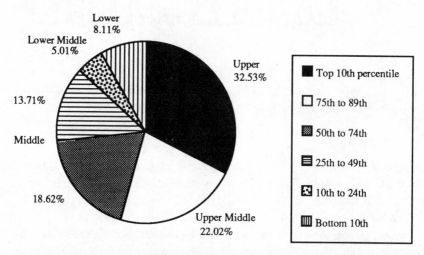

Fig. 5.13. Social composition of UCEDE membership, City of Buenos Aires, 1990. Based on SES level of electoral circuits in which party members live.

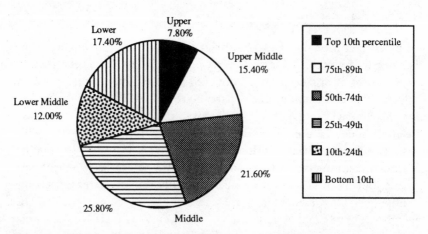

Fig. 5.14. Social composition of UCR membership, City of Buenos Aires, 1990. Based on SES level of electoral circuits in which party members live.

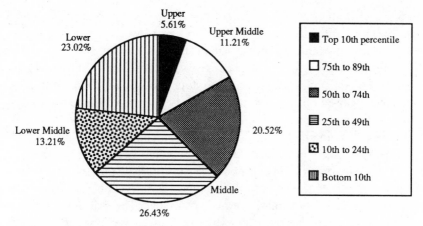

Fig. 5.15. Social composition of PJ membership, City of Buenos Aires, 1990. Based on SES level of electoral circuits in which party members live.

base among unprivileged sectors of the urban electorate. Party building across social sectors was indeed a feature of the party's growth during the 1980s. However, in comparison to the UCR and the Peronists, the UCEDE remained a party whose membership (and voting in internal party elections) was heavily dominated by upper-class voters. This fact appears in sharper relief when the party's 1990 membership is compared with those of the UCR and the Peronist Partido Justicialista. Figure 5.13 shows that fully 54.6 percent of the UCEDE's members resided in the top 25th SES percentile electoral circuits. In contrast, figures 5.14 and 5.15 show that only 23.2 percent of UCR members, and 16.8 percent of PJ members resided in those circuits.

Conclusion

Between 1983 and 1989, a new conservative electoral coalition was forged in Buenos Aires. The Unión del Centro Democrático grew from an ideological party of notables, overwhelmingly dependent on upper-class support, to a multiclass party that contested the long-standing UCR-Peronist dominance of local electoral politics.

Three developments specific to the 1983–89 period contributed to the UCEDE's growth. The first was the political context engendered by democratization. The armed forces were discredited as political actors and internally torn by lingering post-Proceso and post-Falklands resentments. This political climate rendered civil-military coalition building unviable as a political strategy for the leaders of Buenos Aires conservatism. Organization by political leaders in the electoral arena was needed to give the conservative movement a presence in the political debate.

Another factor that propelled conservative elites into the task of party building was that virtually all access to state power and technocratic influence were closed off to them in the administration of President Raúl Alfonsín. Economic policy-making institutions, their traditional hunting-grounds, were dominated by policy makers who had long been intellectual adversaries of economic liberalism. There would be no room in the key policy-making institutions of the Radical-controlled state for Alvaro Alsogaray, Roberto Alemann, or the legions of mid-level liberal economists who had served in previous governments. Influence over decision making would have to be exerted from without, from as-yet-untested areas of political society.

As a result of these developments, a new conservative political elite was formed in the Buenos Aires region. Thereafter, the growth and democratization of conservative party politics were forged by struggle. They did not emerge from the design or democratic vision of its historic leaders. From the moment that free electoral competition was reintroduced into Argentine political life, internal struggle became the driving force of conservatism's reorganization and transformation. It was this struggle that gave impetus to the UCEDE's strategies of popularization. The quest to build an electoral majority by appealing to the urban middle and lower classes was also driven by the efforts of individual political leaders to bolster their positions within a party tightly controlled by its established leadership. Internal struggle, as well as the broader political contest, thus played an important role in shaping the UCEDE's emergence as a contender in Argentine urban politics.

The UCEDE's electoral advances confirmed that there was nothing inherent in the urban social structure of the region that made it impossible for political leaders to forge an electoral coalition linking the dominant strata to the large middle and lower-middle classes. The party's growth demonstrated that social cleavages are matters to be manipulated through ideological mobilization and political organization. It also demonstrated that given the incentives, the time, and the resources, a conservative political class could emerge that was capable of building significant electoral support for its agenda of free-market reform.

The mass base forged by the UCEDE was also facilitated by the changes undergone by the Argentine social structure in previous years, notably the growth of informality and urban poverty, and the softening of the social bases of long-standing populist coalitions. Most of the UCEDE's mass base lay in the middle classes. Yet heterogeneity was also key to the growth of its electoral coalition. In 1987, the party's anti-inflationary message generated new support in the middle and informal sectors. In 1989, its more populist appeal showed signs of penetration among the urban poor.

The most important social constraints on the party's growth lay in core-constituency dynamics. The party's support among the most prosperous sectors of the urban electorate did, of course, provide it with important resources. Privately owned media outlets provided willing and effective channels of dissemination for the party's message of antistatism and free-market reform. In addition, the party's connections to circles of wealth and influence gave clout to its participation in the national debate and provided it with intellectual and financial resources that allowed it to expand its appeal beyond its initial constituencies of well-to-do urban dwellers. Nevertheless, problems in the organization of core-constituency support abounded. The UCEDE's most important shortcoming was its inability to become the primary electoral vehicle for the advancement of the class and sectoral interests of the Argentine business community. Corporatist and technocratic ties to the state continued to be the most important avenues for the political action of Argentine business, and this left little room for strategies of party-based opposition that would have given major impetus to the UCEDE's coalitional efforts. While the UCEDE managed to tap into the ideological commitment of individual business groups and individuals, the *pragmatic* bases of business community support were absent. Without the convergence of ideological and pragmatic support from business, the UCEDE's strategy of opposition failed to generate the momentum that conservative parties in other countries in the region were experiencing during those years of social change and economic decline.

Chapter Six

Shifting Arenas of Political Action:
Conservatives and the State during the Menem Presidency

The very impermanence of political institutions in developing areas underscores the degree to which these institutions are themselves chosen.

ROBERT BATES

I feel I cannot participate in this process of transformation burdened by the obligations of political militancy, which means belonging to a political party.

MARIA JULIA ALSOGARAY, UCEDE leader and Menem government cabinet member, on resigning from the UCEDE

Whether conservative parties did well or poorly in the elections that swept Latin America in the late 1980s, their agendas of free-market reform were implemented by governments that came to power. In some key cases, despite their loss at the polls, conservative leaders occupied ministerial and technocratic positions in governments controlled by other parties. After defeating the conservative FREDEMO coalition led by Mario Vargas Llosa (by vowing not to enact the economic policies promised by Vargas Llosa), Peruvian President Alberto Fujimori promptly appointed a top member of the FREDEMO coalition as his economics minister.[1] In Argentina, the economic policy-making institutions of the Peronist government of Carlos Menem became a veritable revolving door of entering and exiting UCEDE appointees.

Even where such high-visibility conservative participation in the executive branch did not take place, the embrace of free-market agendas by state elites gave conservatives a prominent role in the governing process. In Mexico, the policies and coalition-building strategies pursued by the Salinas government gave rise to a "collaborationist" relationship between the conservative Partido Acción Nacional (PAN) and the ruling PRI. They also fostered a rapprochement between the state and national business sectors that had mobilized behind the PAN in earlier years.

On the one hand, these developments point to the success of conservative parties in shaping the terms of the debate and in gaining public acceptance of their prescriptions for solving the economic crisis. "We lost the election, but we won the battle of ideas," boasted José Piñera, leader of Chile's Unión Democrática Independiente (UDI), and architect of Pinochet's privatization of the national social security system.[2] In a similar vein, Alvaro Alsogaray dismissed pre-election polls that showed his party trailing a distant third in the 1989 presidential elections by remarking, "We have already won the intellectual battle."[3] There is little doubt that structural constraints played a major part in pushing nonconservative governments toward economic reform. But their reforms were greeted with high levels of popular support, much of it generated in the rough-and-tumble of conservative electoral mobilizations that marked the region's "lost decade" of development.

It is also not insignificant to democratic politics that the intellectual battles won by conservatives were waged in democratic arenas. The experience demonstrated that in contrast to earlier pessimism about the compatibility of democracy and elite interests, the organizational labors of conservative party leaders, coupled with the structural power of their core constituencies, can shape the debates and outcomes of mass electoral politics.

On the other hand, developments since the late 1980s raise questions about the institutional future of conservative parties in the region. In most cases their agendas, leaders, and even core constituencies were weaned away by a state controlled by another party. Demobilization of conservative parties was usually the result. The problem may not be serious for well-institutionalized parties, whose sunk costs and legacies of institutional history give them resiliency against such pressures. But conservative party politics in most Latin American countries is largely an uninstitutionalized phenomenon. The electoral movements that burst onto the scene in the 1980s lacked institutional legacies to help them weather political fluctuations. They possessed weak organizational networks and forged tentative social coalitions against an economic model whose demise was subsequently promised by governments in power. The turn to economic reform by nonconservative governments created important problems of identity and practice for the newly mobilized parties of Latin American conservatism. They also strained their ability to hold their new coalitions together in the face of government overtures to their leaders and constituencies.

Just as conservative leaders can choose to enter party politics, to devote time and resources to institution building, and to nurture the active mobilization and commitment of powerful social constituencies, so can they choose to abstain from these activities. Where conservative parties are weakly institutionalized, dependent upon the charisma or authority of small groups of leaders, or supported by newly formed coalitions and fluid voter loyalties, the slackening of leadership commitment can have serious short-term consequences. The volatility of voter loyalties that gave birth to their movements can also unravel those movements once their leaders have set their sights on other political horizons, or when shifting state strategies render electoral mobilization unnecessary for the realization of their agendas. PAN's internal dilemmas in Mexico since the 1988 elections; the fragmentation of conservative forces in Peru under the Fujimori administration; and, as seen in this chapter, the UCEDE's dramatic decline after 1989, provide examples of this. Gains made by conservatives in party politics were jeopardized, in the period of state-led reform that followed the lost-decade mobilizations, by the emergence of new opportunities in nonparty arenas for conservative leaders and their core constituencies.

National Conservative Politics and the Regional Question in Argentina, 1983–1989

The dust had barely settled from the struggles of the first democratic elections of 1983 when the issue of building a national conservative party returned to the fore of conservatism's internal debates. "La unidad del centro," the elusive goal that had dominated conservative aspirations for decades, once again became the clarion call for Argentina's dispersed conservative forces. Within the UCEDE's own ranks, the issue of building a national conservative party was a source of acrimonious internal debates. The party was split between proponents of a single-party (*partido único*) strategy and those of *aliancismo,* building a coalition with existing conservative parties in the interior. Proponents of a partido único stressed the advantages of the internal discipline and ideological coherence that would come from building a new party from the ground up throughout the country. Many were long-time followers of Alvaro Alsogaray's and veterans of previous failed national alliances. They called upon the party to heed the lessons of past coalition building with provincial parties. Advocates of aliancismo shared their adversaries' insistence on liberal dominance of a future conservative movement, but they were willing to sacrifice ideological coherence and organizational discipline for realistic possibilities of capturing national power in the 1989 presidential elections.

By the mid 1980s, the advantage in the UCEDE's internal struggle had clearly shifted to the proponents of aliancismo. As the UCEDE consolidated its hold on the Buenos Aires conservative electorate and saw its influence in the national debate grow, party leaders dared increasingly to speak of capturing political power through elections. But "power" in Argentine politics ultimately meant control over the national executive branch. This required nationwide organization. By the mid 1980s, few in the liberal-conservative movement were willing to endure the long wait that building new party organizations throughout the country's interior provinces would entail. Even fewer were willing to wage the uncertain battles against locally entrenched provincial parties that such a strategy would require. The provinces of the interior possessed ready-made party networks for local conservative mobilization. These, linked for the first time since the 1930s with a consolidated Buenos Aires party, would be the new basis for conservative unity.

Aliancismo thus became the centerpiece of the UCEDE's national political strategy after the mid 1980s. The chief architect of this strategy was María Julia Alsogaray, Alvaro's daughter, a congresswoman-elect in 1985. In 1987, she forged the UCEDE's parliamentary alliance with provincial parties in the congress, known as the Interbloque de Centro. The Interbloque, which anointed conservatism as the third force in the national congress, was widely seen as a first step toward a national electoral alliance in the 1989 presidential elections. In 1987 and 1988, María Julia Alsogaray also piloted the party's negotiations with the conservative parties of the interior for creating a UCEDE-led coalition in the 1989 presidential elections.

National conservative politics between 1983 and 1989 thus became dominated by unending negotiations among provincial conservative parties. Throughout the local and congressional elections of the period, alliances were made and unmade as conservatives vainly sought to counter their organizational fragmentation. At no time did a national alliance emerge that brought conservatives together for the congressional races. Rather, local or regional alliances were made between individual parties that were generally unconnected with larger efforts at integration.

Ironically, the struggles within the conservative movement were taking place against a backdrop of growing ideological convergence. As the crisis of the developmentalist state gathered steam, there were fewer and fewer leaders in the conservative movement openly advocating state-centered models of development. Even among federalists, who in the 1970s had mobilized in opposition to the Proceso's economic policies, calls for privatization and deregulation gained momentum as the economic crisis deepened. The federalist shifts toward more economically liberal postures can be seen in policy platforms advanced by the governor of Corrientes, Romero Feris, who in the 1980s organized a rival conservative party project, the regional axis of which would have been the interior provinces. Partisan attacks against liberal rivals reflected the decades-long liberal-federalist ideological animosity: "We believe in a state of reasonable dimensions, an arbiter and promoter, while the state proposed by orthodox liberalism is a virtually nonexistent state."[4] However, Feris's platform reflected little of past federalist attachment to the developmentalist state. Federalists would, he promised, "reprivatize the economy, and will only allow the existence of three state monopolies: justice, defense, and security."[5] There was little in this federalist "night watchman" conception of the state, or in federalist calls for economic deregulation and export-led growth, that their "orthodox" liberal adversaries would have quarreled with.

The evolution of Argentina's economy in the 1980s, and, specifically, the state's increasingly evident economic deterioration, had narrowed the distance between federalist and liberal economic prescriptions considerably since the days of the Proceso. State-shrinking and deregulation had become the common prescription of both contenders for the leadership of Argentine conservatism. While differences existed in the details of each sector's preferred solutions (and in the potential regional distribution of the costs of those solutions), these were no longer rooted in advocacy of fundamentally divergent economic development models.

The divisive element of conservatism's regional cleavage in the 1980s therefore resided far less than before in the economic realm. It was now located primarily in the organizational realm. The conflict was not between regional political parties with opposing socioeconomic agendas but between political parties eager to protect and advance their individual organizational interests. It was the *organizational* legacy of Argentine conservatism's historic regional fragmentation that confounded national unity in the 1980s, and that ultimately thwarted hopes for a unified conservative ticket in the presidential elections of 1989.

The fragmentation of conservative political organization was compounded by an additional development: the reemergence of the UCR as a pragmatic electoral vehicle for anti-Peronist voters. Struggles within the UCR during the crisis-ridden 1980s resulted in the ascendance of ideologically conservative currents, many based in the interior, over the beleaguered Center-Left currents loyal to President Alfonsín. The Radical candidate for the presidency in 1989 was Eduardo Cesar Angeloz, governor of Córdoba province, the seat of one of the UCR's most ideologically conservative party organizations.[6] His proposals for wide-scale privatizations, budget cutbacks, and economic deregulation marked a sharp rhetorical departure from the Alfonsín government, and once again thrust the UCR into the role of Center-Right opposition to the Peronists.

The emergence of Angeloz's candidacy caused problems for the UCEDE's national campaign. The differences between the local campaign in Buenos Aires and the national campaign were striking. In Buenos Aires the Radical congressional ticket was headed by Center-Left Alfonsinista candidates, a fact that gave the UCEDE's Buenos Aires campaign momentum as a local conservative alternative. Nationally, however, the UCR's rightward turn hurt the UCEDE's campaign in two ways. First, it gave conservative voters a Center-Right alternative to Peronism. It also provided conservative parties in the interior with a coalition-building alternative to the UCEDE. Such parties could now run candidates in local elections but resort to the time-tried strategy of supporting the UCR presidential candidate in return for the promise of postelection rewards from a future Radical presidency.

In late 1988, that was exactly what happened. A group of important provincial parties from the interior, led by the Unión Provincial, of Salta, and the Movimiento Popular Jujeño, of Jujuy, organized the Confederación Federalista Independiente (CFI), an alliance of provincial parties that supported Eduardo Angeloz for president, while running their own local tickets. They did so by setting up a CFI presidential slate with Angeloz as its presidential candidate. His vice-presidential candidate on the CFI slate was María Cristina Guzmán, a leader of the Movimiento Popular Jujeño. Angeloz thus ran on two presidential tickets: the UCR ticket, and the conservative CFI ticket organized by federalist parties. Should one of those slates not give him a majority in the election, the two could be combined in the Electoral College. Voters wishing to support a Center-Right presidential candidate with realistic prospects of winning, but reluctant to support the UCR, which for the previous six years had been dominated by a Center-Left leadership, now had an alternative to the more uncertain prospect of an independent conservative bid. They could cast their vote for the Angeloz-led CFI ticket, giving Angeloz an additional crop of votes in the Electoral College without rewarding the UCR.

The emergence of a Center-Right Radical alternative thus cut into the UCEDE's base horizontally as well as vertically. It threatened to slice away supporters in the upper classes by waving the banners of anti-Peronism and liberal economic reform. It also cut into the UCEDE's regional coalition building by splitting off potential allies in the federalist-conservative movement. In so doing, the UCR displayed its historical abilities to exploit the regional divisions of its conservative adversaries. Faced with a conservative electoral challenge, the UCR availed itself of its own ideological duality to neutralize that challenge. Center-Right forces in the party bubbled to the surface, opening up new coalition-building opportunities with conservative parties in the interior previously opposed to the Alfonsín-dominated UCR. In the process, they consigned the long-sought conservative third-party challenge to oblivion.[7]

The 1989 Presidential Election

The Peronist presidential candidate, Carlos Saúl Menem, handily won the 1989 election with over 47 percent of the vote. Thanks to conservative fragmentation, the presidential election of 1989 was largely a two-party contest. Nearly 80 percent of votes cast nationwide were divided between the UCR and the Peronist Party. The UCEDE-led Alianza de Centro suffered a particularly dismal setback in those elections. Only 6.2 percent of the national vote went to the Alianza's Alsogaray-led presidential ticket.

Because of conservative national divisions, voters resorted once again to ticket-splitting between local conservative and national majoritarian parties: 21 percent of those who voted for a conservative congressional ticket cast their votes for another party in the presidential race. In addition, conservative disunity split the conservative vote right down the middle in the presidential race. The UCEDE-led Alianza de Centro only garnered 47 percent of the conservative vote for president. The remaining 53

Table 6.1
National Election Results in Argentina, 1989 (%)

	Presidential election	Congressional election
Alianza de Centro	6.2	9.5
CFI	4.5	3.7
Other provincial parties	2.5	3.5
UCR	32.4	28.9
PJ	47.3	44.6
United Left	2.4	3.4

Source: Rosendo Fraga, *Argentina en las urnas* (Buenos Aires: Editorial Sudamericana, 1990), 14.

Table 6.2
Ticket-Splitting by Alianza de Centro Voters, 1989 (%)

	Presidential	Congressional	Difference pres.(−)cong.
City of Buenos Aires	12.3	22.0	−9.7
Buenos Aires Province	6.8	9.9	−3.1
Catamarca	0.9	0.9	0.0
Córdoba	3.7	7.6	−3.9
Corrientes	27.5	39.0	−11.5
Chaco	1.9	1.7	−0.2
Chubut	6.9	6.7	−0.2
Entre Ríos	5.9	8.2	−2.3
Formosa	0.2	0.2	0.0
Jujuy	1.3	1.3	0.0
La Pampa	4.5	5.1	−0.6
La Rioja	0.7	0.9	−0.2
Mendoza	16.7	20.3	−3.6
Misiones	4.6	6.5	−1.9
Neuquén	3.8	3.2	−0.6
Rio Negro	6.7	5.0	−1.7
Salta	3.2	2.2	−1.0
San Luis	3.8	3.8	0.0
San Juan	6.2	7.0	−0.8
Santa Cruz	3.9	4.8	−0.9
Santa Fe	5.9	9.1	−3.2
Santiago del Estero	0.7	0.8	−0.1
Tierra del Fuego	8.3	7.3	1.0
Tucumán	1.1	1.4	−0.3

Source: Reproduced from Rosendo Fraga, *Argentina en la urnas* (Buenos Aires: Editorial Sudamericana, 1990), 21.
Note: The city of Buenos Aires is a federal district.

percent was divided between the CFI and independent provincial parties.
Similarly, in the congressional race nationwide, the Alianza only mobilized 57 percent of the conservative vote.

For the UCEDE-led Alianza de Centro, ticket-splitting was particularly
damaging. Its congressional vote total nationwide exceeded the presidential vote total by over 50 percent. We can see this dynamic more clearly
in the data in table 6.2, which show the impact of ticket-splitting on a
province-by-province basis.

The national electoral dynamics were damaging to the UCEDE-led
Alianza de Centro in virtually all provinces. In numerical terms, the greatest cost to the Alianza from ticket-splitting came in the provinces where its
local tickets did best. In the city of Buenos Aires, 44 percent of voters who

Table 6.3

Ticket-Splitting, Social Status, and Party Gains and Losses, City of Buenos Aires, 1989
(correlation matrix)

	Status	UCEDE P.(−)C.	Radical P.(−)C.	Peronist P.(−)C.	CFI P.(−)C.	CFI/Radical P.(−)C.
Status	1.000					
UCEDE: P.(−)C.	−.672*	1.000				
UCR: P.(−)C.	.439*	−.406*	1.000			
PJ: P.(−)C.	−.227*	.022	−.036	1.000		
CFI: P.(−)C.	.629*	−.764*	.261*	−.151	1.000	
CFI/UCR: P.(−)C.	.648*	−.696*	.862*	−.105	.715	1.000

Note: P.(−)C. = presidential total minus congressional total. "Status" (in other tables and figures sometimes referred to as "SES level") is a composite of three socioeconomic status indicators used by the 1980
Argentine census: % of population with a university education, % of population whose occupation is listed
as "employer or partner," and % of the population classified as living in poverty. "Status" is the average
of the three indicators in each of the city's 209 electoral circuits. The poverty indicator was inverted to
reflect the percentage of the population *not* living in poverty. The 209 electoral circuits were then grouped
into five levels of stratification. "Upper" represents the top 10th percentile, "Upper middle" represents the
75th to 90th percentiles, "Middle" represents the 25th to 75th percentiles, "Lower middle" represents the
10th to 25th percentiles, and "Lower" represents the bottom 10th percentile.
*Significant at the .01 level (one-tailed). N = 209.

supported the congressional ticket headed by Adelina de Viola did not
vote for the presidential ticket headed by Alsogaray. This gave the presidential ticket a loss of almost 10 percentage points citywide. In Corrientes
province, where the local conservative congressional ticket actually defeated all other party tickets, the presidential ticket came in third, 11.5
percentage points short of its congressional ticket — a difference of over 30
percent. In Buenos Aires province, 31 percent of voters for the Alianza
congressional ticket did not support the presidential ticket. Similar patterns were repeated throughout the country. Only in Mendoza, the Alianza's third-best performance in the local races, did the presidential ticket
manage to limit its shortfall vis-à-vis the congressional ticket. Only 18
percent of voters supporting the local ticket there did not support the
presidential ticket.

The data in table 6.3 give an indication of the winners and losers as a
result of conservative ticket-splitting in the city of Buenos Aires, revealing the damaging effects of national conservative divisions on the local
UCEDE-led presidential campaign. In general, the results suggest that
when the UCEDE-led presidential ticket suffered from ticket-splitting, the
CFI/UCR alliance gained. The UCR candidate was the clear beneficiary of
a pragmatic upper-class division of support between congressional and

presidential tickets. In one sense, this seemed a repeat of 1983, when conservative and upper-class ticket-splitting favored the Radical candidate, Raúl Alfonsín. However, in 1989 the Radical candidate's gain was due more to his ad hoc alliance with federalists. The correlation coefficients suggest that the UCEDE's presidential ticket losses benefited the Radical candidate, but especially so when he was linked to the federalist CFI ticket. The federalists' decision to ally themselves with Angeloz rather than the UCEDE-led Alianza de Centro was thus very damaging to the latter's presidential campaign. Furthermore, the negative coefficient for the correlation between "status" and "UCEDE presidential minus congressional" totals suggests that ticket-splitting against the party's presidential ticket was greatest among affluent voters. Similarly, the highly positive coefficient for the correlation between "status" and the CFI and combined CFI/UCR totals indicate that the ticket-splitting by affluent voters that damaged the UCEDE's campaign was very beneficial to the temporary marriage between federalists and Radicals. In fact, the correlation coefficients suggest that Radicals gained far more from ticket-splitting by affluent voters when linked to the federalists than when they ran alone in the city of Buenos Aires.

Argentina: A Two-Tier Party System

The 1989 elections also confirmed an additional reality of Argentine politics: the existence of a two-tier party system. At the national level, party politics was characterized by a UCR-Peronist two-party hegemony. Provincial party politics did not, however, mirror dynamics at the national level. At the provincial level, many party systems prevailed, and the two-party UCR-Peronist dominance was often checked by the existence of strong local conservative parties. Conservative provincial parties controlled the governorships of Corrientes, Neuquén, and San Juan, and in each of those provinces, the delegations to the national senate were from the local conservative parties. In addition, individual conservative parties in Rio Negro, Tucumán, and Salta had in 1987 contested local gubernatorial elections, averaging 20 percent of the vote.[8]

As the aggregate congressional vote totals in table 6.4 show, support for conservative parties also grew considerably at the provincial level between 1983 and 1989. In 1983, only three provinces had registered a total vote of over 20 percent for local conservative parties. By 1989 that number had risen to nine. In several provinces, therefore, a multiparty

Table 6.4

Aggregate Congressional Vote Totals for Argentine Conservative Parties by Province, 1983 and 1989 (%)

	1983	1989
Above 20%	Corrientes: 35.8	Corrientes: 41.6
	Neuquén: 34.5	Tucumán: 36.0
	San Juan: 25.3	Neuquén: 32.9
		City of Buenos Aires: 29.1
		Salta: 28.4
		Chubut: 24.9
		Jujuy: 22.1
		San Juan: 21.7
		Mendoza: 21.0
Above 15%	Jujuy: 16.2	
Above 10%	City of Buenos Aires: 10.7	Chaco: 13.8
		Río Negro: 13.4
		Buenos Aires Province: 12.9
		Córdoba: 12.4
		Santa Fe: 10.1
Above 5%	Salta: 7.5	San Luis: 9.2
	San Luis: 7.1	Misiones: 8.8
	Chubut: 5.4	Tierra del Fuego: 8.5
		Entre Ríos: 8.2
		La Pampa: 7.1

Sources: Ezequiel Gallo and Esteban Thomsen, "Electoral Evolution of the Political Parties of the Right: Argentina, 1983–1989," in *The Right and Democracy in Latin America*, ed. Douglas Chalmers et al. (New York: Praeger, 1992), 144; and Rosendo Fraga, *Argentina en las urnas* (Buenos Aires: Editorial Sudamericana, 1990).

competitive dynamic was at work, and while Peronist or Radical control of local government tended to be the rule, their two-party hegemony was challenged by local conservative parties.

The figures in table 6.4 capture the regionally driven nature of conservatism's national electoral plight. In 1989, the Buenos Aires region had the makings of a competitive conservative party. The UCEDE had succeeded in the dual task of mobilizing the support of a core constituency in the upper classes and building a mass base among the region's middle and lower classes. Similarly, conservative provincial party politics in several provinces had evidenced a comeback since 1983. The failure of 1989 was the failure of conservatism as a national electoral force. In spite of the resurgence of a conservative parties at the provincial level, Argentine conservatism failed to overcome the tendency to fragmentation that had shaped its evolution throughout the age of mass politics. Fragmentation continued to be the dominant organizational characteristic of national conservative party politics. This reality would weigh heavily on the minds of conservative leaders as they faced the return of Peronism to the presidency after 1989.

The Postelection Menem Overtures: Conservatives Brought Back into the State

The Milagro Menem

The immediate aftermath of the 1989 elections was a tumultuous period for the UCEDE. The disappointing election results unleashed a bitter struggle within the party, which culminated in Alvaro Alsogaray's resignation as party president. The party's leadership passed to the "renovator" wing of the party linked to the popularization efforts of previous years. Federico Clérici, a Buenos Aires province congressman known for his dedication to political liberalism and parliamentarianism, assumed the party presidency. The UCEDE's national committee was also staffed with Alsogaray opponents. María Julia Alsogaray was removed from the pivotal party office of secretary of political action, and was replaced in that position by Adelina de Viola, who also solidified her control over the UCEDE in the city of Buenos Aires. The party's new leaders immediately announced an official posture of "democratic opposition" to the Peronist government, a stress on party building, and the consolidation of the UCEDE's evolution from an ideological party of notables to a mass conservative party.[9]

Alsogaray's eclipse was short-lived. No sooner had the initiative in conservative politics passed to his rivals than a surprising change on the national scene returned him to the center of events. The Peronist president-elect, Carlos Menem, who had built a winning electoral coalition on a vague platform of "productive revolution," social justice, and redistribution, made an abrupt turnabout after the election.[10] To the surprise of virtually all observers, particularly his supporters in the labor movement and the Peronist Party, he announced that his government would implement a program of economic adjustment, privatization, and deregulation.

In order to implement this program, Menem quickly sought to build an alliance with those who had most forcefully advocated its implementation, and whose confidence would be required to make it work. Alvaro Alsogaray was appointed special advisor to the president for dealings with the international financial community. María Julia Alsogaray was appointed president of the National Telephone Company — whose advanced state of deterioration had made it the supreme target of liberal calls for privatization — with a mandate to privatize. Alberto Albamonte, a UCEDE congressman, was appointed secretary of internal commerce. In a masterful touch of symbolism, Menem made his more momentous announcements on the television news show *Tiempo Nuevo,* hosted by the conservative journalists Bernardo Neustadt and Mariano Grondona, which had served as the UCEDE's most important anti-Menem forum during the election campaign.

The UCEDE was to be given a policy-making role on issues that had been central to the national economic debate, a debate whose terms had been powerfully influenced by the new conservative party. The ambiguous Peronist campaign slogan promising to launch a "productive revolution" was reformulated by the influential conservative newsweekly *Somos.* Featuring a beaming María Julia Alsogaray posing next to the Peronist president-elect on its cover, *Somos* proclaimed the coming of a "liberal and popular revolution."[11] With a mere 6 percent of the national vote, the UCEDE was now a highly visible member of the configuration of forces that would shape the politics of the Peronist government of Carlos Menem.

Menem's overtures dashed the ambitions of those embarked upon renewing the UCEDE as a democratic opposition party. By inviting the UCEDE's collaboration with his government, Menem sought not its numerical strength as a party or parliamentary force but its power in the realm of elite politics. He thus tapped those leaders who most inspired the confidence of the wealthiest and most influential sectors of the UCEDE's electorate. As a result, the locus of power and initiative within the party passed from the renovator leadership back to Argentine liberalismo's historic leader. Responding to the president's overture, Alsogaray described the new situation as a "political accord" between the party and the new Peronist government, consigning the formal UCEDE leadership's claims of "democratic opposition" to oblivion.

Bringing the UCEDE on board his new political project was central to Menem's political strategy. But there was a two-track logic to his overtures to the leaders of Argentina's social elite. The Ministry of the Economy was assigned to a leader of Argentina's business community. The business sector approached by Menem was not, however, the domestic-market-oriented sector that had traditionally provided Peronism with its chief base of business support. Menem approached Bunge y Born, Argentina's sole multinational corporation, a company associated with the most anti-Peronist sectors of the business community. In July 1989, Menem appointed Miguel Roig, Bunge y Born's recently retired president, as minister of the economy. When Roig died just weeks after assuming office, Menem turned to Bunge y Born once again for his replacement, Nestor Rapanelli, then the company's chief executive officer. Rapanelli's top aide in the ministry, Orlando Ferreres, was also a Bunge y Born executive.

Menem's objective was to build an alliance with economic power. While approaching the UCEDE was vital to mobilizing the confidence of the party's upper-class supporters, his strategy was indicative of the ambivalent state of relations between the country's most important business enterprises and the conservative party leadership. Bringing a conservative party into his coalition was not enough. A two-track strategy was needed for building support among Argentina's socioeconomic elite: Alvaro Alsogaray mobilizing the confidence of his affluent and influential electorate, and Argentina's most important industrial concern in charge of the Economics Ministry to guarantee business support.[12]

However, during the government's first six months, Alsogaray became locked in struggles with the business executives running the Economics Ministry. The conflict was rooted in the old liberal-business tensions that had marred the UCEDE's efforts to mobilize business support for its electoral campaigns. To Alsogaray's chagrin, the business executives in the Economics Ministry expressed strong preferences for "gradualist" approaches to economic reform, and availed themselves of many of the heterodox inflation-containment policies that had marked the Radical government's policy making in its final years. Early in Minister Rapanelli's administration, Alsogaray warned the president against the dirigista proclivities of the minister and his staff. He also embarked upon a public and behind-the-scenes effort to counter the Rapanelli economic team's influence over policy making that was reminiscent of his intratechnocratic struggles of years past. In fact, as the conflict unfolded, it was clear that this was the type of bureaucratic power struggle in which Alsogaray possessed far greater experience than his business adversaries in the Economics Ministry. He availed himself of the usual forums. In newspaper columns, television programs, speeches to influential business audiences, and memoranda to the president, he cast doubt over the viability of the Bunge y Born economic program. He criticized the Bunge y Born executives' resort to price and exchange controls, denounced the issuing of money by the central bank, and complained about the slow progress of the privatization program. He also alluded cryptically to impending high-

level changes in the government's economic policy-making team, statements that when officially denied only added to the climate of uncertainty
hovering over Economics Ministry officials.[13]

In December 1989, the Bunge y Born plan foundered, with a run on the
austral and a new inflationary outburst. The Menem government then
took a more orthodox economic turn, implementing a sudden and severe
contraction in the money supply, and removing price and exchange controls. Alsogaray was widely given credit for proposing and designing the
plan (although reports of his authorship were never officially confirmed).
At this point, he was given a more prominent role in the decision-making
process.[14] He also became a prominent and officially sanctioned spokesman for the government's program. On January 3, 1990, in an act normally reserved for ministers of state, Alsogaray gave an address to the
nation that was broadcast by television and radio nationwide. In his address, Alsogaray, whose life-long campaign against populism and the interventionist state had demanded nothing less than "a total change of the
system," gave his reasons for embracing his erstwhile Peronist foes:

> For more than thirty years I have represented a line of thinking in Argen-
> tina that in these moments is coinciding with the economic policies
> implemented by this government. What we are witnessing are not minor
> repairs. It is not a band-aid approach. It is a total change of the sys-
> tem. . . . What the president intends to do is to change this system down
> to the roots and evolve to what he calls a "popular market economy."
> This is what I have always called a "social market economy." It is the
> same thing.[15]

Alsogaray's participation in the Peronist government caused serious
problems for the formal leadership of the UCEDE. Officially, they controlled the party and determined its strategy, but the Menem overtures to
Alsogaray and his followers had seriously undermined their authority and
marginalized them in conservative decision making. Striving to protect the
UCEDE's identity as a democratic opposition force, the party's leaders
repeatedly denied the existence of any "co-governing" arrangement between the UCEDE and Peronism.[16] But their assertions were countered
by the increasingly visible participation of individual members of the
UCEDE, aside from the highly prominent Alsogarays, in the Menem government. The press spoke openly during this period of a division in the
UCEDE between *el poder formal,* held by the party's top officeholders,
and *el poder real,* held by Alsogaray and the UCEDE leaders who had
accompanied him into the government.

This characterization was quite accurate. One of the more striking features of the alliance was the marginal role played by party institutions themselves on the sides of both the UCEDE and the Peronist Party. Menem was once quoted during this period as saying that "alliances between men are generally preferable to alliances between parties."[17] The UCEDE-Peronist union reflected the president's preferred modus operandi. It was an alliance based on personal pacts between Menem and Alsogaray's entourage. It was forged and implemented in complete isolation from, and over the opposition of, the formal leaderships of both parties. Furthermore, and most damaging to the party leadership's denials of "co-government," it was consummated by the participation of UCEDE-affiliated technocrats at all levels of economic policy making in the executive branch.

The pattern that emerged under Menem's government was strongly reminiscent of older times. Ricardo Zinn, a UCEDE fund-raiser and political leader, drew an interesting comparison between liberal involvement in government during the 1960s and 1970s and the UCEDE collaboration with Menem's government. Zinn himself had occupied the powerful position of secretary of economic planning and coordination in Isabel Perón's government in 1975. He was the reputed architect of an economic stabilization program attempted by Celestino Rodrigo, then Isabel Perón's economics minister. The package, widely and infamously remembered to this day as the Rodrigazo, sparked a major crisis in the Peronist government, as well as powerful countermobilizations by organized labor. It also caused the fall of the economics minister and the withdrawal of his economic team from the government. Asked how he would compare that experience with his collaboration with the Menem government, Zinn responded:

> In reality there are strong similarities between the two experiences. But there is also a major difference. In the first experience, nobody was really aware of what we were trying to do: that we were trying to apply a liberal scheme. The only ones who realized were the unions. So it was really a clash between the hidden liberal scheme and the unions. In the second case, it was a clash between a nonhidden liberal scheme and the unions. The only difference is whether it was hidden or not. And it is a difference of power. In the first case, it was hidden, and Isabel Perón didn't know what she was doing. In this case, as Menem knows — knows in some degree — what he's doing, there is really some coefficient of power behind the scheme.[18]

Power was indeed what conservatives had gained from their collaboration with the Menem government, and while that power lay in different institutions of the executive branch, it was most conspicuous in economic policy making, where liberal technocrats and politicians held sway. The list appended to the end of this chapter, compiled from official government organizational charts during the 1989–91 period, gives an indication of the extent of conservative technocratic involvement in the Peronist government of President Menem.

The UCEDE Deflates

The technocratic convergence between the Peronist government and UCEDE took the wind out of the sails of the leaders formally in charge of the UCEDE's party organization, who now had to grapple with several problems. On the one hand, the UCEDE could hope to gain little from the possible success of the Menem economic program. The electoral benefits would flow largely to the Peronists. Its failure, however, would lead to the discredit, not of the Peronist Party itself, but of Menem and his "liberal" allies, who were carrying out their program over the opposition of much of the Peronist Party and the union movement.[19] With the UCEDE's most important leaders in the government helping to implement the UCEDE's own preelection platform, however, any attempt by the party's formal leadership to pursue a strategy of "democratic opposition" lacked credibility with the public. It also generated little support from the most influential sectors of the party's membership, most of which were strongly behind the UCEDE's collaboration with the government.[20]

The "renovator" leadership also faced problems within the party organization. Some of the party's most capable and influential leaders were in senior government positions. In addition, younger and less prominent UCEDE militants, sensing the shift in prospects for career advancement, had followed them into lower-level government positions. The UCEDE's formal leaders were thus unable to give momentum to their own efforts to expand the party's organizational networks. Furthermore, with national political decision making taking place in the state, the party's formal leaders had trouble gaining visibility through their forums in Argentine political society. As a result of these factors, the UCEDE's organizational activities declined significantly in the years following Menem's assumption of the presidency. Party leaders complained repeatedly of a general "demobilization" taking hold of the party.[21]

The first evidence of such demobilization came in internal elections for party positions for the city of Buenos Aires in June 1990. Only 20 percent of the party's members bothered to vote in that election, most of them in the party's traditional strongholds in the affluent districts. The internal election results gave a resounding victory to Alvaro Alsogaray and his followers, who regained control of the capital city's party organization. These developments left few incentives for other sectors of the party to dedicate themselves to party building. Many activists not linked to the party's dominant faction withdrew from party activities.[22] Announcing his retirement upon conclusion of his term, a UCEDE congressman gave a grim assessment of the state of local conservative party politics: "The party in the city of Buenos Aires no longer exists. This is the truth. There are no neighborhood committees. There is no internal mobility. And this is so because the party has compromised its own identity. It has become an appendage of the government."[23]

The UCEDE's decline as an electoral force was steady after that. In the two succeeding elections, the party virtually disappeared from the electoral map. The Peronist government, riding the tide of a successful economic stabilization program, went to the 1991 and 1993 elections at the peak of its popularity. In both congressional elections, the Peronist Party gained 42 percent of the national vote, against 30 percent for the UCR. The UCEDE trailed far behind, with 6.5 percent in 1991, and 2.6 percent in 1993. In the city of Buenos Aires, the UCEDE's decline was cataclysmic; its total vote shrank from 22 percent in 1989 to 8.6 percent in 1991, and plummeted further to 3 percent in 1993. As the bar chart in Figure 6.1 indicates, the party's losses occurred at all social levels.[24] In absolute num-

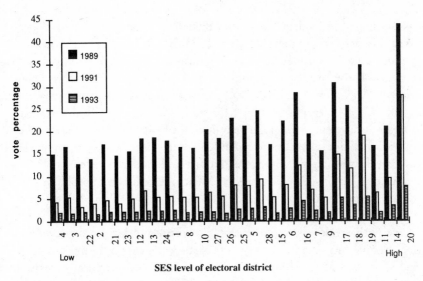

Fig. 6.1. UCEDE vote in the City of Buenos Aires, 1989, 1991, and 1993 congressional elections.

bers, the party's loss of support among affluent voters was devastating. In the 20th electoral district of Socorro, the city's most affluent electoral district and the UCEDE's traditional stronghold, the UCEDE's vote total declined from 43.7 percent in 1989 to 7.8 percent in 1993. In the city's poorest neighborhoods, where the UCEDE's electoral support and organizational networks were of more recent origin, the losses were proportionally even greater. For example, in 1989 the UCEDE had mobilized 13 percent of the vote in the 22d electoral district of Villa Lugano. In 1993, this total was reduced to 2.2 percent.

The UCEDE's alliance with the Menem government seems to have been a Faustian bargain for the young conservative party. Access to state power had been attained. A visible role in the implementation of a program of economic liberalization had also been achieved. But in the process the party withered. Its leaders exchanged the long-term promise of organization in political society for the immediate power of presence within the state. In the short run, this did reduce the uncertainty of Argentina's crisis-ridden democratic politics for conservative leaders and their core constituencies. But in the long run it rendered the future of conservative party politics very uncertain.

A New Scenario for Argentine Conservatism: The Conservatization of Populism?

No sooner had President Menem warmed the presidential chair than speculation began to circulate about a definitive realignment of Argentine politics under his leadership. His overtures to Peronism's traditional adversaries in the business community and the liberal political establishment were warmly approved by the more affluent sectors of Argentine society. Exultation over the postelection Milagro Menem soon evolved into widespread discussion of the popular potential of Menemismo, a new movement that might fuse the powerful Buenos Aires upper-class constituencies of liberalismo with a ready-made Peronist national mass base.

Among Peronism's political elite, Menem was not an improbable candidate for pulling off such a shift. He was governor of the interior province of La Rioja, and was primarily supported by leaders within the Peronist Party with weak ties to Peronism's powerful and largely metropolitan labor union movement. The Peronist party apparatus in the interior provinces, as well as its large, poor, and nonunionized electoral base, was overwhelmingly in his camp. He controlled the party apparatus and possessed a sufficiently strong independent base within the movement to split the party's labor constituencies and neutralize opposition to his reforms.[25] If willing to follow him through the travails of economic reform, the Menemista party apparatus and its large electorate might prove attractive to Buenos Aires elites hungry for a national mass base and willing to shift their support to a "modernized" Peronist Party.

The first sign of such a realignment—beyond the giddy displays of support for the new president by conservative leaders and journalists— came in a Peronist-style mass demonstration in the Plaza de Mayo on April 6, 1990. The rally expressed support for President Menem and his reform programs and was organized in response to a series of anti-Menem rallies organized by Peronist labor groups and opposition parties. The president claimed not to have had a hand in organizing the demonstration. Credit went to the popular conservative journalist Bernardo Neustadt, who had launched a radio and television campaign to encourage Argentina's "silent majority" to express its support for the president by demonstrating in the Plaza de Mayo. An estimated half-million demonstrators heeded Neustadt's call, although many had also been organized by Peronist Party and labor leaders loyal to the president. A survey of participants in the rally revealed that its social composition differed markedly from traditional Peronist demonstrations. Labor union members were in attendance and visible because of their banners, drums, and columns, but the rally seemed largely to bring together two disparate elements: poor, nonunionized Peronist supporters and affluent city dwellers attending their first Peronist rally.[26] The press quickly seized upon this as the beginnings of a new "popular conservative" social coalition that might give electoral continuity to the technocratic coalitions forged by Menem with conservative and business leaders.[27]

Party leaders, both Peronist and conservative, attempted to capitalize upon this budding alliance in the party realm. The first surprising move in this direction was shortly after Menem assumed office in 1989. The senatorial election in the city of Buenos Aires had not produced a majority winner, and the decision was transferred to the Electoral College. María Julia Alsogaray, the third-place UCEDE senatorial candidate, decided to cast her party's votes in the Electoral College for the second-place Peronist Party candidate. The UCEDE move thus gave a majority of Electoral College votes to the Peronist Party, depriving the first-place UCR candidate of a senate seat. This maneuver was followed, two years later, by a formal electoral alliance between Peronism and its conservative former adversaries. In 1991, the Peronist Party nominated a conservative, Avelino Porto, as its candidate for a senate seat in the city of Buenos Aires. The UCEDE and other conservative parties endorsed their Peronist-nominated candidate. Nevertheless, the UCR candidate won, dampening public optimism about Menemismo's potential as a long-term popular conservative electoral scenario. The ideologically moderate UCR candidate even drew significant support from affluent voters, dispersing the hemorrhage of votes from the UCEDE between the Peronists and the radicals.

However, in spite of fits and starts, there is evidence that the "popular conservative" scenario is more than just a chimera of creative political minds. The Menem government's economic successes greatly bolstered its popularity, especially among the country's economic elite. It also gave it maneuvering room to enact political reforms that altered the country's institutional and electoral landscape.[28] These could well be used to refashion social alliances and make the technocratic alliances forged in the early years of the Menem administration effective in the electoral realm.

The second half of Menem's presidential term gave indications that important electoral shifts were in the making. In the city of Buenos Aires, the Peronist Party was the primary beneficiary of the UCEDE's electoral collapse. This was made evident in the 1993 congressional election, when the PJ won a plurality of the city's votes. Electoral data indicate that the PJ's growth between 1989 and 1993 was due, not to its traditional constituencies in the lower social strata, but to the addition of upper-income voters to its electoral coalition. The scatterplot in figure 6.2 compares the changes in vote totals in congressional elections for the UCEDE and the PJ between 1989 and 1993. The scatterplot in figure 6.3 shows the correlation between socioeconomic status and Peronist Party growth in the same

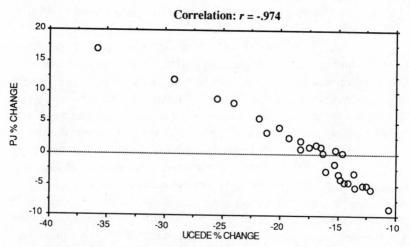

Fig. 6.2.   Percentage vote change, 1989–93, UCEDE, and PJ, City of Buenos Aires congressional elections. N=28 electoral districts.

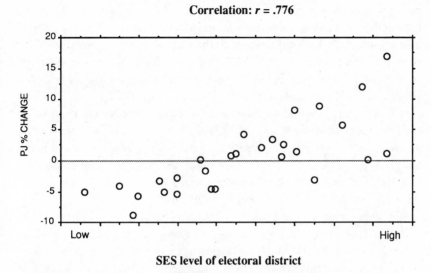

Correlation: *r* = .776

Fig. 6.3. Socioeconomic status and PJ percentage vote change between 1989 and 1993, City of Buenos Aires, congressional elections. N=28 electoral districts.

period. These results reveal a striking association between the UCEDE's decline and the Peronist Party's growth, as well as a clearly positive association between social status and PJ growth.[29] They suggest that important segments of the UCEDE's core constituencies shifted their support to the PJ during this period.

The PJ's 1993 successes sparked a wave of leadership unions between conservatives and Peronists. Throughout 1994, federalist leaders discussed alliance possibilities with Peronist leaders for President Menem's 1995 reelection bid. In Buenos Aires, the injuries suffered by the UCEDE from its October 1993 electoral debacle were soon followed by the insult of Adelina de Viola's flamboyant and highly publicized defection to the Peronist Party. Like many of her UCEDE colleagues, de Viola had served as a high-level official in the Menem government. Between 1991 and 1993, she was vice-minister of the interior. At the end of 1993, she consummated her courtship with Peronism by joining the party. Until that time, the Peronist government's UCEDE collaborators had kept their association with the government at a technocratic level. Even María Julia Alsogaray, who rapidly ascended the bureaucratic hierarchy of the Menem government and resigned from the UCEDE,[30] stayed clear of formal entanglements with the Peronist Party. However, at a large public event staged for her formal induction into the PJ's ranks, Adelina declared herself to be "in love" with Peronism and proclaimed complete loyalty to her new political party. Standing next to a beaming President Menem, she held her arms high in the air in a Peronist victory salute, to wild ovations from the crowd. The president of the local chapter of the PJ then ceremoniously read her name and those of the long list of UCEDE politicians who were making the transfer with her to Peronismo.[31] The event ended, appropriately, with the singing of the Peronist March.

The 1995 presidential election campaign gave further confirmation of the Peronist eclipse of conservative parties in national politics. No conservative party or alliance of conservative parties presented candidates for the presidential election. The UCEDE endorsed President Menem's reelection bid, and limited itself to running candidates in local and congressional elections. Most federalist parties followed suit.[32]

The conservative gamble on President Menem's reelection bid paid off. The president won an impressive victory against two opponents, the UCR and the Frente del País Solidario (Frepaso), a new Center-Left party led by dissident Peronist politicians. The president received nearly 50 percent of the vote against a distant 29 percent for Frepaso, and a dismal showing of 17 percent for the UCR. The presidential ticket won in every province, scoring its biggest successes in the poorer provinces of the interior. In the city of Buenos Aires, the presidential ticket came in a close second to Frepaso, making this the only electoral district not won by the PJ.

The 1995 congressional election in the city of Buenos Aires provided an important local instance supportive of a conservatization-of-populism scenario. The trend of Peronist absorption of the UCEDE's electoral base seen in 1993 was confirmed in 1995, in spite of the local decline in support for the Peronist Party and a modest recovery for the UCEDE. The PJ vote total declined from its 1993 level of 32 percent to 23 percent. The UCEDE received 9 percent of the vote, returning it to the level it held in 1983. However, as the correlation coefficients in table 6.5 indicate, the trend between 1989 and 1995 appeared to be Peronist absorption of much of the UCEDE's electoral base. Furthermore, it appears that the dissident Peronist Frepaso coalition grew at the expense of both the UCR and the PJ, although its negative impact on the UCR was greatest. In this electoral district, where Menem's opponents scored their greatest gains, a realignment joining conservative voters to the PJ, and UCR and dissident Peronist voters to a new Center-Left party, was one plausible electoral outcome of the first six years of Menem's presidency.

Regarding a possible merger between the UCEDE and Peronism, Alvaro Alsogaray once remarked that "an emotional union with Peronism is very difficult for us. We cannot call ourselves Peronists as long as Peronism does not renounce a past that we cannot by any means approve of. And

Table 6.5
Vote Percentage Changes for Selected Parties between 1989 and 1995,
Congressional Elections, City of Buenos Aires (correlation matrix)

	Status	UCEDE	PJ	UCR	Frepaso
Status	1.000				
UCEDE	−.590*	1.000			
PJ	.717*	−.853*	1.000		
UCR	−.148*	−.254*	−.099	1.000	
Frepaso	−.249**	.351*	−.272*	−.742*	1.000

*Significant at the .01 level (one-tailed).
**Significant at the .05 level (one-tailed).
Note: N = 28.

that they will not do."[33] His statement captures the resistance the "conservatization of populism" scenario will face from conservative quarters as a replacement for the long-sought independent conservative party. For conservatives steeped in their long and implacable struggles against Peronism, the idea of Argentina's historic populist party becoming their electoral representative is difficult indeed. Political traditions die hard, and much will have to be overcome before Peronism gains the unreserved support of the country's well-to-do voters.

If resistance from Argentina's hard-pressed conservative movement to this scenario is to be expected, then resistance from Peronist quarters will be even fiercer. Peronism has a long institutional legacy. It has also had a deep core-constituency relationship with one of Latin America's most powerful labor movements. Both legacies can be expected to challenge the fundamental institutional and coalitional transformations the "conservatization of populism" scenario would bring to the party, because this scenario would imply nothing short of a core-constituency shift for the Peronist Party. The party's strategic relationship with its labor constituencies would give way to a new core-constituency relationship with the country's socioeconomic elite. Core-constituency shifts are always traumatic, especially for parties with long traditions and deep emotional ties to their historic constituencies.

However, much has changed in Argentina since Peronism first burst on the political scene. The working class is not what it used to be. Structural changes in recent decades have weakened its economic clout, and this has been followed by a clear decline in its political clout. Furthermore, Peronism has always been a dual movement: proletarian and radical in some parts of the country, polyclassist and conservative in others.[34] As one pillar of the movement declines, the balance within the party is shifting to the other, a fact that may give the Menemista leaders who today control the party maneuvering room to recast its coalitional landscape. As architects of Argentina's free-market miracle, they will be in good position to strengthen their links with a grateful business community. And business, still an unclaimed party constituency, may well be willing to build lasting party ties as its economic links to the state fade in a postdevelopmentalist economic context.

Ultimately, the conservatization of populism scenario may be as vital to the long-term survival of the current Peronist leadership as it is to conservative prospects for electoral representation. This may be the strongest argument in its favor. The shifts in economic policy may well have imposed new coalitional imperatives for President Menem and his followers in the Peronist leadership. What started out as policy measures to deal with a severe economic crisis have now become an economic model requiring maintenance. What started out as pragmatic alliances with socioeconomic elites may now become a social coalition that will permit Peronist leaders to counter internal opposition and reap the electoral dividends of successful economic reform. The party's traditional labor constituencies will not be suitable vehicles for such ambitions. A turn to the beneficiaries of the economic reform program may be necessary to give social clout to Menemista hopes of inheriting a postreform Peronist movement. Thus, while the obstacles to the conservatization of populism scenario are formidable, so are the forces pushing for its realization.

Conclusion

National conservative aspirations were thwarted by two developments in the late 1980s and early 1990s. The first of these was the continuing effect of regional cleavage on national conservative party organizations. The 1989 elections demonstrated just how enduring early legacies of core-constituency divisions can be when perpetuated by their effects in the organizational realm. The organizational fragmentation of conservative parties once again became the central issue of national conservative party politics in the 1989 election, and ultimately dashed hopes for a credible conservative challenge to Peronist and radical dominance. While the economic divisions that had once shaped conservative party alignments showed clear signs of abatement during the latter part of the 1980s, their effect was perpetuated by conflicting organizational interests and rivalries between the leaders of different regional party organizations.

The second setback to conservative party development was the opportunity offered by the Menem government to the conservative party leadership for a shift toward state-centered strategies of political action. In Buenos Aires, the country's most important electoral region, the Faustian nature of the conservative leadership's bargain with the Peronist government was clearly manifested in the UCEDE's dramatic organizational and electoral collapse. Access to state power provided the UCEDE's leaders with a degree of influence in national affairs that was unimaginable a few years earlier. It also, however, led to the deflation of a long process of institution building in political society.

The UCEDE's collapse provides eloquent testimony of the costs to conservative party development of the mobility of its political leadership between polity arenas. As conservative leaders shift their sights from party building to state-centered strategies of political influence, they produce a drain of talent, resources, and constituent support from conservative party politics. In the short term, this permits the realization of agendas they have long pushed for in party politics. In the long run, however, it jeopardizes the labors of political organization that will ensure their continuity as democratic actors should their marriage of convenience with a state controlled by other political forces come to an end.

The impact of these events on Argentine conservatism's development is difficult to foretell. The coalitional and institutional aspects of party politics in Argentina are in a state of flux, as Peronists, conservatives, and Radicals struggle to harness the political winds unleashed by economic reform. It is to be expected that the crafting of new forms of upper-class political representation will be central to these efforts. It may well be that these changes signal a shift in conservative party development away from autonomous party building. This would be the significance of the much-heralded union between conservatism and Peronism. Weary of failed negotiations between fragmented party institutions, conservative leaders may yield to the attraction of absorption into an existing mass party. The object would now shift from building new political institutions to securing upper-class political representation in an existing national party with a ready-made mass base. To Buenos Aires conservatives, it would provide the link to electoral organization and mass support throughout the country that unification with regional conservative parties once promised.

If this scenario is to yield anything new in Argentine politics, it will have to be more than a repetition of past patterns of pragmatic, and temporary, alliances with nonconservative mass parties. And here is the rub. In its current Peronist version, the conservatization of populism scenario would imply a profound transformation not only of conservative party politics, but of Peronism as well. It would imply a core-constituency shift for the Peronist Party, as the addition of upper-class voters and mobilization of business support create a new strategic relationship between the party and its new constituencies. The party's traditional labor constituencies would give way to its newfound elite supporters, and the Peronist masses would provide electoral majorities while the new core constituencies shape policy agendas.

Should this realignment scenario not come to pass, the UCEDE-Peronist alliance might amount to no more than a transitory bargain, serving the immediate interest of the leaders of both movements, but leaving a withered conservative party establishment in Buenos Aires, with little more than its upper-class base of support. If so, Argentine conservatism would return to its historic patterns of class-based pressure politics, regional logrolling, and ad hoc national electoral alliances, seeking power through governments controlled by other political forces, regardless of the popular will expressed through the electoral process.[35]

Adelina de Viola is fond of recounting a conversation she had with Domingo Cavallo in 1982, when Argentine conservatism first contemplated its future in the impending democratic order. Cavallo, a prominent liberal economist who became President Menem's economics czar in 1991, was then the departing military government's Central Bank president. According to Adelina de Viola, they discussed two options: "Either we popularize a liberal party or we liberalize a populist party."[36] The preceding chapters of this book have focused primarily on the quest for the first option, which had its day in the democratic period of 1983–89. Whether the current embrace of the second option by the UCEDE will lead to new "popular conservative" formulas with one of the country's historic mass parties, or merely perpetuate time-tried patterns of conservative political action, will only be known as events unfold. Argentina's political evolution will be closely tied to which of these paths is chosen.

APPENDIX: CONSERVATIVE LEADERS APPOINTED TO EXECUTIVE BRANCH POSITIONS BY CARLOS MENEM'S PERONIST GOVERNMENT, 1989–1991

Presidential Advisors

Alvaro Alsogaray (UCEDE): ad honorem, 1989–90; listed officially as "collaborator of the president" (the only presidential advisor so listed)
Rodolfo Rossi (UCEDE): on salary, 1989 and 1990

Appointees to Economic Policy-making Institutions

Ministry of the Economy

Minister of the Economy: Domingo Cavallo (Independent Liberal), 1990

Undersecretary of Public Enterprises: Diego Estevez (UCEDE; formerly Unión Liberal), 1990

Undersecretary of Internal Commerce: Raúl Ochoa (UCEDE; formerly Unión Liberal), 1989; Pablo Marón Challú (UCEDE), 1990

Director of Communications: German Kammermath (UCEDE), 1991

Director of the National Tax Revenue Service (Dirección General Impositiva): Ricardo Juan Cossio (UCEDE), 1989; deputy director: Venancio Arango (UCEDE), 1990

President of the National Development Bank: Jorge Peyeyra de Olazabal (UCEDE), 1991

Director of the National Mortgage Bank: Oscar Martínez (UCEDE)

Central Bank

President of the Central Bank: Rodolfo Rossi (UCEDE), 1989; Roque Fernandez (UCEDE), 1989; Javier González Fraga (Independent Liberal), 1989, 1990; Enrique Folcini (Independent Liberal), 1990

Directors of the Central Bank: Roque Fernandez (UCEDE), 1990; Rodolfo Rossi (UCEDE), 1990; Pedro Pou (UCEDE), 1991; Carlos Tombeaur (UCEDE), 1991

Ministry of Public Works

Paid Advisors to the Minister of Public Works: Alfredo Expósito (UCEDE), 1990; Roberto M. Van Helderen (UCEDE), 1990

Public Enterprises

Director, National Communications Directorate: José Palazzo (UCEDE), 1990

President, National Telecommunications Corporation: María Julia Alsogaray (UCEDE), 1989; financial advisor: Ricardo Zinn (UCEDE)

President, SOMISA (National Steel Corporation): María Julia Alsogaray (UCEDE), 1990

President, Argentine Railroads: Hector Ludeña (UCEDE), 1991

Special auditors appointed by the Ministry of the Economy in June 1989:
General Ports Administration — Mario Pérez Latorre (UCEDE); National Mines Corporation (YCF) — Patricia Gómez Aguirre (UCEDE); National Petroleum Corporation (YPF) — Marcos Victorica (UCEDE); Obras Sanitarias de la Nácion — Marcello Mastellanes (UCEDE)

Appointees to Noneconomic Policy-making Institutions

Ministry of the Interior

Undersecretary of the Interior (equivalent of vice-minister): Adelina Dalesio de Viola (UCEDE), 1991
Undersecretary for Institutional Affairs: Santiago Lozano (UCEDE), 1991
Deputy Undersecretary of the Interior: María del Carmen Prado (UCEDE), 1991
Director, National Directorate for Provincial Affairs: Gustavo Brignone (UCEDE), 1991
Director, National Electoral Directorate: Francisco Dolci (UCEDE), 1991

Ministry of Defense

Undersecretary of Defense: Luis Gonzáles Estevez (UCEDE; formerly Unión Liberal), 1991

Secretariat of State for the Environment

Secretary of State (with rank of minister): María Julia Alsogaray (UCEDE), 1991

Secretariat for Social Security

Secretary: Santiago de Estrada (CFI), 1989

Government of the Province of Corrientes

Interventor (surrogate governor appointed by the president after federal intervention): Francisco de Durañona y Vedia (UCEDE), 1990

Federal District of Buenos Aires

Director, Central Market of the Buenos Aires Urban Area (appointed by the president): Raúl Scialaba (UCEDE), 1989; Juan Levit (PDP), 1991
Director, Buenos Aires Subway System: Tulio Michellucci (UCEDE), 1990
President, Municipal Privatizations Commission: Francisco Siracusano (UCEDE), 1990

Chapter Seven

Conclusions:
Problems of Conservative Party Development in Latin America

A basic question drives this book: what are the conditions that foster or inhibit the formation of conservative parties in Latin America? The significance of this question is that it addresses the institutional forms of upper-class political representation. Conservative parties are vital institutions for mobilizing privileged social constituencies in the democratic struggle for power. Other institutions and political arenas play an important role in representing the interests of the socially privileged. Only parties, however, are explicitly organized for the capture of political power in democratic regimes. How the upper strata of society are integrated into democratic political life is intimately connected to their relationship to party politics.

A related consideration driving this study is the importance of conservative parties to the stability of democracy. Representation of upper-class interests through conservative parties has historically been associated with higher levels of democratic stability in Latin America. The historical evidence for the region does not support the statement "No conservative parties, no democracy." It does, however, support the contention that the longevity of democratic government has been far more problematic in countries with histories of weak conservative party organization than in countries with strong conservative party organization. This provides the normative basis for this study. The development of conservative parties is a desirable outcome for democracy.

A minimal definition of conservative parties has also been advanced in this book. Conservative parties are defined according to the social coalition that supports them. Specifically, conservative parties are defined as parties that draw their core constituencies from the upper strata of society. The minimal definition identifies conservative parties by their relationship to upper-class constituencies. However, description and analysis of conservative parties should also take their role as forgers of multiclass electoral coalitions into account. The distinction made in this book between "core constituencies" and "mass base" makes this possible. It provides a conceptual basis for highlighting the protagonism of key social constituencies, while addressing the multiclass coalition-building aspects of party politics in mass electoral competition.

The social definition of conservative parties highlights the importance of constituency-based factors in the evolution of conservative party politics. An assumption underlying this definition is that a party's relationship to its constituencies, particularly its core constituencies, provides the most important constraints and opportunities facing party leaders. This relationship is usually an evolving one, and its study reveals much about the interactions between social structure, institutions, and political leadership that shape patterns of party development over time.

The definition of conservative parties by their social base rather than their ideology is also necessary because of the ideological diversity of conservative parties. This diversity exists within nations as well as across history and national contexts. A social definition of conservative parties makes the comparative study of such parties possible regardless of ideological variations. It also facilitates the study of ideological change and conflict, between and within conservative parties.

The preceding chapters of this book identified the determinants of Argentina's troubled patterns of conservative party development. The argument presented was that the failures of conservative party organization in Argentina since the advent of mass politics in the twentieth century were due, not to mass-base dynamics, but to dynamics at the elite level: core-constituency and political leadership dynamics. The actors referred to here are socioeconomic elites and party elites. The two groups often have different interests and are driven by different goals and expectations, yet the process of conservative party development is profoundly shaped by the interaction between them, as well as by their separate patterns of political action.

Two sets of elite-level factors shaped conservative party development in Argentina. The first was intra-elite dynamics: core-constituency divisions, specifically regional economic cleavages among Argentina's upper classes, obstructed the formation of cross-regional upper-class alliances during the formative stages of conservative party development. Economic divisions continued to obstruct core-constituency unity until the 1980s. Furthermore, regional partisan alignments bequeathed a legacy of national organizational fragmentation. Thus, economic core-constituency divisions were compounded by institutional rivalries and divisions between political leaders, and perpetuated the regionally driven nature of Argentine conservative party development through the 1990s.

The second elite-level factor that shaped conservative party development was the relationship between elites and the state. At the leadership level, they were between party elites and the state. At the core-constituency level, they were between business and the state. In the uninstitutionalized context of Argentine party politics, the key incentives for participation in electoral arenas by conservative leaders and their core constituencies have been provided by their relationship to the state. When opportunities exist for direct access by conservative leaders to state power or policy making, they abstain from party-building efforts. Similarly when opportunities exist for business elites to gain access to state policy making and patronage, they abstain from active support of party politics. Conservative party development thus advances or retreats as a function of the relationship between party leaders and their core constituencies with the state. This book's comparison of these relationships across historical periods in Argentina, and at both the national and local levels, suggests that they best explain that country's troubled pattern of conservative party development.

Beyond clarifying the specifics of the Argentine case, the generalizability of these arguments can be extended to other countries in Latin America. In the following pages of this conclusion, specific arguments for Argentina are recapitulated. In addition, a shift in the comparative emphasis to other countries in the region is undertaken to develop the comparative implications of these findings.

Political Leadership and Democratization

The question that bedeviled the Latin American Left in the early 1980s, as it mused over its role in the postauthoritarian order, might well have been asked by Latin American conservatism: "Why participate?"[1] Both Right and Left faced formidable tasks of organization and ideological mobilization in political arenas that were relatively new to them. Both forces were linked to constituencies whose own experience with democratic institutions had historically been problematic. They were also unsure of the type of mass coalitions they would need to mobilize if they took the plunge into electoral politics.[2]

Conservatives might have faced even greater dilemmas than the Left as they calculated their options during the return to democracy. In contrast to the Left, neither the leaders nor the core constituencies of conservatism had traditionally needed the protection of democratic institutions to prosper as political or economic actors. Their control over economic influence, and the privileged access they enjoyed to state power, raised doubts about their need to participate in democratic institutions, as well as about the advantages of devoting resources to the tasks of party building and electoral mobilization.

In Argentina, two factors played a role in changing the incentives for conservative political action. The first was the negative impact of authoritarian rule on conservatives' relationship with the military. The second was exclusion from state power during the early periods of democratic government.

The authoritarian experience that preceded the 1983 transition to democracy raised doubts about the certainty of benefits from military rule for the leaders and constituencies of Argentine conservatism. One of the distinguishing features of this authoritarian period was that it produced important strains in the system of quid pro quos that governed conservative-authoritarian alliances in the past. Conservative political leaders had accepted military control of the state in exchange for privileged access to its most important policy-making institutions. Similarly, business leaders abstained from autonomous political action in exchange for the benefits discretionary state power under authoritarian rule could provide: the repression of competing claims from labor, and privileged business access to the state.[3]

For conservative politicians, the 1976–83 experience demonstrated that abdication to military partners entailed growing risks. They saw their influence checked by the increasingly autonomous military. Even those civilian leaders who gained access to economic policy making during that period found themselves incapable of shaping the military government's political course or of countering the deleterious impact of internal military crises on the policy-making process. In addition, Argentina's conservative leadership found that after 1976, it, too, was a target of the military regime's agenda of political transformation. In the end, the regime's collapse and the massive discredit suffered by the armed forces left Argentine conservatives isolated from the political process. Deprived of possibilities for alliances with the military, conservatives turned to party politics to gain influence over the political process.

The incentives to continue strategies of party building during the first six years of democratic rule were provided by the fact that during the government of the UCR president Raúl Alfonsín, access to state power was completely closed off to conservative leaders. There was no room in the top institutions of economic policy making for the technocratic elite that had filled the leadership functions of the Argentine conservative movement. If influence was to be exercised over governmental decisions, it would have to be from without, through the mobilization of opinion and the construction of coalitions. Party politics thus emerged as an important arena for the political action of conservative leaders, as well as a viable route for the pursuit of personal advancement and political influence.

This pattern of disenchantment with authoritarian rule and exclusion from state power also spurred conservative party building in other countries in the region. The experience of authoritarian rule, however different from country to country, did provide a common lesson to conservative leaders and their constituencies in the upper classes: discretionary state power under authoritarian rule can be a double-edged phenomenon. While providing an effective check on popular challenges, it had also proven to be a growing threat to the interests of political and economic elites.

In Peru, the leftist turn of the armed forces during the 1968–75 period of rule by General Velasco Alvarado introduced a major rupture in the conservative civil-military relationship. The country's first elected president after the transition, Fernando Belaúnde Terry, had himself been overthrown by the armed forces in 1968, and had based his comeback campaign in the founding elections of 1980 on a platform of opposition to the military regime.[4] In 1985 a populist, the APRA leader Alan García, came to power. The exclusion of conservatives from his government led, not to conservative civil-military coalition building, but to new strategies of conservative electoral mobilization. During the late 1980s, party politics became a major arena for conservative political action in the country's chaotic democratic regime. This was bolstered by the mobilization of business behind party politics in the late 1980s, as business elites turned to the electoral arena in opposition to a government that exhibited growing hostility to business interests.

The Mexican transition from one-party rule had a similar effect in pushing conservative leaders toward strategies of electoral mobilization. For conservative political leaders, the embrace of the Partido Acción Nacional's agenda of political democratization was vital to challenge the ruling party's monopoly on political decision making. It also became important to business elites made wary by government-sponsored antibusiness campaigns and increasingly systematic use of discretionary state power against business interests during the 1970s and 1980s. Electoral politics thus became an arena for political leaders and business elites alike in which to build alternative vehicles by which to counter the power of the state.[5]

In all these cases, therefore, the impetus for conservative party building lay in a change in state-elite relations. The rationale for submitting to democratic competition was provided by the new uncertainties associated with authoritarian rule. The embrace of party politics under democratic government was precipitated by the exclusion of conservative leaders from state decision making. Party politics became a means of countering the autonomy and unpredictability of the authoritarian state and building independent bases of power for civilian conservative elites in a context of exclusion from state decision making in democratizing regimes.

These developments had an important impact on the development of leadership cadres in the conservative movement. They opened the way for the emergence of a more diverse conservative political class, which saw in the manifold ideological and organizational tasks of party politics a route to influence and political advancement. In Argentina, the internal pluralization of conservatism sparked challenges to established leaders and set internal struggles in motion that transformed the UCEDE's power structure and its appeals to the electorate. The new leaders who flocked into conservative party politics gave it a new ideological content. They introduced agendas and discourses that permitted the UCEDE to appeal to a broader cross-section of supporters. Their interest in gaining access to tightly controlled leadership structures also made them advocates of internal democratization and increased the importance of political liberalism as an ideological banner for rallying their followers. Similarly, they sought to challenge established leaders by building new bases of support outside the party's traditional electorate through strategies of electoral popularization.

The combination of ideas, organization, and political practice that came to be known as *la nueva derecha* in Argentina was thus an outgrowth of internal struggle. New conservative movements in other countries were similarly the product of intraleadership struggles. The transformation of Latin American conservatism was not generally carried out by its established leaders. It was the synthesis of a clash between old and new, between traditional leaders and new activists contesting primacy. In Argentina, this struggle was two-tiered. On the one hand, it was a struggle between the UCEDE, a new party advocating an agenda of liberal economic reform, and traditional parties wedded to nonliberal ideologies. On the other hand, it was a struggle within the UCEDE, between Alsogaray and new adherents of conservative party politics, whose ideological agendas pushed the appeals of Argentine *liberalismo* well beyond the bounds intended by the party's founder.

In Mexico, the protagonism in the democratization process of the Partido Acción Nacional attracted new activists and business elites into the party. Catholic *solidarista* currents that had dominated the PAN were displaced by *neo-panista* currents that gave the party's ideological orientation a far more liberal content.[6] They also expanded the party's pro-democracy platforms with new antistatist appeals and agendas of liberal economic reform. The Peruvian electoral Right's transformation in the late 1980s was marked by struggle between new activists and liberal intellectuals who rallied behind Vargas Llosa's Movimiento Libertad and established party leaders in Acción Popular and the Partido Popular Cristiano (PPC), which had dominated conservative party politics for decades. Libertad's activists were generally new to party politics. They brought new agendas of antistatism and "popular liberalism" that clashed with the "social-Christian" doctrines of the PPC, and with the paternalistic orientations of Belaúnde's Acción Popular.[7] The new activists eventually came to shape Peruvian conservatism's appeals to the electorate in the late 1980s, but before reaching that stage, they first had to impose their agenda on a resistant conservative movement.

Core-Constituency Dynamics and Conservative Party Development

Business and Conservative Parties

Historic patterns of business collective action in Latin America constitute one of the most problematic dimensions of conservative party development in the region. However, the link between business and political parties has not been a major focus of the literature on business collective action in the region. This is due largely to the empirical fact that business-party ties have been weak and unstable. Historically, Latin American business has remained an aloof ally in the electoral struggles of conservative parties. At election time, conservative parties may do well among the upper social strata; as individuals, business executives may vote for such parties and contribute financial support to their campaigns. But the organizational expressions of Latin American business, such as trade associations, large companies, or even prominent business elites, have rarely identified themselves with electoral politics. The political action of Latin American business has been focused directly on the state, either through firm-state contacts or through corporatist institutions.

The most important reason for this lies in the historical evolution of Latin American business, particularly the region's industrial sectors. In

Argentina, as in most countries in Latin America, business development has taken place under the protection and tutelage of the state. This has been particularly pronounced for the industrial sector, although the commercial, financial, and agricultural sectors have also had their development closely patterned by state intervention and have channeled their political action through corporatist channels. This state-dependence has strongly conditioned business patterns of collective action, and has made business elites wary of identification with partisan political action.

Argentine democratization after 1983 suggests that subordination to democratic rule does not imply active business support for political party organization. It often simply provides a new institutional context in which business elites can seek to reestablish privileged channels of access to the state. Strong incentives must therefore exist to induce organized business to shift its political strategies and resources to party politics. If its interests in a democratic society can be guaranteed without resort to this somewhat messy task, it will tend to be unwilling to devote energy and capital to the support of conservative party politics.

In spite of the depth of the economic crisis in the 1980s, the Alfonsín government guaranteed business access to economic policy-making institutions throughout its term in office. The most important state-business crisis during this period, between economic policy makers and the agricultural sector, was settled in 1987 by the appointment of representatives of the agricultural sector to key economic policy-making institutions.[8] The continuity of state-business ties hindered the UCEDE's efforts to mobilize active business support for its agenda of economic reform. Conservative party politics and business collective action thus proceeded on separate paths. After 1989, this was dramatized by the two-track logic of President Menem's overtures to the Argentine upper classes when he sought their support for his program of economic reform. Business was approached directly, through the virtual concession of the Economics Ministry to executives of the powerful Bunge y Born company, while prominent leaders of the UCEDE were offered technocratic and advisory positions in other economic policy-making institutions.

The absence of a contrasting example of business electoral mobilization in Argentina makes it difficult to stipulate the conditions under which such mobilization would occur. It also makes it difficult to gauge just how harmful the political aloofness of business was to the party-building efforts of the UCEDE. A shift in the comparative emphasis to other countries in the region does, however, provide some answers to these questions. Three democratizing countries experienced significant business electoral mobilization during the 1980s: Peru, Mexico, and El Salvador. In each of these cases, the cause of that mobilization was a break in relations between business and the state. In addition, this mobilization helped to make conservative parties national electoral contenders. It catapulted Peru's new Frente Democrático (FREDEMO) coalition and Mexico's Partido Acción Nacional to the fore of national politics. It also led to the capture of national power by El Salvador's Alianza Rebublicana Nacionalista (ARENA).

Long-standing ties between the state and the business community deteriorated progressively in each of these countries in the years preceding the business mobilization of the late 1980s. In Peru, relations between President Alan García and the business community, initially cordial when García came to power in 1985, became marked by open hostility as the government intensified its populist policies and business groups became increasingly reluctant participants in the government's plans for industrial development.[9] In Mexico, the business community had historically acted stealthily in the nation's politics, abstaining from open political activity in exchange for regular informal access to policy-making elites within the state, and to the rent-seeking opportunities such access could provide. Political autonomy was sacrificed to the benefits provided by preferential access to state power. This arrangement came under strain during the 1970–76 administration of President Luis Echeverria, whose populist orientation and antibusiness rhetoric marked a change from the collaborative stance of earlier governments toward business. Business-state tensions continued into the 1976–82 government of President Lopez Portillo, whose nationalization of the banking system in 1982 sparked open political mobilization by business through interest associations and support for the opposition Partido Acción Nacional.[10] In El Salvador, previously close ties between the state and business were broken by the reformist turn of the state after 1982 and the advent of the reformist Christian Democratic government of Napoleón Duarte in 1984. In an effort to consolidate popular support, and to counter growing support for the leftist opposition, the Christian Democratic government initiated socioeconomic reforms that, while imperfectly implemented, put business and agricultural elites on the defensive. Under siege by a powerful leftist movement demanding radical change, excluded from a government committed to social reform, and deprived by the contingency of U.S. military aid from ousting the government via military coup, economic elites embarked upon major organizational and ideological mobilization. Business leaders also began to flow toward a party linked to agrarian elites and controlled by paramilitary groups, the Alianza Republicana Nacionalista.

The catalyst of the business-conservative party alliance in all these countries was the attempted nationalization of the banking system by reformist governments, which took place in Mexico and El Salvador in the early 1980s and in Peru in 1987. These actions created a collective sense of threat within the various sectors of the business community and prompted their turn to electoral politics to protect their common class interests against an antagonistic state. In this endeavor, they found willing allies in the once-distant pro–free market politicians who were transforming the conservative party landscape. Antistate party agendas, once in tension with the business community, now became an effective ideological vehicle for challenging discretionary state power. They also provided the ideological glue for linking business concerns to a more diverse set of democratization and economic growth issues capable of generating multiclass support.

The electoral mobilization of business galvanized conservative party politics. The open support of the Peruvian business community for the electoral challenge mounted by Mario Vargas Llosa's Movimiento Libertad endowed the movement with resources and credibility that allowed it to assert its hegemony over other parties in the conservative movement and emerge as a major contender in the 1989 presidential elections.[11] In Mexico, the defection of important national business interests to the Partido Acción Nacional after the 1982 nationalizations solidified neopanista control over the party and gave major credibility to PAN's challenge to the governing party in the name of democracy and free markets. During the 1980s, PAN became a serious electoral contender in a number of regional elections, and, for the first time in its history, presented a national challenge to the governing PRI in the 1989 electoral campaign. In El Salvador, the mobilization of business behind ARENA produced an important leadership change in the party, as Alfredo Cristiani, a figure linked to agricultural and business interests, displaced the party's paramilitary leader, Robert d'Abuisson. After a series of ARENA advances in congressional elections during the 1980s, the party captured the presidency in the elections of 1989.[12]

Just as business-state ties can break, however, they can also be mended. As Soledad Loaeza wrote regarding the later years of Miguel de la Madrid's presidency in Mexico, "All that the de la Madrid government [1983–89] needed to do was to restore harmony between the state and business for the latter to abandon its support for party opposition."[13] Under the presidency of Carlos Salinas de Gortari, state overtures to business intensified, resulting in an open alliance between the government and business groups behind the Salinas administration's program of economic reform. These developments produced a withdrawal of business support from PAN, particularly by the larger business and national industrial interests that had mobilized behind it after the attempted bank nationalizations of 1982. PAN today is sustained largely by regional business support, a fact that has helped it continue its local challenges to PRI hegemony in key states.[14] A renewal of ties between PAN and national business will be vital to any new PAN challenge to the PRI at the national level. Similarly, amid the general deflation of conservative party activity in Peru that followed the rise to power of Alberto Fujimori, there has been a renewal of state-business ties and a dissolution of the business-party links that had characterized the post-1987 period. Only in El Salvador, where ARENA continues to control the national government (having captured the presidency once again in 1994), have the links forged between the conservative party and business during the 1980s endured.

A comparative look at the Latin American experience in the 1980s thus suggests that the potential for business electoral mobilization is negatively associated with the strength of the state-business relationship. Where conservative parties are poorly institutionalized, the electoral fortunes of such parties are particularly sensitive to fluctuations in this relationship.[15] Business can become a powerful force for the expansion of conservative party influence when a rupture in its ties with the state takes place. However, when these ties are mended, the withdrawal of business support can constrain the institutionalization of conservative parties, and can prevent the maintenance of viable strategies of opposition. This vulnerability to the fickleness of business support constitutes one of the most important impediments to the development of conservative parties in the region.

Regional Cleavage and Organizational Alignments

The national organizational fragmentation of Argentine conservatism has its historical roots in regional cleavage. Regional divisions between Argentina's upper classes were economic. They separated the prosperous, agricultural-exporting and ideologically liberal elites of Buenos Aires and the Pampas region from the domestic-market-oriented and antiliberal elites of the interior provinces of the country. Regional conflict shaped the evolution of politics and political institutions in the nineteenth century. At the party level, it resulted in the organizational crystallization of provincially based political parties, rather than cross-regional oligarchic parties that competed with one another nationally. National elite conflict and competition were thus mediated primarily by the state. This legacy of economic division, organizational fragmentation, and state dependence would mar conservative efforts to mount electoral responses to the challenges of mass politics. Regional cleavage thus operated as a historical cause of conservative electoral disunity throughout the twentieth century, thwarting national coalition-building efforts in the first mass-suffrage elections of 1916, and continuing its divisive effects up to the present day. Successful conservative party-building efforts have thus only occurred at the local and provincial level, where the divisive effect of regionalism has been absent. This book has examined conservative party building at both levels: national coalition building in different historical periods and, locally, the growth of the Unión del Centro Democrático in Buenos Aires between 1983 and 1989.

The roots of Argentina's regional cleavage lay in the different production structures, class structures, and economic development models of the coastal and metropolitan areas of the Pampas region and the less-developed interior provinces. They stemmed from a centuries-long struggle by the interior provinces against domination by Buenos Aires province. Regionalism in conservative party politics was, however, a product of both socioeconomic and organizational legacies. Its origins lay in upper-class economic divisions. Its continuity was ensured by the crystallization of party organizations along regional lines, which perpetuated regional divisions independently of the original economic divisions.

Throughout the age of mass politics, Radicalism and Peronism exploited upper-class regional divisions by forging disparate social coalitions at the national level. The social coalitions of the UCR and the Peronist Party differed markedly between the coastal metropolitan region and the interior provinces. In the former region, the UCR was built on networks of urban middle-class support. In the less developed interior, it consisted of alliances between elite-controlled multiclass party networks. Similarly, in the economically advanced parts of the country, Peronism's social coalition was dominated by its working-class constituencies, while in the interior provinces it was supported by more heterogeneous, often elite-dominated coalitions. The glue that held these coalitions together under single institutional umbrellas was the common opposition of Buenos Aires's lower strata and the upper strata of the interior to the upper classes of the Buenos Aires region. The class threat posed to the Buenos Aires upper classes by Radicalism between 1916 and 1930 and the proletarian threat posed by Peronism in the 1940s were not felt by interior elites. The regional dichotomy created a situation of threat duality for the Argentine upper classes. This fact compounded conservative disunity and shaped the electoral alignments of conservatism for most of the twentieth century.

As a result of regional dynamics, Argentina is today characterized by a two-tier party system. At the national level, a two-party competitive dynamic between Radicalism and Peronism dominates electoral politics. Conservatism plays a minor role in this competition, and its impact tends to be manifested in support for one of the large parties in presidential contests through ticket-splitting and provincial party alliances with radicalism or Peronism. At the provincial level, however, a more varied competitive dynamic is at work. In individual provinces, conservative parties dominate electoral politics or contest the hegemony of Radicalism and Peronism in a multiparty competitive setting.

A look at other cases of conservative party development suggests that the Argentine case is not unique. Brazil provides an interesting comparative case. Regionalism there has been a major historical determinant of conservative alignments and has operated as one of the most important impediments to national conservative party development. The organization of Brazil's oligarchic power structures in the nineteenth century was in many ways similar to that in Argentina. During the oligarchic "Old Republic" (1889–1930), regionally varied oligarchies established firm control over local politics through clientelistic elite-controlled parties. Strong local party organization was a major instrument of oligarchic political control.[16] These local organizations failed, however, to develop into a system of nationally competitive oligarchic parties. The state thus became the mediator of conflict and bargaining at the national level between regional oligarchies.[17]

Brazil's first sustained experiment with democratic politics, from 1945 to 1964, was also marked by the national electoral decline of conservative parties. This process is traced in Maria do Carmo Campello de Souza's landmark book on Brazilian political parties.[18] De Souza notes that one of the most visible trends of the party system's evolution during this period was the fragmentation of national conservative parties and the decline of conservatism as a national electoral force. This development led, as in Argentina between 1916 and 1930, to prolonged institutional conflicts between an executive branch controlled by reformist or populist parties and a legislative branch that served as an institutional bastion for regionally fragmented conservative parties.[19] National conservative strategies thus eventually focused on capturing state power by nonelectoral means.

If we look to politics at the regional level, however, we find that the national conservative electoral decline was not mirrored by a decline in individual states. In fact, the Brazilian pattern was similar to that in Argentina. As the work of Olavo Brasil has shown, in spite of a generalized conservative decline nationally, "conservatism was most strongly manifested at the state level." He goes on to write:

In truth, the party system varied across time and political levels . . . there were marked differences in party system structure from state to state, as well as between the federal and state levels of competition. . . . The process of coalition building produced varied electoral results, depending on the level [federal or state] of competition. Hypotheses advanced about the decline of conservative parties are simply not true at both levels."[20]

One of the goals of Brazil's 1964–85 military rulers was to counter the national fragmentation of conservatism by engineering the creation of a national two-party system, much as their counterparts in the 1976–83 Argentine military regime attempted to do. They were successful in this endeavor, although they lifted many of the restrictions on multiparty organization once they recognized its unifying effect on nonconservative parties.[21] The impetus for national unity came to Brazilian conservatism in the presidential elections of 1989, not from any state efforts at institutional engineering, but from a national electoral challenge from the Left. The rise of the Workers' Party gave Brazilian conservatism its first relatively homogeneous national class-based challenge, a challenge that, unlike the more regionally heterogeneous populist challenges of the past, drove Brazilian conservatives into an anti–Workers' Party front behind the candidacy of Fernando Collor de Mello.[22] The "regional duality–threat duality" dynamic discussed earlier in connection with Argentine conservatism was overcome in Brazil by this national challenge from the Left. It was overcome once again in 1994, when conservatives mobilized behind the free-market candidacy of the Social Democratic leader Fernando Henrique Cardoso to defeat the Workers' Party's second presidential bid.

Comparison of the Brazilian case with Argentina's suggests something about regionalism's impact on conservative unity. Its effect is not only a function of endogenous factors. It is also a function of the relationship of conservative parties to nonconservative parties. Changes in threat duality will alter the divisive effect of regionalism on conservative electoral organization. Conservative regional divisions will be greatest where class threats posed by other parties to their core constituencies are nationally heterogeneous. The more uniform that threat across regions, the more likely the prospect of national conservative unity. Argentine conservatives remained divided because of conflicts among their core constituencies and among their party organizations. But they also remained divided because of the varied nature of their opponents' social coalitions across regions. Brazilian conservatives had been divided for similar reasons, but when they were confronted with a common national threat in 1989 and 1994, they found formulas for electoral unification.

Regionalism is not categorically bad for conservative party organization. It does provide a way for conservative leaders and their constituencies to retain a grip on local power. It resolves a number of problems, especially when national electoral mobilization is problematic. Regional mobilization fits in well with the vertical, cross-class ideological appeals of conservatism. Regional, religious, ethnic, and even linguistic bases of electoral mobilization at the local level help to dilute the impact of national class-based challenges from opposing parties and to forge alternative sources of collective identity for conservative electoral mobilization. In a context of regional cleavage, the vertical logic of conservative electoral mobilization thus finds more fertile ground in local electoral strategies than in national-level strategies that require unity among regional elites. Having failed to project themselves as carriers or guardians of a national project that supersedes class divisions, conservative leaders claim custodianship over regional sources of collective identity.

This, however, is only a second-best strategy. In Latin America, presidentialist systems make the presidency the supreme prize of politics and often render legislative institutions and gubernatorial positions vulnerable to the encroachments of presidential power. As the Latin American experience has shown, regionally based conservative electoral power does little to contribute to the stability of national democratic politics. It may preserve the grip of regional elites on local politics, but it provides a fragile institutional basis for advancing and organizing conservative interests democratically at the national level.

Changing Social Structures, State Crisis, and Conservative Mass Mobilization

In the 1980s, Latin America underwent the deepest and most generalized socioeconomic crisis since the Great Depression. At issue in this crisis was the decline of the state-centered models of development that had emerged as a regional response to the depression and the postwar push for economic development. As state-centered models of development were called into question, the only ideological force — on either the Right or the Left — historically linked to non-state-centered models of development was liberalismo. Long dormant as an electoral force, it took the initiative in the 1980s in shaping the debate and political agendas of democratic politics in several countries. This development had a profound impact on Latin American conservatism. It facilitated the rise of new leaders advocating free-market reform, reshaped the internal power structures of conservative movements, and transformed their strategies of mass mobilization.

Mass coalition-building opportunities were provided by the changing structures of Latin America's societies. In Argentina, secular trends in the evolution of the economy, as well as the more recent changes caused by state-centered economic decline, had altered the demographic and occupational makeup of society. Atomization and heterogeneity were the most visible long-term effects of the country's social evolution. Informality and urban poverty were among the fastest-growing trends in the Argentine economy. So, too, was the relative expansion in the number of people employed in the service and financial sectors relative to the previously dominant industrial sector.

The effect of these changes was to soften the social bases of long-standing political coalitions. The class-based collective identities forged at the workplace and in the labor unions in an industrial and proletarianized urban society were subjected to the individualizing and atomizing strains of the country's evolving occupational structure. New bases for political mobilization were emerging from these social changes, and they were to be found in social sectors vulnerable to the effects of a crumbling state and marginalized from the corporatist system that had shaped prior coalitions.

As objective social conditions, these changes remained politically latent in the early years of the consolidation period. But they had imparted volatility to voter loyalties that proved particularly susceptible to new forms of mass mobilization. Conditions for the manufacturing of new collective wills in the Argentine urban electorate had emerged, and these became reflected in conservative mass mobilization strategies during the mid 1980s. Middle-class voters formed the most important mass component of the new urban coalition built by the Unión del Centro Democrático in the Buenos Aires region. However, this coalition was expanded as the popularizers of liberalismo chipped away at social sectors traditionally outside conservatism's reach and patched together the bits and pieces crumbling from the edges of the long-standing urban constituencies of Radicalism and Peronism. The result was not the massive capture of those constituencies but the piecing together of a heterogeneous coalition held together by concern over the disintegration of Argentina's interventionist state. Self-employed workers, the unorganized urban poor, and middle

sectors ravaged by inflation and declining real wages were the most important social sectors targeted by Argentine conservatism for the construction
of its antistate, anticorporatist alliance.

A glance at the experiences of other countries strongly suggests that
these developments were not unique to Argentina. In Peru, the explosive
growth of the informal sector shifted the social bases of electoral politics
in the 1980s. Census data indicate that in Lima, the home of the country's
most important urban electorate, wage-earning and salaried populations
remained relatively stable between 1981 and 1986. During this period,
however, the informal sector grew by over 65 percent.[23] While these occupational shifts complicated the Peruvian Left's class-based strategies of
electoral mobilization, they also provided opportunities for new conservative strategies of electoral mobilization. The new conservative electoral
movements of the 1980s made the informal sector a major target of antistate mobilization, seeking to link informal workers with urban middle
classes buffeted by declining living standards in a pro-free-market electoral coalition.[24] In Mexico, the Partido Acción Nacional's growth in the
1980s was facilitated by the expansion of social sectors not linked to
Mexico's system of state-corporatist intermediation. The economic crisis
of the 1980s galvanized support in these sectors for PAN, and strengthened the position of leaders committed to bringing a broader *anti-estatista*
agenda of liberal economic reform to the party's political agenda. A growing informal sector, expanding middle sectors, and small and medium-
sized business sectors not linked to the corporatist apparatus provided the
stuff of the mass coalition building behind PAN's antistate agenda in the
1980s.[25] Additional empirical research into each of these countries would
provide a clearer sense of the actual impact of these newly mobilized
sectors on the growth of the new conservative coalitions. However it is
quite apparent that the socioeconomic crisis of Latin America's "lost decade" of development reshaped the ideological and coalitional content of
conservative party politics. The weakening of the state's capacities for
economic management and social organization and the withering of class-
based bonds of solidarity provided fertile ground for the vertical, cross-
class, individualizing appeals of conservative electoral movements.

Shifting Arenas of Political Action: Possible Futures for
Conservative Party Politics in Latin America

In an earlier chapter, Robert Bates was quoted as saying that the impermanence of institutions in developing countries "underscores the degree to

which these institutions are themselves chosen."[26] His observation captures both the promise and the plight of conservative party politics in Latin America. The promise lies in the fact that institutions and electoral coalitions are the products of political agency. They are objects to be crafted by political leadership. Their absence or instability are not immutable, but conditions that can often be overcome with investments of resources, manpower, and political skill. The plight of conservative party politics lies in the tentativeness of leadership and core-constituency commitment in the rapidly changing opportunity contexts of Latin American politics. The experience of the 1980s and early 1990s placed this situation in sharp relief. Important advances were made in the realm of electoral mobilization, but far fewer in the realm of party building.

Given this fluid state of affairs, speculation on the possible futures of conservative party organization in the countries discussed above might seem foolhardy. However, trends in the evolution of state-elite relations since the end of the lost decade mobilizations do give some hints of possible changes in conservatism institutional makeup. The consolidation of new conservative parties as influential and regular players in democratic politics should by no means be ruled out. El Salvador's ARENA has shown signs of moving in this direction. Its hold on power since 1989, reaffirmed by its comfortable victory in the presidential and local elections of 1994, has given it the opportunity to evolve beyond its preelectoral status as an elite-based opposition movement.[27] As the fragile and socially polarized peace process has evolved, power has permitted ARENA to solidify its position as the most important electoral representative of the country's socioeconomic elite. However, in most of the countries discussed in these pages, the likelihood of such an institutionalization scenario developing seems more remote. Three other scenarios might thus be advanced as plausible futures for conservative political organization.

The first of these is merely a return to the time-tried pattern of state-centered pressure politics. In this case, the state-conservative coalitions of the 1990s would have served only as temporary marriages of convenience, leaving no lasting legacies in the party realm other than the erosion of the party institutions built in the 1980s. Economic power, technocratic influence, and civil-military alliances would continue to be the main political currencies for conservative leaders and core constituencies in national political life.

However, things have changed in much of Latin America, and there are reasons to hope that the current disarticulation of conservative party politics does not merely represent a return to old historical patterns. The combined experiences of disastrous military rule and lessons learned from the lost-decade mobilizations have left their mark on the structure of politics and the incentives guiding conservative political action. The de-institutionalization of existing conservative parties might thus well be part of a transition to "something else" in the electoral realm rather than a return to past patterns of electoral marginalization.

A second and more hopeful scenario for the consolidation of Latin American democracies might be termed the "conservatization of populism." It would be a sequel of sorts to the policy-making shifts of populist parties in the aftermath of the lost decade mobilizations. Where this leads to successful economic policies and favorable electoral dividends, it may help to bring about deeper changes at the institutional and coalitional levels. The "populist conservatization" scenario, as it appears to be unfolding in Argentina, would involve the absorption of conservatives into the leaderships of populist parties. More fundamentally, however, it would be driven by a core-constituency shift for these parties.

At one level, the lessening of the mutual dependence of business and the state as developmentalism yields to new economic models would lead to new patterns of upper-class political representation. In this scenario, the formerly populist parties could become the electoral carriers of conservatism — modern guarantors of market stability with a ready-made popular base. Historic state-business ties would yield to more stable party-business ties. The ideological and pragmatic convergences that have brought populist leaders together with business groups today would thus lead to longer-lasting institutional unions.

In this scenario, the electoral base of populist parties would become increasingly transformed by the addition of upper- and upper-middle-class voters. At the interest-group level, the support of business groups for populist parties would become solidified and increasingly open, making business a pivotal base of financial and political support and displacing the parties' traditional social constituencies. In effect, this development would constitute a core-constituency shift for populist parties, rendering them effective advocates of upper-class political agendas while maintaining mass support for those agendas. The Peronist Party in Argentina has succeeded in mobilizing important electoral support from upper-income voters and has deepened its ties with big business, once the nemesis of the Peronist movement. This budding core-constituency shift appears now to be prompting a leadership union, inasmuch as prominent conservative party leaders have joined the Peronist Party. In Mexico, the PRI seems on its way toward fulfilling a populist conservatization scenario. In Chile, the reformist Christian Democratic Party's promarket and probusiness stand in the past few years has lessened support among both the electorate and businesspeople for the country's traditional conservative parties. The election to the presidency in 1994 of the Christian Democrat Eduardo Frei, an economic conservative with close ties to the business community, leaves open the possibility of an eventual shift in the party's social bases of support. In Bolivia, the ideological and coalitional shifts experienced by the Movimiento Nacional Revolucionario in the past decade may provide another instance of populist conservatization.[28]

However, the realization of a populist conservatization scenario is frought with obstacles. Any such transition would be marked by considerable conflict. Old-guard elements on both the populist and conservative sides stand ready to undermine the union at every turn. Victory by radical populist leaders in internal elections could split the alliances apart. In addition, loyalties to old party labels and standards can prove surprisingly resilient. In these situations, economic success might not be a strong enough glue to keep the pragmatic alliance from unraveling when faced with entrenched ideological and institutional legacies.

A third scenario would thus fall between the two mentioned above: a new "rapid deployment" model of conservative party politics. The 1980s taught conservatives important lessons. In a very short period of time, they proved able to change the terms of the political debate and gain support for their agendas through the electoral process. They did so without the help of their erstwhile uniformed allies, and in many cases without prior party structures. Given the structural power of their core constituencies, control of vital mass-media outlets, contacts with influential intellectual circles, international ties, and the now tested financial power of a mobilized business community, conservatives have found themselves quite adept at mobilizing national electoral movements quickly and when crisis conditions warrant them.

That they have proven equally willing to abandon party building when the possibility of state-centered strategies emerges does not preclude a return to electoral mobilization if conditions change. In a future post-Fujimori crisis in Peru, a new conservative coalition might well emerge from the ashes of the short-lived FREDEMO and Movimiento Libertad, with familiar leaders wearing new and unfamiliar party labels. Rapid deployment in presidential elections might be an effective conservative response to the intractability of regional fragmentation. It would offer a viable national strategy for conservatives unable to build lasting national parties but with strong regional parties that safeguard their interests between presidential elections.[29] If the populist conservative scenario fails in Argentina, rapid deployment may well emerge as the only feasible strategy for the fragmented federalist and liberal parties of Argentine conservatism. Rapid deployment seems once again to have saved Brazilian conservatism from a Workers' Party victory in the 1994 presidential elections, when conservatives mobilized behind the successful Center-Right electoral bid of Fernando Henrique Cardoso. In the future, a new fresh face, propelled across the country by the omnipresent Rede Globo media network, may rise as the newborn embodiment of the Brazilian electoral Right. Knitting together the familiar constellation of regional party networks and business interests behind a new institutional façade, conservatives may continue their check of the Brazilian Left's long and hard-fought bid for national power.

As a model of conservative political action, "rapid deployment" might blend the old and the new of conservative party politics in Latin America. It remains true to its historic institutional fluidity in much of the region, yet it also incorporates the significant changes in political practice that came with the lost decade mobilizations. Its impact on democratic development in the region, however, is hard to foretell. On the one hand, it would be an advance on previous military-coup models of conservative political action. On the other, it is just as much a crisis-driven form of political action, one that does little to solidify the institutional bases of democratic politics. Rapid deployment is, after all, about electoral mobilization, not party building.

The 1980s were a period of major conservative transformation in Latin America, fueled by new agendas and marked by unprecedented electoral mobilization. These advances have produced changes that will be very difficult to reverse. It can be said that conservatives "discovered" party politics in many countries during the 1980s. It might be too much, however, to expect stable patterns of party development to result from this throughout the region. At this stage in Latin America's tentative reencounter with democracy, the only certainty is that conservative party politics will continue to be a fluid and often unstructured affair. Although sustained by the gains made in the first decades of democratic politics, it will continue to be hindered by conservative preference for the immediacy of technocratic politics and ad hoc electoral mobilization, as opposed to the more uncertain, and laborious, option of party building.

Appendix

Argentine Heads of Government since 1862

1862–1868	Bartolomé Mitre (Partido Liberal, Buenos Aires)
1868–1874	Domingo F. Sarmiento (Partido Autonomista Nacional)
1874–1880	Nicolás Avellaneda (Partido Autonomista Nacional)
1880–1886	Julio A. Roca (Partido Autonomista National)
1886–1990	Miguel Juarez Celman (Partido Autonomista National)
1890–1892	Carlos Pellegrini (Partido Autonomista National)
1892–1895	Luis Sáenz Peña (Partido Autonomista National)
1895–1898	José Evaristo Uriburu (Partido Autonomista National)
1898–1904	Julio A. Roca (Partido Autonomista National)
1904–1906	Manuel Quintana (Partido Autonomista National)
1906–1910	Roque Sáenz Peña (Partido Autonomista National)
1913–1916	Victorino de la Plaza (Partido Autonomista National)
1916–1922	Hipólito Yrigoyen (Unión Cívica Radical)
1922–1928	Marcelo T. de Alvear (Unión Cívica Radical)
1928–1930	Hipólito Yrigoyen (Unión Cívica Radical)
1930–1932	José F. Uriburu (Military)
1932–1938	Agustín P. Justo (Military-Concordancia)
1938–1940	Roberto M. Ortiz (Concordancia)
1940–1943	Ramón S. Castillo (Concordancia)
1943	Arturo Rawson (Military)
1943–1944	Pedro P. Ramirez (Military)
1944–1946	Edelmiro J. Farrel (Military)
1946–1955	Juan Domingo Perón (Partido Justicialista)

1955	Eduardo Lonardi (Military)
1955–1958	Pedro E. Aramburu (Military)
1958–1962	Arturo Frondizi (Unión Cívica Radical Intransigente)
1962–1963	José María Guido (Military-dominated interim president)
1963–1966	Arturo Illía (Unión Cívica Radical del Pueblo)
1966–1970	Juan Carlos Onganía (Military)
1970–1971	Roberto M. Levingston (Military)
1971–1973	Alejandro A. Lanusse (Military)
1973	Héctor Cámpora (Partido Justicialista)
1973	Raúl Lastiri (Partido Justicialista)
1973–1974	Juan Domingo Perón (Partido Justicialista)
1974–1976	Maria Estela Martínez de Perón (Partido Justicialista)
1976–1981	Jorge Rafaél Videla (Military)
1981	Roberto Viola (Military)
1981–1982	Leopoldo F. Galtieri (Military)
1982–1983	Reynaldo B. A. Bignone (Military)
1983–1989	Raúl R. Alfonsin (Unión Cívica Radical)
1989–	Carlos S. Menem (Partido Justicialista)

Notes

Chapter One / Conservative Parties and Democratic Politics

Epigraph: Max Weber, "Parties," in *From Max Weber: Essays in Sociology,* ed. H. H. Gerth and C. Wright Mills (1946: Oxford University Paperback, 1958), 195.

1. Guillermo O'Donnell and Philippe C. Schmitter, *Tentative Conclusions about Uncertain Democracies,* vol. 4 of *Transitions from Authoritarian Rule: Prospects for Democracy,* ed. Guillermo O'Donnell, Philippe C. Schmitter, and Laurence Whitehead (Baltimore: Johns Hopkins University Press, 1986), 62–63.

2. I employ the phrase *electoral movements,* instead of *parties,* to maximize inclusiveness. The fluidity of many party systems in Latin America often produces the appearance of movements vying for power through the electoral process that do not have formal party status (like Vargas Llosa's Movimiento Libertad in Peru), are structurally inchoate and thus not entirely worthy of the label *party* (like Collor de Mello's Partido de Reconstrução Nacional), or are shifting alliances of several parties (like Izquierda Unida in Peru). The term *electoral movements* permits inclusion of such phenomena alongside parties in this analysis.

3. Some portions of this chapter appeared in Edward L. Gibson, "Conservative Electoral Movements and Democratic Politics: Core Constituencies, Coalition-Building, and the Latin American Electoral Right," in *The Right and Democracy in Latin America,* ed. Douglas Chalmers, Atilio Boron, and Maria do Carmo Campello de Souza, (Westport, Conn.: Praeger, 1992).

4. Giovanni Sartori, "Guidelines for Concept Analysis," in *Social Science Concepts,* ed. id. (Beverly Hills, Calif.: Sage Publications, 1984), 74.

5. Ibid.

6. Clinton Rossiter, "Conservatism," in *International Encyclopedia of the Social Sciences,* ed. David Sills (New York: Free Press, 1968), 3: 290.

7. R. A. H. Robinson, "Political Conservatism: The Spanish Case, 1875–1977," *Journal of Contemporary History* 14 (1979): 561, 578 (special issue, "A Century of Conservatism").

8. Martin Greiffenhagen, "The Dilemma of Conservatism in Germany," *Journal of Contemporary History* 14 (1979): 611.

9. Kenneth Medhurst, "Spanish Conservative Politics," in *Conservative Politics in Western Europe,* ed. Zig Layton-Henry (New York: St. Martin's Press, 1982), 292.

10. Edgar Grande, "Neoconservatism Without Neoconservatives? The Renaissance and Transformation of Contemporary German Conservatism," in *The Transformation of Contemporary Conservatism* ed. Brian Girvin (London: Sage Publications, 1988), 56–57.

11. David Noble, "Conservatism in the USA," *Journal of Contemporary History* 13 (1979): 732 (special issue, "A Century of Conservatism").

12. Hans Geerd Schumann, "The Problem of Conservatism: Some Notes on Methodology," *Journal of Contemporary History* 13 (1979): 805.

13. Zig Layton-Henry, "Introduction," in *Conservative Politics in Western Europe,* ed. id., 1.

14. Stig-Björn Ljunggren, "Conservatism in Norway and Sweden," in *Transformation of Contemporary Conservatism,* ed. Girvin, 127.

15. Robinson, "Political Conservatism," 577.

16. Clinton Rossiter, *Conservatism in America* (Cambridge, Mass.: Harvard University Press, 1955), 5.

17. Russell Kirk, *The Portable Conservative Reader* (New York: Penguin Books, 1982), xiv–xv.

18. Samuel Huntington, "Conservatism as an Ideology," *American Political Science Review* 51 (June 1957): 461.

19. Ibid., 456.

20. Robert Nisbet, *Conservatism: Dream and Reality* (Minneapolis: University of Minnesota Press, 1986), 1.

21. Kirk, *Portable Conservative Reader,* xiii.

22. The work by Edmund Burke that has most influenced modern conservative thought is his assault on the French Revolution, published as *Reflections on the Revolution in France* in 1790.

23. Russell Kirk, *A Program for Conservatives* (Chicago: Chicago University Press, 1954), 22, 39.

24. Huntington, "Conservatism as an Ideology," 468.

25. See, e.g., the introductory chapters to the volumes edited by Layton-Henry and Girvin cited in nn. 9 and 10 above, as well as the introduction by Robert Nisbet to the special issue of the *Journal of Contemporary History* cited in n. 7.

26. In this sense, conservatism can be distinguished from "the Right," which is an ideological label, and refers to space on one end of a Left-Right continuum. Conservative movements can be considered one type of movement generally found on the "Right" end of that ideological spectrum, but they often share that space with movements with different sociological bases.

27. The distinction between "defining" and "variable" properties is taken from Sartori, "Guidelines for Concept Analysis."

28. See Otto Kirscheimer, "The Transformation of Western European Party Systems," in *Political Parties and Political Development,* ed. Joseph LaPalombara and Myron Weiner (Princeton, N.J.: Princeton University Press, 1966), 177–200.

29. In many parts of the world, the first successful multiclass parties were

conservative parties. The case of the Conservative Party of Great Britain is paradigmatic in this sense.

30. In his study of Latin American business, for example, Carlos Acuña suggests that "parties are not the actors on which to focus the analysis of capitalist class political organization under democratic regimes" (Acuña, "The Bourgeoisie as a Political Actor" [Ph.D. diss., University of Chicago, forthcoming]).

31. Peter Mair argues that it is more feasible to think in terms of structural change in *party systems* than in *parties,* since it is virtually impossible to identify the structural "essence or core" of an individual party. See Mair, "The Problem of Party System Change," *Journal of Theoretical Politics* 1, 3 (1989). If we analyze a party's relationship to society in addition to its institutional and organizational dimensions, however, we can look to its social base to distill its "essence or core." This would help us do what Mair considers problematic: distinguishing between changes in *aspects* of a party and changes in a party *tout court.*

32. David Rock, *Politics in Argentina, 1890–1930: The Rise and Fall of Radicalism* (London: Cambridge University Press, 1975), 267, 58, 97–98, 266.

33. Ibid., 111, 222.

34. See Max Weber, "The Distribution of Power Within the Political Community: Class, Status, Party," in *Max Weber: Economy and Society*, ed. Guenther Roth and Claus Wittich (Berkeley and Los Angeles: University of California Press, 1978), 926–40.

35. Coercive and institutional resources have, of course, often meshed with socioeconomic power. Landowners in Latin America, for example, control coercive resources in the countryside as well as political institutions. However, their control over these resources is derived from their socioeconomic power. For analytical purposes, only those groups or individuals whose power or authority is rooted in the social order would be identified as potential core constituencies of a conservative party.

36. This is not a random example. As later chapters will reveal, it captures the historic plight of conservative parties in much of Latin America.

37. Weber, *Economy and Society,* quoted in Giovanni Sartori, "The Sociology of Parties: A Critical Review," in *Party Systems, Party Organizations, and the Politics of New Masses,* ed. Otto Stammer (Berlin: Institute for Political Science, Free University at Berlin, 1968); reprinted in *The West European Party System,* ed. Peter Mair (Oxford: Oxford University Press, 1990), 166.

38. Schumpeter, *Capitalism, Socialism and Democracy* (1942; New York: Harper & Row, 1976), 270.

39. Ibid., 263.

40. Adam Przeworski and John Sprague, "Party Strategy, Class Organization, and Individual Voting," in Adam Przeworski, *Capitalism and Social Democracy* (New York: Cambridge University Press, 1985), 99–101.

41. Quoted in the *New York Times,* Sunday, Jan. 20, 1991.

42. Przeworski and Sprague, "Party Strategy, Class Organization, and Individual Voting," 100–101.

43. See Maurice Duverger, *Political Parties: Their Organization and Activity in the Modern State,* trans. Barbara and Robert North, (1954; London: University Paperbacks, 1972), xiii.

44. See M. Ostrogorski, *Democracy and the Organization of Political Parties in the United States and Great Britain* (Garden City, N.Y.: Doubleday, Anchor Books, 1964, abridged); Robert Michels, *Political Parties: A Sociological Study of the Oligarchical Tendencies of Modern Democracy,* trans. Eden and Cedar Paul (New York: Free Press, 1962); Giovanni Sartori, *Parties and Party Systems: A Framework for Analysis* (Cambridge: Cambridge University Press, 1976).

45. Angelo Panebianco, *Political Parties: Organization and Power* (Cambridge: Cambridge University Press, 1988).

46. Ibid., 3. The other prejudice criticized by Panebianco is what he calls the "teleological prejudice," which he describes as "attributing *a priori* 'goals' to parties which in the observer's mind represent the *raison d'être* of the party in question" (4). As the earlier discussion in this chapter on ideology should indicate, this is a criticism with which I agree.

47. Ibid., 276.

48. We may, of course, be interested in a type of party for reasons other than its relationship to social conflict. It could be for ideological reasons, whereby we would analyze Right or Left parties according to their ideology and relationship to ideological competition. In any case, the analysis of interparty conflict will generally require a basis for comparison that lies outside the organizational realm.

49. Alfred Stepan, *Rethinking Military Politics: Brazil and the Southern Cone* (Princeton, N.J.: Princeton University Press, 1988), 3.

50. Ibid.

51. Ibid., 4.

52. Ibid.

53. Max Weber, "Politics as a Vocation," in *From Max Weber: Essays in Sociology,* ed. H. H. Gerth and C. Wright Mills (1946; Oxford University Paperback, 1958), 99.

54. Karen L. Remmer, *Party Competition in Argentina and Chile: Political Recruitment and Public Policy, 1890–1930* (Lincoln: University of Nebraska Press, 1984), 222.

55. Dietrich Rueschemeyer, Evelyn Stevens, and John Stevens, *Capitalist Development and Democracy* (Chicago: Chicago University Press, 1992), 274. For another major comparative historical study whose findings support this argument, see Ruth Berins Collier and David Collier, *Shaping the Political Arena: Critical Junctures, the Labor Movement, and Regime Dynamics in Latin America* (Princeton, N.J.: Princeton University Press, 1991).

56. The figures for Costa Rica skew the average for the first group of countries considerably. In this case, the median ratio is probably a fairer measure. The median ratio for the group of countries with strong conservative parties is 4.2, while the median ratio for countries with weak historical legacies of conservative party organization is .6. If only the South American cases are taken into account

(Central America and Mexico providing the extreme values on both ends), the average ratios are 3.4 and 0.9. Whatever measure is chosen, however, the conclusion remains the same: countries with viable national conservative parties in place at the start of democracy experienced far greater democratic stability throughout the twentieth century than countries that did not.

57. The notion of "historical cause" comes from the work of Arthur Stinchcomb, *Constructing Social Theories* (New York: Harcourt, Brace & World, 1968), 101–29. Historical causes are events that occur at a specified point in time, and their legacy or effects are felt throughout subsequent historical periods without the recurrence of the original event. They leave distinctive legacies, usually institutional, which perpetuate the effect of the original cause in subsequent periods. Stinchcomb distinguishes historical causes from "constant causes," which are not single-shot events, and are predicted to have the same effect with each iteration. They correspond to the more familiar concept of causation employed in the social sciences.

Chapter Two / Region, Class, and Conservative Parties

Epigraph: Carlos Ibarguren, *La historia que he vivido* (Buenos Aires: Ediciones Peuser, 1955), 249.

1. Comparative historical evidence for this proposition is provided by Seymour M. Lipset and Stein Rokkan, "Cleavage Structures, Party Systems, and Voter Alignments: An Introduction," in *Party Systems and Voter Alignments: Cross-National Perspectives,* ed. id. (New York: Free Press, 1967), 1–64. See also Maurice Duverger, *Political Parties: Their Organization and Activity in the Modern State,* trans. Barbara and Robert North (1954; London: University Paperbacks, 1972).

2. This is not to say that the state was an unimportant instrument for political domination in countries where national competitive party systems were established. The point here is that in some countries, political parties were important vehicles for capturing national power, and competition between elite-dominated parties at the national level played a major role in determining who would control the state and its vast resources for patronage and political control. Where national networks of competing parties did not exist, party competition did not play such a role.

3. For the distinction between "historical causes" and "constant causes," see Chapter 1, n. 57, as well as Arthur Stinchcomb, *Constructing Social Theories* (New York: Harcourt, Brace & World, 1968).

4. A collection of historical essays that address how the regional question shaped social institutional, and ideological developments in Latin America is *La unidad nacional en América Latina: Del regionalismo a la nacionalidad,* ed. Marco Palacios (Mexico City: El Colegio de México, 1983).

5. Throughout this book the term *liberal* will be employed in its classical, most widely used sense internationally, to denote doctrines or ideologies of the limited

state, or as a label for parties or movements espousing such doctrines or ideologies. It is not employed in its contemporary U.S. usage, to denote Center-Left ideologies or movements. Conflict between socioeconomic elites in much of nineteenth- and twentieth-century Latin American politics has often been structured by movements espousing such liberal causes as free-market development, anticlericalism, individualism, and political liberty against elite movements (often adopting "conservative" as an ideological label) opposed to such positions. "Liberalism" is thus one of several possible ideologies or movements competing for primacy in parties that are socially, but not ideologically, defined as "conservative" in this book.

6. In a 1967 study of Colombian politics, Robert Dix presented ecological data that revealed the twentieth-century continuity of rural-urban biases in electoral support for the Liberal and Conservative parties, in spite of their overall composition as multisectoral, cross-regional, and multiclass parties. The Liberal Party tended to dominate electoral politics in cities, while the Conservative Party tended to be stronger in rural areas. See Dix, *Colombia: The Political Dimensions of Change* (New Haven, Conn.: Yale University Press, 1967), 239–45.

7. Ruth Berins Collier and David Collier, *Shaping the Political Arena: Critical Junctures, the Labor Movement, and Regime Dynamics in Latin America* (Princeton, N.J.: Princeton University Press, 1991), 124–25.

8. The Radical Party was founded in 1861 on a strong anticlerical platform. Socially, however, it was closely linked to new mining interests in northern Chile. "Socially and economically, then, the Radical Party was at first the expression of the political demands of the new wealthy bourgeoisie produced by the development of mining in the north and subsequently became the focus of resistance by the agricultural provinces of the south to the centralization of power in Santiago" (Federico Gil, *The Political System of Chile* [Boston: Houghton Mifflin, 1966], 43). Thus, while anticlericalism served as an important banner for the Radicals, and separated them ideologically from the Conservatives, the underlying common interest in opposing the expansion of state authority overrode the church-state issue and brought the Radicals into convergence with conservatives against the Liberals in Santiago.

9. For a discussion of the 1874 electoral reform bill, see Timothy R. Scully, "Reconstituting Party Politics in Chile," in *Building Democratic Institutions: Party Systems in Latin America,* ed. Scott Mainwaring and Timothy R. Scully (Stanford, Calif.: Stanford University Press, 1995).

10. Gil, *Political System of Chile,* 48.

11. Dietrich Rueschemeyer, Evelyn Stevens, and John Stevens, *Capitalist Development and Democracy* (Chicago: Chicago University Press, 1992), 216.

12. Events of these periods in Colombia are addressed in Richard Sharpless, *Gaitán of Colombia: A Political Biography* (Pittsburgh: Pittsburgh University Press, 1978); Miguel Urrutia, *The Development of the Colombian Labor Movement* (New Haven, Conn.: Yale University Press, 1969); and Ronald Archer, "Party Strength and Weakness in Colombia's Besieged Democracy," in *Building Democratic Institutions,* ed. Mainwaring and Scully. For Uruguay, see José Barrán and

Benjamín Nahum, *Batlle, los estancieros, y el imperio británico*, vols. 1–6 (Montevideo: Ediciones de la Banda Oriental, 1979–85). For a comparative treatment of Colombia and Uruguay, see Collier and Collier, *Shaping the Political Arena*.

13. Collier and Collier, *Shaping the Political Arena*, 106–7.

14. As the Colliers note, in contrast to Chile's more programmatic, parliament-based parties, "Brazilian parties were personalistic, local organizations with an ephemeral existence at the level of national politics and the national legislature" (ibid., 107–8).

15. For an influential book on Brazilian political parties arguing that the historic dominance of the state in the organization and mediation of conflict has been a decisive obstacle to party formation, see Maria do Carmen Campello de Souza, *Estado e partidos políticos no Brazil, 1930–1964* (Sao Paulo: Alfa-Omega, 1983).

16. As Miriam Kornblith and Daniel H. Levine point out, the Gomez dictatorship, through repression and oil-induced structural change, effected major changes in the social and political characteristics of the Venezuelan elite, further eliminating the legacies of earlier party organization: "The political parties whose conflicts dominated nineteenth century politics left no trace at all" (Kornblith and Levine, "Venezuela: The Life and Times of the Party System," in *Building Democratic Institutions*, ed. Mainwaring and Scully).

17. Collier and Collier, *Shaping the Political Arena*, 131.

18. For discussions of party politics in Peru during this period, see Hugo Garavito Amézaga, *El Perú liberal: Partidos e ideas políticas de la ilustración a la república aristocrática* (Lima: Ediciones El Virrey, 1989). For an article-length overview of Peruvian party politics, see Julio Cotler, "Political Parties and the Problems of Democratic Consolidation in Peru," in *Building Democratic Institutions*, ed. Mainwaring and Scully.

19. One of the first writers to highlight the issue and implications of conservative electoral weakness in twentieth-century Argentina was Torcuato Di Tella in his much discussed article, "La búsqueda de la fórmula política argentina," *Desarrollo Económico* 42/44 (1971): 317–25.

20. Peter Smith, *Argentina and the Failure of Democracy: Conflict Among Political Elites, 1904–1955* (Madison: University of Wisconsin Press, 1974).

21. Ramón J. Cárcano, *Mis primeros ochenta años* (Buenos Aires: Editorial Sudamericana, 1943), 303.

22. Quoted in ibid., 303, and in David Rock, *Politics in Argentina, 1890–1930* (Cambridge: Cambridge University Press, 1975), 35.

23. The notion of "genetic defects," and their impact on the development of party institutions, is discussed in Angelo Panebianco's work on the organizational dynamics of party development. See Panebianco, *Political Parties: Organization and Power* (Cambridge: Cambridge University Press, 1988).

24. See Oscar E. Cornblit, Ezequiel Gallo, and Alfredo O'Connell, "La generación del 80 y su proyecto: Antecedentes y consecuencias," in *Argentina, sociedad de masas*, ed. Torcuato S. Di Tella, Gino Germani, and Jorge Graciarena (Buenos Aires: Editorial Universitaria de Buenos Aires, 1965), 30. Growth rates in per-

capita wealth in other countries during that period were: United States, $29; United Kingdom, $24; Australia, $44.

25. Ibid.

26. Roberto Cortés Conde, "Problemas del crecimiento industrial, 1870–1914," in *Argentina, sociedad de masas,* ed. Di Tella, Germani, and Graciarena, 82.

27. Miron Burgin, *The Economic Aspects of Argentine Federalism, 1820–1852* (Cambridge, Mass.: Harvard University Press, 1946), 82–83.

28. For accounts of the political process that led to the development of the interior's sugar and wine industries, see Jorge Balán, "Una cuestión regional en la Argentina: Burguesías provinciales y el mercado nacional en el desarrollo agroexportador," *Desarrollo Económico* 18 (Apr.–June 1978): 49–87.

29. James R. Scobie, *Argentina: A City and a Nation* (New York: Oxford University Press, 1971): 147–50.

30. Ibid., 149–50.

31. Karl Mannheim, "Conservative Thought," in *From Karl Mannheim,* ed. Kurt H. Wolff (New York: Oxford University Press, 1971), 159.

32. Scobie, *Argentina,* 154.

33. One of the most eloquent exponents of policies to foster immigration as a "civilizing" measure was Domingo Faustino Sarmiento, president of Argentina in the 1860s, a Freemason, and one of the Argentine republic's liberal founding fathers. His literary magnum opus, subtitled *Civilization or Barbarism,* is an eloquent celebration of the struggle to bring European civilization to the backwaters of Argentina's interior.

34. Marcelo Sanchez Sorondo, *La Argentina por dentro* (Buenos Aires: Editorial Sudamericana, 1987).

35. For an account of the economic development of the Pampas region, see James R. Scobie, *Revolution on the Pampas: A Social History of Argentine Wheat, 1860–1910* (Austin: University of Texas Press, 1964).

36. Karen L. Remmer, *Party Competition in Argentina and Chile: Political Recruitment and Public Policy, 1890–1930* (Lincoln: University of Nebraska Press, 1984), 28.

37. Natalio Botana, *El orden conservador: La política argentina entre 1880 y 1916* (Buenos Aires: Editorial Sudamericana, 1977).

38. Smith, *Argentina and the Failure of Democracy,* 9.

39. Botana, *El orden conservador,* 173.

40. Quoted in Ibarguren, *La historia que he vivido,* 213.

41. Paraphrased in Oscar Cornblit, "La opción conservadora en la política argentina," *Desarrollo Económico* 56 (1975): 631.

42. For a listing of the key founding members of the PDP, see Ibarguren, *La historia que he vivido,* 301. For a listing of the provincial parties that joined the alliance, see Cornblit, "La opción conservadora," 62.

43. The Argentine presidential election system until 1994 was based on the U.S. system. The popular vote was formally cast for nominees to an Electoral

College, which subsequently cast the official vote for president. If no majority was obtained in the Electoral College, the vote passed to the national congress.

44. Cornblit, "La opción conservadora," 628. A similar line of argument is provided by Remmer in the comparative study of party competition in Argentina and Chile cited in n. 36 above.

45. Most of these proposals, Ibarguren noted with pride in his memoirs—published under the 1946–55 Peronist government—"are now being implemented" (Ibarguren, *La historia que he vivido*, 305).

46. Ibid., 305–6. (Italics added). A complete text of the Partido Demócrata Progresista's platform was published in *La Nación* (Buenos Aires), Sept. 11, 1915.

47. Panebianco, *Political Parties*, 51.

48. Congress similarly provided a forum for the representation of regional interests and an arena in which regional elites could come together to check the power of the national executive branch in other regionally divided countries, such as the United States.

49. Ana María Mustapic, "Conflictos institucionales durante el primer gobierno radical, 1916–1922," *Desarrollo Económico* 24 (Apr.–June 1984). See also Liliana de Riz and Catalina Smulovitz, "Instituciones y dinámica política: El presidencialismo argentino," Centro de Estudios de Estado y Sociedad, Documento CEDES 37 (Buenos Aires, 1990).

50. For accounts of the institutional dimensions of the struggles of the period, see Ana María Mustapic, "El Partido Conservador de la provincia de Buenos Aires ante la intervención federal y la competencia democrática 1917–1928," Instituto Torcuato Di Tella, Documento de Trabajo No. 95 (Buenos Aires, 1987); id., "Conflictos institucionales"; and Anne Potter, "Political Institutions, Political Decay, and the Argentine Crisis of 1930" (Ph.D. diss., Stanford University, 1978).

51. Mustapic, "Conflictos institucionales," 94–95.

52. This can be seen in the wording of Article 6 of the national constitution, which authorizes the president to replace elected provincial authorities with federally appointed authorities whenever he deems it necessary to "guarantee the republican form of government, or repell foreign invasions, as well as at the request of the [provincial] constituted authorities to support them or restore them to office if they have been dislodged by sedition, or by invasion from another province" (quoted in Botana, *El orden conservador*, 122).

53. Ibid., 127, 133.

54. The conservative provinces intervened in were Buenos Aires (Apr. 1917); Corrientes (Nov. 1917); Jujuy (Dec. 1917); La Rioja (Apr. 1918); Catamarca (Apr. 1918); Salta (Apr. 1918); San Luis (May 1918); Santiago del Estero (Oct. 1918); and San Juan (Oct. 1919). See Mustapic, "Conflictos institucionales," 101.

55. Mustapic, "El Partido Conservador de la provincia de Buenos Aires," 10.

56. A detailed presentation of this argument may be found in de Riz and Smulovitz, "Instituciones y dinámica política."

57. Richard J. Walter, *La provincia de Buenos Aires en la política argentina, 1912–1943* (Buenos Aires: Emecé Editores, 1987), 91.

58. Rock, *Politics in Argentina*, 228–40.

59. For an account of the intervention-centered strategies of the Buenos Aires conservatives, see the chapter aptly entitled "Alvear y la no intervención," in Walter, *La provincia de Buenos Aires*, 89–108. See also Mustapic's article, "El Partido Conservador de la provincia de Buenos Aires."

60. Walter, *La provincia de Buenos Aires*, 265.

61. For an engaging account of the elite dynamics of the political selection processes and the widespread use of fraud during this period, see Felix Luna, *Ortiz: Reportaje a la Argentina opulenta* (Buenos Aires: Editorial Sudamericana, 1986).

62. In his history of Buenos Aires politics, Richard Walter provides a detailed analysis of the decline of the Buenos Aires Conservative Party after the 1930 coup. See Walter, *La provincia de Buenos Aires*, 257.

63. Ibid., 258.

64. For accounts of the economic reforms undertaken by the governments of the period, see David Rock, *Argentina, 1516–1982: From Spanish Colonization to the Falklands War* (Berkeley and Los Angeles: University of California Press, 1985), and Fernando Henrique Cardoso, *Ideologías de la burguesía industrial en sociedades dependientes: Argentina y Brasil* (Mexico City: Siglo XXI Editores, 1982).

65. Two works by social scientists that detail the origins and evolution of Argentine nacionalismo are Marysa Navarro Gerassi, *Los nacionalistas* (Buenos Aires: Editorial Jorge Alvarez, 1968), and Cristián Buchrucker, *Nacionalismo y peronismo: La Argentina en la crisis ideológica mundial, 1927–1955* (Buenos Aires: Editorial Sudamericana, 1987). Also interesting are works by nacionalista writers themselves. These include Carlos Ibarguren's memoir cited earlier, *La historia que he vivido*, and his *La inquietud de esta hora* (Buenos Aires: Juan Roldán, 1934), as well as Federico Ibarguren, *Orígenes del nacionalismo argentino, 1927–1937* (Buenos Aires: Editorial CELCIUS, 1969).

66. Ibarguren, *La historia que he vivido*. Ibarguren himself, arguably nacionalismo's most important ideologue, was from a prominent aristocratic family from Salta province.

67. Among the more prominent conservative defections to the Peronist camp were those of Ramón J. Cárcano, former governor of Córdoba and eminent member of the Generation of 1880, and Manuel Fresco, governor of Buenos Aires province.

68. Two studies, based on electoral data from the 1946 election, confirm the conservative-Peronist electoral shift. Ignacio Llorente, in a study of the 1946 election in Buenos Aires, and Luis González Estevez, in a study of the Córdoba election, reported significant positive correlations between the decline of the conservative vote and the emergence of Peronist electoral support. Only in industrially developed areas, where the working class was mostly congregated, did middle- and upper-class vote shifts benefit the UCR. See Ignacio Llorente, "Alianzas políticas en el surgimiento del peronismo: El caso de la provincia de Buenos Aires," and

Luis González Esteves, "Las elecciones de 1946 en la provincia de Córdoba," both in *El voto Peronista: Ensayos de sociología electoral argentina,* ed. Manuel Mora y Araujo and Ignacio Llorente (Buenos Aires: Editorial Sudamericana, 1980).

69. In the province of Buenos Aires, the conservative hemorrhage was dramatic. The conservative party (locally named the Partido Demócrata Nacional since the Concordancia) garnered only 3.3 percent of the vote in the presidential election, compared to the 74.1 percent it had received in 1937, in the more hospitable days of the Concordancia. In congressional elections, its vote share declined from 72 percent in 1942 to 6 percent in 1946. Darío Cantón, *Materiales para el estudio de la sociología política en la Argentina* (Buenos Aires: Centro de Investigaciones Sociales, Instituto Torcuato Di Tella, 1968), 1: 132–33.

70. Rock, *Politics in Argentina,* 62.

71. The most important contemporary cleavage lies between Raúl Alfonsín's Buenos Aires–based "Coordinadora" faction and the followers of the governor of Córdoba province, Eduardo Cesar Angeloz.

72. The best-known early case of this is provided by the "Radicales Disidentes" of Santa Fe province, a conservative splinter of the UCR, whose defection almost cost Hipólito Yrigoyen the 1916 election.

73. Smith, *Argentina and the Failure of Democracy,* 79.

74. Manuel Mora y Araujo, "La estructura social del peronismo: Un análisis electoral interprovincial," *Desarrollo Económico* 56 (1975). Mora y Araujo presented this as a preliminary study, intended to identify directions for future research. Amazingly, in light of the provocativeness of his findings, his call for additional research on this subject has not been heeded. An indication of the general indifference that permeates scholarship on Argentina toward the interior, and toward the importance of regional cleavage (most notably by *Porteños* themselves), is provided by the fact that there has not been a single study analyzing the social and political characteristics of Peronism in the interior provinces. This has made a fundamental pillar of that intriguing and perplexing movement one of the black holes of Argentine studies.

75. Ibid., 717.

76. The exception to this rule is the case of Alvaro Alsogaray, whose ability to shift his political activities from the state to the arenas of party politics is described in detail in Chapter 4.

77. Max Weber, "Politics as a Vocation," in *From Max Weber: Essays in Sociology,* ed. H. H. Gerth and C. Wright Mills (1946; Oxford University Paperback, 1958), 83.

78. For a fascinating case study of this process of intratechnocratic competition, see Guillermo O'Donnell, *Bureaucratic Authoritarianism: Argentina, 1966–1973, in Comparative Perspective,* trans. James McGuire in collaboration with Rae Flory (Berkeley and Los Angeles: University of California Press, 1988).

79. Rosendo Fraga (with Gabriela Malacrida), *Argentina en las urnas, 1916–1989* (Buenos Aires: Editorial Centro de Estudios Unión para la Nueva Mayoría, 1989), 13.

80. This list was compiled from information contained in Ricardo Balestra and Jorge Luis Ossona, *¿Qué son los partidos provinciales?* (Buenos Aires: Editorial Sudamericana, 1983); Ezequiel Gallo and Esteban F. Thomsen, "Electoral Evolution of the Parties of the Right: Argentina, 1983–1989," Columbia University / New York University Consortium, Conference Paper No. 28 (New York, 1989); "Los partidos políticos: El conservadorismo," *La Nación,* May 10, 1983: sec. 3, 1); and Emilio J. Hardoy, *¿Qué son los conservadores en la Argentina?* (Buenos Aires: Editorial Sudamericana, 1983).

81. See, e.g., Gallo and Thomsen, "Electoral Evolution of the Parties of the Right."

82. For a brief historical background of the MPN, see Balestra and Ossona, *¿Qué son los partidos provinciales?*

Chapter Three / Authoritarian Crafting of Conservative Democracies

Epigraph: Albano Harguindeguy, quoted in *Clarín,* Nov. 27, 1980.

1. In Chile, the regime was quite effective in its institutional redesign of political life. Most of its changes were embodied in a new constitution drafted by the regime's political architects in 1980. The constitution is today in force under the postauthoritarian regime.

2. For an analysis of the Spanish transition that takes into account the long-term socioeconomic transformations undergone by Spain under the Francoist regime, see Edward Malefakis, "Spain and Its Francoist Heritage," in *From Dictatorship to Democracy: Coping with the Legacies of Authoritarianism and Totalitarianism,* ed. John Herz (Westport, Conn.: Greenwood Press, 1982), 215–30. The political objectives of the Chilean authoritarian regime's socioeconomic transformations are analyzed in Hector Schamis, "Market Reform as State Crafting: Chile and Great Britain in Comparative Perspective" (Ph.D. diss., Columbia University, 1994).

3. On the Brazilian regime's difficulties in legitimizing a permanent project for authoritarian rule, see Juan Linz, "The Future of an Authoritarian Situation or the Institutionalization of an Authoritarian Regime: The Case of Brazil," in *Authoritarian Brazil: Origins, Policies, and Future* ed. Alfred Stepan (New Haven, Conn.: Yale University Press, 1973), 233–54.

4. The laws inhibiting the multiplication of parties were repealed when the government perceived they had provided too great a stimulus for the unification of opposition forces. For accounts of this process, see Thomas Skidmore, "Brazil's Slow Road to Democratization," and Bolivar Lamounier, "*Authoritarian Brazil* Revisited: The Impact of Elections on the *abertura*," in *Democratizing Brazil: Problems of Transition and Consolidation,* ed. Alfred Stepan (New York: Oxford University Press, 1989).

5. For accounts of the management of the Spanish transition by Adolfo Suarez and his supporters, see José María Maravall and Julián Santamaría, "Political Change in Spain and the Prospects for Democracy," in *Southern Europe,* vol. 1 of

Transitions from Authoritarian Rule: Prospects for Democracy, ed. Guillermo O'Donnell, Philippe C. Schmitter, and Laurence Whitehead (Baltimore: Johns Hopkins University Press, 1986). For a comparison of the Spanish and Brazilian transitions, which are analyzed as examples of "transitions from above, " see Donald Share and Scott Mainwaring, "Transitions from Above: Democratization in Brazil and Spain," Kellogg Institute for International Studies, University of Notre Dame, Working Paper No. 13 (Notre Dame, Ind.: December 1984).

6. Hereafter referred to simply as the Proceso, as the regime came commonly to be labeled during this period.

7. See, e.g., Scott Mainwaring and Eduardo J. Viola, "Transitions to Democracy: Brazil and Argentina in the 1980's," *Journal of International Affairs* 38 (Winter 1985): 195.

8. The concept "transition period" used here follows the one provided by Philippe C. Schmitter and Guillermo O'Donnell: "Transitions are delimited, on the one side, by the launching of the process of dissolution of an authoritarian regime and, on the other, by the installation of some form of democracy, the return to some form of authoritarian rule, or the emergence of a revolutionary alternative" O'Donnell and Schmitter, *Tentative Conclusions about Uncertain Democracies,* vol. 4 of *Transitions from Authoritarian Rule: Prospects for Democracy,* ed. Guillermo O'Donnell, Philippe C. Schmitter, and Laurence Whitehead [Baltimore: Johns Hopkins University Press, 1986], 6). In this case, the beginning of the transition is seen to be the start of formal discussions between the military government and actors in civil and political society over the regime's liberalization. Its conclusion is seen as the "founding elections" of October 1983, which inaugurated the current democratic regime.

9. Alfred Stepan, "State Power and the Strength of Civil Society in the Southern Cone of Latin America," in *Bringing the State Back In,* ed. Peter Evans, Dietrich Rueschemeyer, and Theda Skocpol (New York: Cambridge University Press, 1985), 320.

10. An analysis of the military interpretation of the political crisis can be found in Inés Gonzalez Bombal, "El diálogo político," a manuscript that it is to be hoped will eventually be published in book form, which contains the most complete and valuable examination of the Argentine transition to date. In it, González Bombal analyzes relations between all major forces in political society and the military government from the start of the transition in 1979 to the regime's collapse in 1982.

11. "Proyecto nacional (Documento de trabajo)," internal military document reprinted in Enrique Vázquez, *La Ultima: Origen, apogeo, y caída de la dictadura militar* (Buenos Aires: Editorial Universitaria de Buenos Aires, 1985), 300–301.

12. María Laura San Martino de Dromi, *Historia política argentina, 1955–1988* (Buenos Aires: Editorial Astrea, 1988) 2: 330.

13. David Pion-Berlin, "The Fall of Military Rule in Argentina, 1976–1983," *Journal of Interamerican Studies and World Affairs* 27 (Summer 1985): 59–60.

14. As noted in Chapter 2, *federalist* was the label assigned to the current of

provincial conservative parties located primarily in the interior provinces; "liberals" were their Buenos Aires counterparts.

15. One of Martinez de Hoz's uncles served as governor of Buenos Aires province in the 1930s.

16. The posts held by Martinez de Hoz had included brief tenures as secretary of state for agriculture and livestock and minister of the economy in the 1962 Guido government, as well as service as minister of the economy of the province of Salta, which had been intervened in by the military government of General Aramburu after the 1955 overthrow of the Peronist regime.

17. Liliana de Riz, "Argentina: Ni democracia estable ni régimen militar (conjeturas sobre las perspectivas para la democracia)," in *"Proceso," crisis, y transición democrática,* vol. 2, ed. Oscar Oszlak (Buenos Aires: Centro Editor), 13.

18. For analyses of the political dimensions of the economic program, and the limits imposed on it by the military institution, see Jorge Schvarzer, *Martinez de Hoz: La lógica política de la política económica* (Buenos Aires: Centro de Investigaciones Sociales sobre el Estado y la Administración, Ensayos y tesis CISEA, 1983); id., *Expansion económica del Estado subsidiario, 1976–1981* (Buenos Aires: Centro de Investigaciones Sociales sobre el Estado y la Administración, Ensayos y tesis CISEA, 1981); and Armando Ribas, *El retorno de Luz del Dia: Liberalismo y desarrollo* (Buenos Aires: Editorial Sudamericana, 1988).

19. César L. Mansilla, *Las fuerzas de Centro* (Buenos Aires: Centro Editor, 1983), 78.

20. *La Nación,* June 20, 1979, quoted in Mansilla, *Las fuerzas de Centro,* 79–80.

21. "Producir es libertad," advertisement published in *La Nación* (Buenos Aires), Mar. 22, 1976, reprinted in Mansilla, *Las fuerzas de Centro,* 116–23.

22. See Francisco Manrique, *¿Qué es el Partido Federal?* (Buenos Aires: Editorial Sudamericana, 1983), 83.

23. Ibid., 173.

24. For a discussion of the effect of military-institutional strife on governability during this period of shared military rule, see Andres Fontana, "Fuerzas armadas, partidos políticos, y transición a la democracia en Argentina, 1981–1982," Kellogg Institute for International Studies, University of Notre Dame, Working Paper No. 28 (Notre Dame, Ind., July 1984).

25. "Apreciación de la situación nacional al mes de noviembre de 1978," government memorandum reprinted in Vázquez, *La Ultima,* 94–103.

26. Quoted in San Martino de Dromi, *Historia política argentina,* 415.

27. Ibid., 416.

28. *La Prensa* (Buenos Aires), May 30, 1980, quoted in Carlos Acuña, "El 'diálogo' del gobierno," *Revista del Centro de Investigación y Acción Social-CIAS,* no. 295–96 (Aug.-Sept. 1980): 46.

29. Ibid. 47. Throughout the past half-century of conservative public image problems in Argentina, the term *centrist* has served as a euphemism for *conserva-*

tive. It has generally been used as a label by conservatives themselves when referring to conservative party politics.

30. *Clarín* (Buenos Aires), Apr. 24, 1980, quoted in Gonzales Bombal, "El diálogo político," 15.

31. See Acuña, "El 'diálogo' del gobierno."

32. Statement by Horacio Guzmán, president of FUFEPO and leader of the Movimiento Popular Jujeño, of the province of Jujuy. Quote in Mansilla, *Las fuerzas de Centro*, 80.

33. Mansilla, *Las fuerzas de Centro*, 82.

34. Ibid., 125.

35. Declarations published in *La Nación*, Oct. 19, 1980, quoted in González Bombal, "El diálogo político," 81.

36. Mansilla, *Las fuerzas de Centro*, 83.

37. Fontana, "Fuerzas armadas, partidos políticos," 6.

38. Amadeo Frúgoli, of the Partido Demócrata de Mendoza, was Viola's minister of justice. José Antonio Romero Feris, leader of the Partido Autonomista of Corrientes, and Francisco Moyano, of the Partido Demócrata of Mendoza, and G. Fernandez Gil, of the Partido Federal, were appointed presidential advisors.

39. Horacio Guzmán, of the Movimiento Popular Jujeño, was appointed governor of Jujuy. Ismael Amit, of the Movimiento Federalista Pampeano, was appointed governor of La Pampa. MOLIPO was given the governorship of Entre Rios, and Alberto Natale, of the Partido Demócrata Progresista, was given the mayoralty of Rosario.

40. The contents of "Orientations No. 2" were widely discussed in the press. See, e.g., the political editorial in *La Nación*, Apr. 30, 1981.

41. Also joining the Multipartidaria were the Frondizi-led Movimiento de Integración y Desarrollo (MID), the developmentalist party that had split off from the Radical Party in the 1950s and had collaborated with the Proceso until the formation of the Multipartidaria; the center-left Partido Intransigente (PI), itself a splinter of the Frondizi-led UCRI, the MID's precursor; and the Christian Democratic Party.

42. *la Nación*, editorial, Dec. 6, 1981, quoted in Fontana, "Fuerzas armadas, partidos políticos," 21.

43. Quoted in Alberto Braun, *El boom liberal* (Buenos Aires: Edicones Astro, 1988), 36.

44. The pathos of the federalist position during this period was captured by the following remark by one of FUFEPO's top leaders during the final months of the Galtieri presidency: "The government has brought us on board the boat, and if it sinks we all drown together. This is why we are demanding the right to be given an oar and a little bucket so that we can fight for our lives together" (quoted in Mansilla, *Las fuerzas de Centro*, 89).

45. "La afirmación de un eje central," *La Nación*, Aug. 22, 1982, 8.

46. Fontana, "Fuerzas armadas, partidos políticos," 28–29.

47. Mansilla, *Las fuerzas de Centro,* 94–96.
48. "El complejo control de estatuto," *La Nación,* Aug. 3, 1982, 6.
49. "La afirmación de un eje central," *La Nación,* Aug. 23, 1982, 9.

Chapter Four / Party Leaders and Democratic Transitions

1. Guillermo O'Donnell and Philippe C. Schmitter, *Tentative Conclusions about Uncertain Democracies,* vol. 4 of *Transitions from Authoritarian Rule: Prospects for Democracy,* ed. Guillermo O'Donnell, Philippe C. Schmitter, and Laurence Whitehead (Baltimore: Johns Hopkins University Press, 1986), 62.

2. Argentine Central Bank figures cited in Jorge Schvarzer, *Martinez de Hoz: La lógica política de la política económica* (Buenos Aires: Centro de Investigaciones Sobre el Estado y la Administración CISEA, 1983), 127–46.

3. UCEDE, "Orígenes del partido y documentos relacionados con su fundación," 2.

4. See, e.g., "La mujer y la política: Adelina de Viola (UCD)," *La Nación* (Buenos Aires), Oct. 27, 1983, sec. 3a, 1.

5. UCEDE, "Orígenes del partido y documentos relacionados con su fundación" (Buenos Aires: Party Document, July 1982), 4.

6. Ibid.
7. Ibid.
8. Ibid.

9. Alvaro Alsogaray, interview by the author, Buenos Aires, June 5, 1990. Tape recording.

10. Charles Anderson, "Toward a Theory of Latin American Politics," in *Politics and Social Change in Latin America,* ed. Howard Wiarda (Amherst: University of Massachusetts Press, 1982), 311.

11. His father, Alvaro Alsogaray, was a colonel in the army and in 1930 served as head of the Casa Militar under the government of General Uriburu. His grandfather, an army colonel also named Alvaro, fought in the country's wars against Paraguay alongside Domingo F. Sarmiento, who would later serve as president in the 1860s. His great-grandfather, the first of the Alvaros, was a naval adjutant to Admiral William Brown, the founder and architect of the Argentine navy.

12. Fabián Doman and Martín Olivera, *Los Alsogaray: Secretos de una dinastía y su corte* (Buenos Aires: Aguilar Ediciones, 1989), 40–41.

13. Alvaro Alsogaray, interview by the author, Buenos Aires, June 5, 1990. Tape recording.

14. Ibid.

15. For an interesting account of the politics of the Revolución Libertadora, see Alain Rouquié, *Poder militar y sociedad política en la Argentina,* vol. 2, 1943–1973 (Buenos Aires: Emecé Editores, 1982), 107–48. See also Robert Potash, *El ejército y la política en la Argentina* (Buenos Aires: Editorial Sudamericana, 1984).

16. María Laura San Martino de Dromi, *Historia política argentina, 1955–1988* (Buenos Aires: Editorial Astrea, 1988), 1: 43–48.

17. Alvaro Alsogaray, interview by the author, June 5, 1990.

18. Alvaro Alsogaray, notes from his private archive (prepared for the magazine *Todo es historia*) Buenos Aires, Mar. 14, 1988, 2.

19. Ibid.

20. *Tribuna Cívica,* June 26, 1958, 4.

21. Alvaro Alsogaray, editorial in *Tribuna Cívica,* Feb. 27, 1958, 4.

22. Ibid.

23. Ibid.

24. The alleged "pact" between Frondizi and Perón has been widely written about in scholarly work on Argentina. See, e.g., Rouquié, *Poder militar y sociedad política en la Argentina,* 2: 146–49.

25. "Los grandes responsables del fracaso económico social de la revolución," editorial in *Tribuna Cívica,* Apr. 24, 1958, 1.

26. Ibid.

27. San Martino de Dromi, *Historia política argentina,* 1: 143–44.

28. Potash, *El ejército y la política en la Argentina,* 2: 413–14.

29. Arturo Frondizi, *¿Que es el Movimento de Integración y Desarrollo?* (Buenos Aires: Editorial Sudamericana, 1983), 157.

30. Alvaro Alsogaray, notes from his private archive (prepared for *Todo es historia*), Buenos Aires, Mar. 14, 1988.

31. Alvaro Alsogaray, interview by the author, Buenos Aires, June 5, 1990. Tape recording.

32. Roberto Olivier José Reboursin, *Las gestiones ministeriales del ingeniero Alvaro Carlos Alsogaray en el Ministerio de Economía de la Nación* (Buenos Aires: Instituto de la Economía Social de Mercado y la Democracia Liberal, 1985), 4–5. The author of the monograph then goes on to exclaim that "from this moment — and this is how it was seen by the public — the ingeniero Alsogaray became a virtual 'prime minister' who, in economic and labor matters, 'governed,' while Dr. Frondizi, in these matters, merely 'reigned.' "

33. Potash, *El ejército y la política en la Argentina,* 2: 442.

34. "We were an enclave . . . and that could not be tolerated," Alsogaray noted in our interview. "The strategy was therefore to replace us with a liberal façade and a Frigerista supporting cast." Alvaro Alsogaray, interview by the author, Buenos Aires, June 5, 1990. Tape recording.

35. Alvaro Alsogaray, interview by the author, June 5, 1990.

36. Cesar L. Mansilla, *Las fuerzas de Centro* (Buenos Aires: Centro Editor, 1983), 136.

37. The terms *nationalist* and *paternalist* to describe the main adversarial currents of the liberals are taken from Guillermo O'Donnell's *Bureaucratic Authoritarianism: Argentina, 1966–1973, in Comparative Perspective* (Berkeley and Los Angeles: University of California Press, 1988). O'Donnell provides a detailed and fascinating account of the internal dynamics of the Revolución Argentina, the various internal currents competing for power, their social bases and ideological agendas, and the impact of their struggles on the evolution of Argentina's

bureaucratic-authoritarian regime. The description of Economics Minister Salimei is also borrowed from O'Donnell.

38. O'Donnell, *Bureaucratic Authoritarianism,* 72.

39. O'Donnell reports that in his interviews with military and civilian leaders of the period, they repeatedly mentioned that Krieger Vasena's reputation for "pragmatic" liberalism was a major factor in his selection by Onganía and the paternalist military leadership over the "dogmatic" liberals, of whom Alsogaray was the most prominent. See O'Donnell, *Bureaucratic Authoritarianism,* 72–73.

40. Alvaro Alsogaray, resignation letter presented to President Juan Carlos Onganía, Oct. 31, 1968. Reprinted in Alvaro Alsogaray, *Bases liberales para un programa de gobierno, 1989–1995* (Buenos Aires: Editorial Planeta, 1989), 237–38.

41. I was unable to obtain hard evidence concerning the identity of Alsogaray's corporate supporters, which has never been publicly revealed. Alsogaray refused to go beyond stating that they were a "group of Argentine corporations that had never before been involved in this type of activity" (interview by the author, June 5, 1990). In interviews with several of Alsogaray's followers, however, many of which were involved in Nueva Fuerza, Bunge y Born, Argentina's sole multinational corporation, was identified (without my suggesting it as a possible contributor) as the main contributor to Nueva Fuerza. Bunge y Born's name also came up during the 1973 campaign as the chief suspect. See, e.g., the interview with María Julia Alsogaray published in the magazine *Esquiú,* "Cuando la juventud se mete en la política," Oct. 1, 1972, 4.

42. "Gráfico de organización," *Nueva Fuerza* (official organ of the party), August 29, 1972, 11.

43. Alvaro Alsogaray, interview by the author, June 5, 1990.

44. See the biographical article published in "Chamizo-Ondarts: Estabilidad y Liberación," *Nueva Fuerza,* Dec. 30, 1972, 1.

45. Rosendo Fraga (with Gabriela Malacrida), *Argentina en las urnas, 1916–1989* (Buenos Aires: Editorial Centro de Estudios Unión para la Nueva Mayoría, 1989), 13.

46. "Alsogaray exhortó a no apresurarse con un golpe," *Clarín* (Buenos Aires), March 21, 1976, 2.

47. Alsogaray actually lost a nephew in the military's campaign against leftist insurrection. His brother Julio's son had joined the Trotskyist Ejercito Revolucionario del Pueblo (ERP) and was killed by a military ambush in the province of Tucumán. This incident did not affect either of the Alsogaray brothers' unwavering support for the military's conduct of the campaign.

48. Alsogaray made the statement with his characteristic bluntness: "If, in the final instance, our vote proves to be decisive, we will vote, covering our noses as if we were being forced to take castor oil, for the Radical Party. This will be done, of course, only after extracting the greatest number of guarantees" ("Alsogaray apoyará al la UCR en la Asamblea Legislativa," *La Nación,* Oct. 25, 1983, 4).

49. Mansilla, *Las fuerzas de Centro,* 153.

50. "Opiniones en un mitin de características peculiares," *La Nación,* June 22, 1983, 4.

51. "Alvaro Alsogaray afirmó que 'el desorden actual puede agravarse,' " *La Nación,* June 22, 1983, 4.

52. "Alsogaray previene sobre la demagogia," *La Nación,* Sept. 27, 1983, 18.

53. "Unión del Centro Democrático pide un informe sobre la guerra antisubversiva," *La Nación,* Mar. 4, 1973, 9.

54. See the report on his speech at the Luna Park rally in "Alvaro Alsogaray afirmó que 'el desorden puede agravarse,' " *La Nación,* June 22, 1983, 4.

55. The conservative vote in the presidential elections was atomized among a myriad small, mostly provincial parties. Manrique's Alianza Federal mobilized the highest share of this meager total, 0.38 percent. The alliance between the Demócrata Progresistas and the Partido Socialista Independiente received 0.32 percent. The UCEDE received 0.05 percent. Fraga, *Argentina en las urnas,* 13.

56. Giving conservatism a whopping 3 representatives in congress, out of a total of 254 deputies. Ibid., 26–27.

57. In Corrientes, the Pacto Autonomista-Liberal gained a plurality of 35.1 percent in the 1983 congressional elections, and won the governorship with 46.6 percent of the vote against its nearest rival, the Peronist Party, with 22.9 percent. In Neuquén, the Movimiento Popular Neuquino handily won the governorship with 55.3 percent of the vote. It came in second to the Radical 39 percent with 34.5 percent of the vote in the congressional elections. In San Juan, the Partido Bloquista won the governorship with 39.5 percent of the vote, and received 25.3 percent of the congressional vote. In Jujuy, the FUFEPO leader Horacio Guzman's Movimiento Popular Jujeño garnered a respectable 15.5 percent. In La Pampa, another FUFEPO party, the Movimiento Federal Pampeano, came in with 13.5 percent. The Partido Renovador of Salta received 7.5 percent of the congressional vote. Finally, in the territory of Tierra del Fuego, the local Movimiento Popular Fueguino received 18.7 percent of votes cast for the congress. Sources: congressional races, Ministry of the Interior, Departamento de Estadísticas; gubernatorial races, Fraga, *Argentina en las urnas.*

58. In Buenos Aires province, where neither of the two conservative parties possessed the party organization necessary to cover the province's extensive geography, the UCEDE captured the minuscule portion of the vote received by the electoral Right: 1.12 percent.

59. Unless otherwise noted, statistical analyses are in this book based on unpublished electoral data for the 209 electoral circuits of the city of Buenos Aires and unpublished socioeconomic data from the 1980 Argentine census. Socioeconomic data were obtained from the Argentine census bureau for each of the 266 censal fractions into which the bureau divides the city. Electoral data were obtained from the Juzgado Electoral de la Capital Federal for the city's 209 electoral circuits. The data for the 266 geographic fractions were then adjusted to match the 209 electoral circuits for the purpose of correlating social-status indicators with party vote. Published census data for the 1980 census are aggregated by

the census bureau into 20 larger geographic "sections." Similarly, published electoral results for the city of Buenos Aires are provided by the Juzgado Electoral for the city's 28 electoral districts. My use of the much smaller and more numerous censal fractions and electoral circuits was motivated by a desire to increase the number of cases used in calculations and to maximize the social homogeneity of the geographic units. The analysis presented here thus provides an advance over previous ecological analyses of the vote in the city of Buenos Aires, which have used the larger 20 census sections or 28 electoral districts as the statistical units of analysis. See, e.g., Gino Germani, "Categoría de ocupación y voto político en la Capital Federal," in *El voto peronista: Ensayos de sociología electoral argentina,* ed. Manuel Mora y Araujo and Ignacio Llorente (Buenos Aires: Editorial Sudamericana, 1980), 254–67; Luis Gonzáles Esteves and Ignacio Llorente "Elecciones y preferencias políticas en Capital Federal y Gran Buenos Aires: El 30 de octubre de 1983," in *La Argentina Electoral,* ed. Natalio Botana et al. (Buenos Aires: Editorial Sudamericana, 1985), 39–73; Leticia Maronese, Ana Cafiero de Nazar, and Víctor Waisman: *El voto peronista '83: Perfil electoral y causas de la derrota* (Buenos Aires: El Cid Editor, 1985); and Raúl Jorrat, "Las elecciones de 1983 ¿Desviación o realineamiento?" *Desarrollo Económico* 26, no. 101 (Apr.–June 1986), 89–120 (Jorrat's ecological analysis for the city of Buenos Aires, while using data from the 209 electoral districts, correlates them with socioeconomic data taken from voter registration lists rather than official census data).

Chapter Five / Conservative Party Building

Epigraph: Adelina Dalesio de Viola quoted in Alberto Braun, *El boom liberal* (Buenos Aires: Ediciones Astro, 1988), 174.

1. For an analysis of the Salvadoran process, see Gabriel Gaspar Tapia, *El Salvador: El ascenso de la nueva derecha* (San Salvador: CINAS, 1989), with a prologue by Guillermo Manuel Ungo.

2. For accounts of the impact of business mobilization on the Partido Acción Nacional's growth in Mexico, see Blanca Heredia, "Can Rational Profit-Maximizers be Democratic? Business and Democracy in Mexico" (paper presented at a conference on Business Elites and Democracy in Latin America, Kellogg Institute of International Studies, University of Notre Dame, May 3–4, 1991); Soledad Loaeza, "The Right in Mexico's Political Change," in *The Right and Democracy in Latin America,* ed. Douglas Chalmers, Maria do Carmo Campello de Souza, and Atilio Boron (Westport, Conn.: Praeger, 1992); and Leticia Barraza and Ilán Bizberg, "El Partido Acción Nacional y el régimen político mexicano," *Foro Internacional* 31, no. 3 (Jan.–Mar. 1991). For the Peruvian case, see Francisco Durand, *Business and Politics in Peru: the State and the National Bourgeoisie* (Boulder, Colo.: Westview Press, 1994), and id., *La burguesía peruana: Los primeros industriales. Alan García y los empresarios* (Lima: Cuadernos DESCO, 1988). Gaspar Tapia's account of the rise of ARENA in El Salvador (cited in n. 1

above) also includes a detailed analysis of the role of business mobilization in fueling the party's ascendance.

3. Alvaro Alsogaray, "Soluciones del problema argentino," *La Nación* (Buenos Aires), Economy and Finance section, 1.

4. William C. Smith, "Democracy, Distributional Conflicts, and Macroeconomic Policymaking in Argentina, 1983–1989," *Journal of Interamerican Studies and World Affairs* 32 (Summer 1990): 5.

5. Robert R. Kaufman, *The Politics of Debt in Argentina, Brazil, and Mexico: Economic Stabilization in the 1980's,* Institute of International Studies, University of California, Berkeley, Research Series, No. 72 (Berkeley, 1988), 7.

6. Gary Wynia, *Argentina: Illusions and Realities* (New York: Holmes & Meier, 1986), 176.

7. According to World Bank figures, public expenditures for defense declined by 56 percent in 1984 and 8.5 percent in 1985. World Bank, Country Study, "Argentina: Reforms for Price Stability and Growth" (1990), 257.

8. See *Nunca mas: Informe de la Comisión Nacional sobre la Desaparición de Personas (CONADEP)* (Buenos Aires: EUDEBA, 1984).

9. Smith, "Democracy, Distributional Conflicts, and Macroeconomic Policymaking in Argentina," 7.

10. Ibid.

11. Kaufman, *Politics of Debt in Argentina, Brazil, and Mexico,* 36.

12. Poll by SOCMERC, Buenos Aires, reprinted in Kaufman, *Politics of Debt,* 40.

13. The UCEDE mobilized 920,000 votes nationally in the congressional elections of 1987. This represented a 70 percent growth rate over 1985. It nevertheless made it a distant third after the 6 million votes gathered by the Radicals and 6.6 million gathered by the Peronists. See Edward L. Gibson, "Democracy and the New Electoral Right in Argentina," *Journal of Interamerican Studies and World Affairs* 32, (Fall, 1990): 184.

14. Ezequiel Gallo and Esteban F. Thomsen, "Electoral Evolution of the Political Parties of the Right: Argentina, 1983–1989," in *The Right and Democracy in Latin America,* ed. Douglas Chalmers, Maria do Carmo Campello de Souza, and Atilio Boron (New York: Praeger, 1992), 154.

15. José Nun, "Cambios en la estructura social de la Argentina," in *Ensayos sobre la transición democrática en la Argentina,* ed. id. and Juan Carlos Portantiero (Buenos Aires: Puntosur, 1987), 135.

16. See, e.g., Raúl Jorrat's article on the social bases of the 1983 elections, "Las elecciones de 1983 ¿Desviación o realineamiento?" *Desarrollo Económico* 26, no. 101 (Apr.–June 1986).

17. Mariano Grandona, *Los pensadores de la libertad* (Buenos Aires, Editorial Sudamericana, 1986), and *Bajo el imperio de las ideas morales: Las causas no económicas del desarrollo económico* (Buenos Aires: Editorial Sudamericana, 1987). Grondona never joined the UCEDE, and he maintained a journalistically

proper distance from the party's electoral campaigns. Nevertheless, he was an active participant in the party's debates, was a favored speaker at its events, and gave ample coverage to its views and leaders in his television programs. His son was also a UCEDE party activist.

18. Jorge E. Bustamante, *La república corporativa* (Buenos Aires: EMECÉ Editores, 1988).

19. "Convención de Capital: Habrá elecciones internas," *Tribuna Cívica* (newspaper of the Unión del Centro Democrático), Oct. 31, 1984, 1. For some of the debate surrounding these internal elections see the March through June 1985 issues of *Tribuna Cívica*.

20. "Elecciones internas de la UCD en la Capital," *Tribuna Cívica*, Apr. 1985, 4.

21. The social composition of the UCEDE's membership is addressed in the final section of this chapter.

22. Sergio Crivelli, "El partido de Alsogaray," *La Prensa* (Buenos Aires), May 12, 1987, 9.

23. An example of this was the composition of the Alfonsín wing of the UCR. Most of its leaders, such as Facundo Suarez Lastra, former mayor of Buenos Aires, Enrique Nosiglia, Alfonsín's minister of the interior until early 1989, Jesus Rodriguez, prominent congressman and briefly the minister of the economy in 1989, as well as some of the most important leaders of the "Coordinadora" faction, Alfonsín's main base of support in the party and the congress, first cut their political teeth in the tumultuous arenas of university politics.

24. Carlos Maslatón, interview by the author, Sept. 9, 1988. Tape recording.

25. See, e.g., the Mar. 16, 1988, *La Nación* editorial celebrating UPAU's rise, "Elecciones estudiantiles en la UBA" (8).

26. Manuel Mora y Araujo, interview published in Braun, *El boom liberal*, 174.

27. Interview with Adelina Dalesio de Viola, *Humor*, May 1989, 35. The term *negra*, or *negro*, is used in Argentina to denote people of lower social origins (often without regard to skin or hair color), and is a common disparaging term used by the well-to-do in reference to the working and lower classes.

28. Polls published by *El Heraldo de Buenos Aires* between Aug. 9 and 18, 1988, for example, consistently gave Adelina de Viola a two-to-one margin over her nearest Peronist and radical rivals.

29. Max Weber, "Politics as a Vocation," in *From Max Weber: Essays in Sociology*, ed. H. H. Gerth and C. Wright Mills (1946; Oxford University Paperback, 1958), 96.

30. Neustadt co-hosted the television program *Tiempo Nuevo* with Mariano Grondona, who played the professorial counterpart to Neustadt's histrionic and unerudite style.

31. This was written by Marcos Victórica, director of IDEC and a prominent UCEDE supporter. The book's prologue, written by Bernardo Neustadt, is entitled "In Doña Rosa's Name." Faustino A. Fernandez Sasso, *El estado y yo, por Juan*

García (taxista) (Buenos Aires: Instituto de Estudios Contemporáneos [IDEC] / Grupo Editor Latinoamericano, 1988).

32. Speeches by Adelina de Viola in the Buenos Aires neighborhoods of San Telmo and Agronomía, Nov. 1988, observed by the author. "Southern neighborhoods" refers to the lower-middle and lower-class neighborhoods in the urban area south of Rivadavia Avenue in Buenos Aires.

33. Ticket-splitting can be rather confusing for many voters, especially the uneducated. Separate paper ballots are printed for each party, listing all its candidates for national and local office. Voters wishing to split their vote between candidates of different parties must tear the ballots along printed (but unperforated) lines, and place the pieces of paper from the separate ballots in a common envelope. Instructions for ticket-splitting are not provided on the ballots, and ballots torn incorrectly are automatically annulled by the election authorities.

34. "Un debate malogrado," *La Nación,* May 10, 1980, 6.

35. Data on the social composition of the CFI's support in the city of Buenos Aires are presented in Chapter 6.

36. Mario Vicens and Pablo Gerchunoff, "Gasto público, recursos públicos, y financiamiento de una economía en crisis" (Buenos Aires: Instituto Torcuato Di Tella, 1989), 33.

37. These figures are based on the 1987 quasi-fiscal surplus of the Central Bank, which amounted to 1 percent of GDP. In 1989, the quasi-fiscal deficit rose to 5.5 percent of GDP. See World Bank, "Argentina: Reforms for Price Stability and Growth," 69.

38. Ricardo Zinn, UCEDE campaign finance chairman, interview with the author, Buenos Aires, April 18, 1989.

39. Carlos Dietl, president of PASA Petroquímica Argentina, S.A., and vice president of the Argentine Stock Exchange, interview with the author, Buenos Aires, May 24, 1987.

40. For analyses of the Mexican case, see Heredia, "Can Rational Profit-Maximizers be Democratic?"; Loaeza, "The Right in Mexico's Political Change"; and Barraza and Bizberg, "El Partido Acción Nacional y el régimen político mexicano."

41. This process is detailed and analyzed in Gaspar Tapia's collection of essays, *El Salvador: El ascenso de la nueva derecha.*

42. Raymundo Duharte, ex-president of the National Industrial Society, in an article published in *Actualidad económica del Perú,* no. 95 (Nov. 1987): 6. Quoted in Durand, *La burguesía peruana.*

43. Carlos Acuña and Laura Golbert, "Empresarios y política (parte II): Los empresarios y sus organizaciones: ¿Que pasó con el Plan Austral?" *Boletín Informativo Techint,* no. 263 (May–Aug. 1990): 39.

44. The last-ditch government economic program, the Plan Primavera, launched in 1988, was designed and implemented in close collaboration with industry and commerce and their respective federations, the Unión Industrial Argentina and the Cámara Argentina de Comercio. President Alfonsín was to

label this collaboration an "alliance between production and democracy." Carlos Acuña, "Intereses empresarios, dictadura, y democracia en la Argentina actual (O, sobre porqué la burguesía abandona estrategias autoritarias y opta por la estabilidad democrática)," Centro de Estudios de Estado y Sociedad, Documento CEDES 39, (Buenos Aires, 1990), 51–53.

45. Manuel Mora y Araujo, interview with the author, Buenos Aires, May 21, 1987.

46. Acuña and Golbert, "Empresarios y política," 44.

47. Ricardo Zinn, UCEDE campaign finance chairman, interview with the author, Buenos Aires, Apr. 18, 1989.

48. Ricardo Zinn, UCEDE campaign finance chairman, interview with the author, Buenos Aires, June 1, 1990. Tape recording.

49. Unless otherwise noted, all statistical analyses presented in this chapter are based on unpublished electoral data for the 209 electoral circuits of the city of Buenos Aires and unpublished socioeconomic data from the 1980 Argentine census. Socioeconomic data were obtained from the Argentine census bureau for each of the 266 censal fractions into which the bureau divides the city. Electoral data were obtained from the Juzgado Electoral de la Capital Federal for the city's 209 electoral circuits. The data for the 266 geographic fractions were then adjusted to match the 209 electoral circuits for the purpose of correlating social-status indicators with party vote. See note 59, Chapter 4 for additional information.

50. Departamento de Estadísticas, Dirección Nacional Electoral, Ministry of the Interior.

51. The stratification used in figures 5.7 and 5.8 is the same as that used in earlier tables and figures, which divided the city's 209 electoral circuits into upper, upper-middle, middle, lower-middle, and lower levels, according to the percentiles displayed here for the SES index. In this case, the 25–50th and 50–75th percentiles correspond to the category "Middle" used earlier. They are disaggregated here for a more finely tuned view of that social category's distribution in different parties' voter coalitions.

52. Increases in party membership are mostly a function of neighborhood organization, as opposed to general increases in voter support, which can be more directly attributable to such nonorganizational factors as mass-media influence. The task of registering new members is generally carried out by *punteros,* local party activists operating out of neighborhood party committees, whose own rise in the internal party hierarchy is often tied to their success in obtaining new members. The presence of party organization in neighborhoods is thus generally a prerequisite for the acquisition of new local members.

53. Membership data for 1985 could not be obtained for the 209 electoral circuits of the city of Buenos Aires. Figure 5.12 therefore uses the much larger electoral "districts" of the city as the unit of analysis. Membership data for the 209 electoral circuits were obtained for 1990, however, and they are displayed in

figures 5.14 through 5.16. However, to maximize comparability between 1985 and 1990, I have opted in figure 5.13 to present data for the 28 electoral districts for both years.

Chapter Six / Shifting Arenas of Political Action

Epigraphs: Robert Bates, "Macropolitical Economy in the Field of Development," in Perspectives on Positive Political Economy, ed. James Alt and Robert Shepsle (New York: Cambridge University Press, 1990), 47. María Julia Alsogaray, quoted in La Nación (Buenos Aires), Sept. 30, 1991.

1. Lesser cabinet positions were also given to leftists by Fujimori, but the strategic economic policy-making positions were reserved for the Right.

2. José Piñera, television interview, Santiago, Chile, Sept. 1991.

3. Alvaro Alsogaray, interview in La Nación, May 6, 1989, 8.

4. "José Romero Feris definió las bases de la Nueva Mayoría," La Nación, Aug. 22, 1986, 12.

5. "Anunció Romero Feris las metas de la Nueva Mayoría," La Nación, July 11, 1986: p. 20.

6. The conservative roots of Córdoba's radicalism lie in the struggle between the Catholic Church and the local members of the Generation of 1880's liberal leadership. In Córdoba, the UCR's rise was tied to Catholic opposition to Ramón J. Cárcano, the anticlerical liberal-conservative governor of Córdoba prior to 1916. Although various ideological currents subsequently emerged in the Córdoba Radical Party, its conservative strains have always remained strong.

7. National conservative alignments in the 1989 presidential elections crystallized into several competing clusters: the UCEDE-led Alianza de Centro presented Alvaro Alsogaray as its presidential candidate. His vice-presidential candidate was Alberto Natale, of the Partido Demócrata Progresista. In addition, the Alianza grouped the Partido Autonomista and the Partido Liberal of Corrientes, the Unión Demócrata de Centro of Córdoba, the Partido Demócrata of Mendoza, and the balance of the Concentración Demócrata, a federation of Demócrata parties in a number of provinces. The Alianza also presented joint candidate lists for congressional and local elections in a number of provinces. The CFI, whose presidential–vice-presidential ticket consisted of Eduardo Angeloz and María Cristina Guzmán, was supported by the Partido Federal, the Partido Renovador of Salta, the Movimiento Popular Jujeño, the Movimiento Popular Catamarqueño, and the Partido Acción Chubutense, of Chubut. Other key provincial parties, such as the Movimiento Popular Neuquino of Neuquén, the Partido Bloquista of San Juan, Fuerza Republicana, of Tucumán, and Bandera Blanca, also of Tucumán, ran their own local presidential slates for the purpose of using their votes as leverage in a possible Electoral College vote.

8. Following the 1987 gubernatorial elections, in which the PJ scored major victories, the distribution of governorships was as follows: PJ, 15; UCR, 4; conser-

vative provincial parties: 3. Chief executives for the territory of Tierra del Fuego are appointed by the president. In 1989, these therefore passed from radical into Peronist hands.

9. For newspaper accounts of these developments, see "UCEDE: Alsogaray dejó la presidencia," *La Nación,* June 11, 1989, 1; "UCEDE: la diputada Alsogaray fue el blanco de las críticas," *La Nación,* May 21, 1989, 18; and "La UCEDE sin Alsogaray," *Página/12* (Buenos Aires), June 21, 1989, 5.

10. The Peronist Party's electoral platform can be appreciated in all its vagueness in *Menem/Duhalde: Plataforma Electoral, 1989* (Buenos Aires: Partido Justicialista, 1989).

11. "Revolución liberal y popular," cover of *Somos,* June 28, 1989. The article's title, which outlined Menem's ambitious program of wide-scale privatization, was also exultantly ironic. Alluding to Juan Perón's designation by the Peronist movement as "El primer trabajador" ("The First Worker"), the article's title heralded the sea change in Peronism's leadership by annointing Menem as "El primer privatizador" ("The First Privatizer").

12. Interestingly enough, events just prior to Menem's assumption of the presidency seemed to bear his strategy out. Alberto Albamonte, the UCEDE congressman appointed to head the powerful Secretariat of Internal Commerce, resigned his commission 48 hours before the new government took office. The reason for his resignation was his refusal to administer a price-control scheme designed by the minister of the economy–designate and negotiated with the country's most influential corporations as a centerpiece of the government's economic policy. One of the first internal crises of the conservative-populist coalition concocted by Carlos Menem thus emerged, not between labor and business, but between liberalismo and business.

13. In one instance, Alsogaray is reported to have told a group of bankers that "an economic model for one company is not necessarily suited to the needs of a country." He then added, somewhat ominously, "It is vital for us to prepare for the next phase in this process, hopefully still under the leadership of the present economic authorities." For a report of these statements and other criticisms of the economic team's program, see "A Alvaro Alsogaray no hay plan que le venga bien," *Página/12,* Sept. 1, 1989, 4.

14. According to *La Nación,* Alsogaray was instrumental in the drafting of the plan adopted by the government's new economics minister, Erman González. The newspaper reported that "On Saturday [Dec. 30], the government found itself without any kind of economic plan, and with a country anxious for the announcement of new economic measures. This is when Alvaro Alsogaray, advisor to the president, emerged on the scene. He brought Minister González a plan that attacked monetary expansion as the primary cause of the ongoing inflationary process." See "La política económica signada por contramarchas," *La Nación,* Jan. 3, 1990, 10. In another article, the newspaper said: "Financial analysts with long years of experience do not stop finding similarities between the plan recently announced and [another plan] launched in August 1962. One thing at least is

certain: Presidential Advisor Alvaro Alsogaray is the author of both plans." See "Similitudes con el Plan 9 de Julio," *La Nación,* Jan. 3, 1990, 12. Other reports also give credit for the formulation of the economic plan to another liberal technocrat, Foreign Minister Domingo Cavallo, a long-time rival of Alsogaray's, who would become economics minister in mid 1991.

15. Alvaro Alsogaray, nationally broadcast address, Jan. 2, 1991, transcribed in "Alsogaray: Estamos abandonando el estatismo y el intervencionismo," *La Nación,* Jan. 3, 1990, 1.

16. "La UCEDE intenta borrar la imagen de que cogobierna," *La Nación,* Dec. 31, 1989, 8.

17. Carlos Menem interview, "El análisis de Menem," *Somos,* Oct. 3, 1990, 9.

18. Ricardo Zinn, interview with the author, Buenos Aires, June 1, 1990. Tape recording.

19. Federico Clérici, president of the UCEDE National Committee, interview with the author, Sept. 22, 1989.

20. Ibid.

21. One of the most vociferous denouncers of this state of "demobilization" at the end of 1989 was Carlos Maslatón, a UCEDE city council member and founder in the early 1980s of the UPAU university student movement. See "La relación Menem-Alsogaray divide a la UCEDE," *La Nación,* Jan. 21, 1990, and "Somos una empresa en quiebra," *Página/12,* Nov. 21, 1990, 6.

22. The general state of disillusionment among the party's rank and file and younger militants, and the withdrawal of many from political life, was confirmed to me in repeated interviews and conversations with party activists between January and June 1990.

23. Héctor Siracusano interview, "El Francotirador," *Somos,* Apr. 15, 1991, 16.

24. Socioeconomic data for all the analyses provided in Chapter 6 were drawn from the 1980 census. More precise results for the late 1980s and early 1990s would have been obtained using results from the 1991 Argentine census, which were released in 1993. Unfortunately, however, in many instances socioeconomic data provided in the 1980 census were not released in the results published in 1993, or could not be recoded in time for these analyses. While I do not expect any significant variation from the measured relationships between socioeconomic status and electoral results provided here, these findings should be confirmed by future analyses based on more up to date socioeconomic data.

25. This Menem did early in his term by elevating Luis Barrionuevo and other conservative union leaders to high positions in the government. This was followed in subsequent years by a series of labor law reforms that weakened union power by decentralizing union organization, finance, and collective bargaining arrangements. For an analysis of the Menem labor reforms, see María Victoria Murillo, "Union Responses to Economic Reform in Argentina: Organizational Autonomy and the Marketization of Corporatism" (paper presented at the American Political Science Association Annual Convention, Sept. 1994).

26. Fundación para el Cambio en Democracia (FUCADE), *Encuesta de Opinión Pública, realizada durante el acto en Plaza de Mayo el 6/4/1990* (Buenos Aires: FUCADE, May 1990).

27. See, e.g., "Pasos hacia un partido conservador popular," *Página/12*, Apr. 8, 1990.

28. Major constitutional reforms were approved in 1994. In addition to electoral law changes and legislative and executive branch reforms, they included a change in the presidential term to four years, as well as a reelection clause. This permitted President Menem to run, successfully, for a second, four-year term.

29. The 28 electoral districts of the city of Buenos Aires used as the ecological units of analysis for figures 6.2 and 6.3, and for table 6.5.

30. At one point, María Julia Alsogaray held three portfolios in the government: president and privatizer of the National Telephone company; president and privatizer of the national steel company; and cabinet secretary for the environment.

31. The list of UCEDE defectors included Carlos Maslatón, city councilman and founder of the conservative student movement, UPAU; Santiago Lozano, a former UCEDE youth leader and congressional candidate; Francisco Siracusano, leader of the UCEDE block in the Buenos Aires city council; and several other local party leaders.

32. Among the federalist provincial parties endorsing President Menem's reelection in 1995 were the Movimiento Popular Neuquino, of Neuquen, the Partido Renovador, of Salta, Accion Chaqueña, of Chaco, the Partido Bloquista, of San Juan, the Partido Demócrata Progresista, of Santa Fe, and the Movimiento Popular Fueguino, of Tierra del Fuego. The Pacto Autonomista-Liberal de Corrientes and other federalist parties only ran in local contests and did not endorse any presidential tickets.

33. Alvaro Alsogaray, interview with the author, Buenos Aires, June 5, 1990. Tape recording.

34. The dual nature of Peronism's social coalition is discussed in Chapter 2.

35. This was the future predicted for the party by José Juan Manny, a former UCEDE congressman and long-time follower of Alvaro Alsogaray's: "The UCEDE will no longer be a party. It will be a pressure group, with leaders striving to latch on to power, rather than seeking it through the ballot box" (quoted in *La Nación*, "María Julia y Adelina reflotarán en la UCEDE viejos enfrentamientos," May 24, 1991, 4).

36. "Adelina Dalesio de Viola y sus metas: madre y presidente," *Noticias*, Jan. 28, 1990, 80–81.

Chapter Seven / Conclusions

1. For an exploration of this question by a prominent member of the Brazilian Left, see Francisco Weffort, "Why Democracy?" in *Democratizing Brazil: Problems of Transition and Consolidation*, ed. Alfred Stepan (New York: Oxford University Press, 1989), 327–50.

2. The debates of sectors of the Brazilian Left over coalition-building strategies as they strove to organize the Brazilian Workers' Party are nicely analyzed in Margaret E. Keck, *The Workers' Party and Democratization in Brazil* (New Haven, Conn.: Yale University Press, 1992). The conflicts and debates within the Peruvian electoral Right in the mid 1980s over social coalition-building strategies are analyzed in Mirko Lauer, "Adios conservadurismo, bienvenido liberalismo: La nueva derecha en el Perú," *Nueva Sociedad* 98 (Nov.–Dec. 1988); as well as in Francisco Durand, "The New Right and Poltical Change in Peru," in *The Right and Democracy in Latin America,* ed. Douglas Chalmers, Maria do Carmo Campello de Souza, and Atilio Boron (Westport, Conn.: Praeger, 1992).

3. "Authoritarian regimes tend to produce outcomes that are known to some, but whose possibility or likelihood of occurring are uncertain to most," Blanca Heredia writes. "This, paradoxically, makes outcomes unpredictable, yet at the same time, controllable. Under such conditions, the sine qua non condition for advancing one's interests is to assure access to the decision-making process" ("Can Rational Profit-Maximizers be Democratic? Business and Democracy in Mexico" [paper presented at a conference on Business Elites and Democracy in Latin America, Kellogg Institute of International Studies, University of Notre Dame, May 3–5, 1991], 2).

4. For an account of Belaúnde's strategies on his return to power, and the symbolic strength of his campaign as a repudiation of the experience of military rule, see Julio Cotler, "Los partidos políticos y la democracia en el Perú," CEDES/CLACSO Grupo de Trabajo de Partidos Políticos, Documento de Trabajo 9 (Buenos Aires: 1989).

5. Similar patterns were also noted in a study of antistatist business and party mobilization in a number of Central Andean countries, Catherine M. Conaghan, James M. Malloy, and Luis A. Abugattas, "Business and the 'Boys': The Politics of Neoliberalism in the Central Andes," *Latin American Research Review* 25, no. 2 (1990): 3–30.

6. See Ricardo Tirado, "Los empresarios y la política partidaria," *Estudios Sociológicos* 15 (Mexico: El Colegio de México, 1987).

7. Besides Mario Vargas Llosa, the more notable among the new liberal activists were the young intellectuals who participated in the research and writing of Hernando de Soto's blockbuster manifesto of popular liberalism, *El otro sendero* (Lima: Instituto Libertad y Democracia, 1986). *El otro sendero* became a bestseller throughout Latin America, and offered a program of radical socioeconomic transformation along the lines of popular capitalism. It also recast the region's large, and until then perceived as marginal, informal sector as the social agent of this transformation. One of de Soto's co-authors, Enrique Ghersi, who became one of Vargas Llosa's closest political associates, explained *El otro sendero*'s mass appeal to me by describing it as "liberation theology of the Right, with the same degree of illusion" (Ghersi, interview with the author, Aug. 12, 1989; tape recording).

8. These developments are detailed in Chapter 5.

262 / Notes to Pages 218–222

9. The evolution of business-government relations under the García government are analyzed in detail in Francisco Durand, *Business and Politics in Peru: The State and the National Bourgeoisie* (Boulder, Colo.: Westview Press, 1994).

10. See Heredia, "Can Rational Profit-Maximizers be Democratic?"; and Leticia Barraza and Ilán Bizberg, "El Partido Acción Nacional y el régimen político mexicano," *Foro Internacional* 31, no. 3 (Jan.–Mar. 1991).

11. See Lauer, "Adios conservadurismo, bienvenido liberalismo,"; and Durand, *Business and Politics in Peru.*

12. Gabriel Gaspar Tápia, *El Salvador: El ascenso de la nueva derecha* (San Salvador: CINAS, 1989).

13. Soledad Loaeza, "Derecha y democracia en el cambio político mexicano, 1982–1988," Columbia University / New York University Consortium, Conference Paper No. 24 (New York, Apr. 1990), 47.

14. As Yemile Mizrahi notes in her study of the links between business mobilization and PAN in northern Mexico, "the most important cleavage defining the political behavior of entrepreneurs in 1992 was the degree to which they had economic or personal links with government and/or PRI authorities. Large entrepreneurs supported the PRI, while small and medium size entrepreneurs supported the PAN" (Mizrahi, "A New Conservative Opposition in Mexico: The Politics of Entrepreneurs in Chihuahua, 1983–1992" [Ph.D. diss., University of California, Berkeley, 1994], 267).

15. The institutionalization of conservative parties prior to the consolidation of state-business ties appears to make a difference. In Latin American countries with histories of conservative party organization, such as Uruguay, Colombia, or Chile, or, more recently, Venezuela, conservative parties have appeared far more able to weather these fluctuations in business support, in spite of similar patterns of economic development and business class formation after these parties were formed. Similarly, European conservative parties have continued to play a pivotal role in politics, in spite of the rise of neocorporatist patterns of policy making, and the formation of close ties between business and the state. Conservative party-business ties have not fluctuated as widely as they have in Latin America. While confirmation of this proposition would require further evidence, it seems likely that the prior institutionalization of parties did create mechanisms and relationships that lessened the vulnerability of conservative parties to the state-business relationships that emerged with the advent of the developmentalist state in Latin America and neocorporatism in Europe.

16. Ruth Berins Collier and David Collier, *Shaping the Political Arena: Critical Junctures, the Labor Movement, and Regime Dynamics in Latin America* (Princeton, N.J.: Princeton University Press, 1991), 106–8.

17. One such "bargaining" issue was the selection of the president. Thomas Skidmore describes this process under the "Old Republic": "The presidency was the chief prize in national politics. . . . Once the nomination was agreed upon [by state governors], however, it was tantamount to election because the state gov-

ernments had the power to administer elections and did not hesitate to manipulate the returns to fit their pre-election agreements" (Skidmore, *Politics in Brazil, 1930–1964: An Experiment in Democracy* [New York: Oxford University Press, 1967], 3).

18. Maria do Carmo Campello de Souza, *Estado e partidos políticos no Brasil, 1930 a 1964* (São Paulo: Alfa-Omega, 1983).

19. Ibid., 143–54.

20. Olavo Brasil de Lima Junior, *Os partidos políticos brasileiros: A experiência federal e regional, 1945–1964* (Rio de Janeiro: Edições Graal, 1983), 30, 34.

21. For accounts of these events, see Thomas Skidmore, "Brazil's Slow Road to Democratization," and Bolivar Lamounier, "*Authoritarian Brazil* Revisited: The Impact of Elections on the *abertura*," in *Democratizing Brazil: Problems of Transition and Consolidation,* ed. Alfred Stepan (New York: Oxford University Press, 1989), 5–42, 43–82.

22. And this only during the second, majority runoff round of elections, when the Workers' Party emerged officially as one of the two top vote-getting parties in the first round.

23. Maxwell Cameron notes that between 1981 and 1986, the number of manual workers in the formal sector increased from 330,000 to 350,000, while the number of white-collar employees increased from 510,000 to 540,000. The number of people employed in the informal sector, however, increased from 440,000 to 730,000. See Cameron, "Political Parties and the Worker-Employer Cleavage: The Impact of the Informal Sector on Voting in Lima, Peru," *Bulletin of Latin American Research* 10, no. 3 (1991): 293–313.

24. See ibid. for analysis, as well as statistical evidence, of the impact of the informal sector on the shifting cleavage structures of electoral politics in 1980s Peru. He also provides insights into the factors that limited the new conservative movements' efforts to mobilize the informal sector as a substantial component of their mass electoral base.

25. For an analysis of socioeconomic changes in Mexico that identifies the growth of these social sectors, particularly in the northern regions where PAN was strongest, see Brigida García, *Desarrollo económico y absorción de fuerza de trabajo en México, 1950–1980* (Mexico City: El Colegio de México, 1988). The impact of social and demographic change on the electoral fortunes of the PRI is analyzed in Juan Molinar Horcasitas, *El tiempo de la legitimidad* (Mexico City: Cal y Arena, 1991).

26. Robert Bates, "Macropolitical Economy in the Field of Development," in *Perspectives on Positive Political Economy,* ed. James Alt and Robert Shepsle (New York: Cambridge University Press, 1990), 47–48.

27. For an analysis of factors behind ARENA's performance in the 1994 elections, see Liesl Haas and Gina M. Perez, "Voting with Their Stomachs: 'Las elecciones del siglo' in El Salvador," *LASA Forum* (Latin American Studies Association) 25, no. 3 (Fall 1994): 3–6.

28. For an analysis of recent developments in Bolivian politics, including policy making and coalition building by the MNR under presidents Paz Estensoro and Sanchez de Lozada, see Eduardo A. Gamarra, "Democracy and Governance in Bolivia: A Mid-decade Critique" (paper prepared for Inter-American Dialogue governance project).

29. I am indebted to Jeanne Giraldo for this point.

Author Index

266 / Author Index

Subject Index

Büchi, Hernán, 23
Buenos Aires (city): conversion to federal
district, 45; and 1983 elections, 128–
32; and 1985 elections, 165–67; and
1987 elections, 166–67; and 1989 elections, 188–89; and 1993 elections,
197–98, 200–201; and 1995 elections,
203
Buenos Aires Conservative Party: and federal intervention, 56, 58; and 1946 elections, 243 n. 69; and PDP, 49–50
Buenos Aires province: federal intervention of, 56; importance of, 103; pre-
1880 power of, 45
Bunge y Born, 192–93
Burke, Edmund, 5
Bush, George, 17, 18
business community: and democratic rule,
217; importance of, 158; mobilization
in El Salvador, 217–20; mobilization in
Mexico, 217–20; mobilization in Peru,
217–20; and political involvement, 20,
160, 162, 216–17; problems with
UCEDE, 159, 160; state dependence of,
217; support for conservatism, 220,
262 n. 15
Bustamante, Jorge, 147

Cardoso, Fernando Henrique, 223, 230
Catholic Church, 44
Cavallo, Domingo, 206, 207
centrist, as euphemism for "conservative,"
246 n. 29
Chamizo, Julio, 121–22
Chile, 25, 26, 30, 33, 34, 75–76, 228–29,
244 n. 1
Church-state relations: in Chile, 33,
238 n. 8; and regionalism, 32
Civilista Party (Peru), 36
civil society, 21
class politics, and the Left, 17
Clérici, Federico, 146, 191
Colombia, 25, 26, 30, 32–33, 34, 238 n. 6
Concordancia, 59, 60, 62
Confederación Federalista Independiente
(CFI), 185
conservatism: different meanings of term,
3–4; and Edmund Burke, 5, 234 n. 22;
as ideology, 5–7; and resistance to
change, 5; and social class, 6
conservative parties: and business support, 13, 262 n. 15; and coalition building, 9–11, 170, 225–26; and core

constituencies, 9–14; definition of, xiii,
7–8, 210–11; ideological diversity of,
8, 211; and ideology, 3, 6–7, 8–9; logic
of electoral action of, 17–18; and noncore constituencies, 14–15; polyclass
nature of, 9, 17–18; problems in defining, 3–4; scholarship on, 3–4; and
shaping of collective identities, 15–18;
teleological conceptions of, 8–9
conservative parties, Argentina: and antipersonalist radicals, 57–58, 59–60; and
Concordancia, 59–61; determinants of
development, 27–28; early challenges
by Radical Party, 37–41, 48–49; fragmentation of, 51–53, 62, 88, 184, 186,
190–91, 204; list of, 71–74; and 1946
election, 62–63; and 1983 election, 98–
99, 101, 103–5, 125, 126–32; origins
of, 35, 37–40, 45–48; and Peronism,
61–66; post-1916 logic of organization, 52–59; and the Proceso, 78, 80–
101, 213; and ticket-splitting, 130–32,
157, 186–89. See also Unión del Centro
Democrático
conservative parties, Latin America: business and, 160–61, 216–20, 235 n. 36,
262 n. 15; and the conservatization of
populism, 228–29; and democratic stability, 23–27, 30, 210; formation of, 29–
36; and liberalism, 32, 134–35, 215–
16, 224–25; possible futures for, 227–
30; problems with military rule, 213–
14; rapid deployment model of, 229–
30; regionalism and, 29–36, 220–24
Conservative Party (United Kingdom), 10
conservative transition of 1979–82: contradiction in strategy, 90; divisions
within conservatism over, 90–92;
failure of, 77, 98–99; military hin-
drances to, 94; Multipartidaria's opposition to, 95; need for civilian
support, 87; organizational divisions,
90–91; and provincial party leaders,
87–88; views of, 86–87; Viola's strategy for, 93. See also Proceso
conservatization of populism, 198–204,
205–6, 228–29
core constituencies: and Argentine party
development, 10–11, 27, 39–40, 125–
26, 129–30, 159, 163, 179, 198, 203,
205–6, 216–17, 220–21; and Argentine Radical Party, 10–11; and British
Conservative Party, 10; and "catch-all"

Partido Demócrata Progresista (*cont.*)
  Buenos Aires Conservative Party, 49–
  50; and *nacionalista* movement, 50, 61;
  and 1916 elections, 49–51; and 1922
  elections, 57; origins of, 49–50
Partido Federal, 165–66
Partido Social Cristiano COPEI, 30
party development: in Argentina, 31; in
  Brazil, 31; and Buenos Aires Conservative Party, 58–59; in Chile, 30, 34; in
  Colombia, 29, 30, 34; of conservatism,
  211–12; and conservative electoral
  weakness, 30, 31; and core constituency dynamics, 31; and cross-regional
  oligarchic alliances, 32; divergent paths
  of, 29; effect of genetic legacy on, 29–
  31; hindrance of regional divisions, 34–
  35; in Peru, 31; and regionalism, 31–
  36; and territorial diffusion, 52; in
  Uruguay, 29, 30, 34; in Venezuela, 30,
  31
Pellegrini, Carlos, 49
Perón, Isabel, 122, 195
Perón, Juan Domingo, 62, 63, 66, 103,
  114
Peronism: absorption of conservatism's
  mass base in 1946, 62–63; Alsogaray's
  views on, 110, 112, 136, 194, 202–3;
  coalition shifts by Menem, 191–96,
  198–206; and conservatization of populism, 198–204, 205–6, 228; core-
  constituency shift in, 228; electoral
  coalition, composition of, 129, 130,
  165, 169, 172, 173, 201; membership,
  composition of, 177; national coalition
  building of, 63–65; and 1946 elections,
  63; and 1983 elections, 126–28, 130–
  32; and 1985 elections, 165; and 1987
  elections, 166–67; and 1989 elections,
  186, 188; and 1993 elections, 197, 200,
  201; and 1995 elections, 202, 203; opposition to Buenos Aires upper classes,
  65; origins of, 61–63; and Proceso, 79,
  82, 89, 93, 95; as proletarian movement, 65; regional duality in, 64–66;
  and Revolución Libertadora, 111, 114;
  significance of 1983 defeat, 126, 132,
  136; successes in 1987 elections, 140–
  41; and "threat duality" to upper
  classes, 65–66; and ticket-splitting,
  131, 188; and UCEDE, 191–96, 199–
  204, 206–9
Peronist Party. *See* Peronism

personalist-antipersonalist split, 57
Peru, 25, 26, 31, 35–36, 161, 180, 182,
  214, 216, 217–20, 226, 229
Piñera, José, 181
Plan Austral, 139, 162, 164
Plan Primavera, 255 n. 44
Plaza de Mayo demonstration, 199
political parties: organizational approaches to, 19–20; and political leadership, 15–16, 21; relationship to social
  base, 9–15; and shaping of collective
  wills, 15–16; study of, in Latin America, 20–23. *See also* conservative parties; party development
political society, definition of, 22
polity arenas: definition of, 21–22; movement between by Latin American
  leaders, 22–23; shifting balance between, 22
populism, 78, 145–46, 158. *See also* Peronism
Prebisch, Raúl, 111–12, 114
Proceso de Reorganización Nacional: and
  Alvaro Alsogaray, 107, 122, banish-
  ment of party leadership, 79; collapse
  of, 96–97; conception of populism, 78;
  and conservatism, 90, 98–99, 101, 213;
  and dialogue with society, 86; economic
  performance during, 104–5; economic
  reform under, 81–82; failure of leadership in, 107–8; and federalists, 80, 82–
  83, 100; and FUFEPO, 82, 83, 89–90,
  98; internal instability of, 85; isolation
  from society, 79–80; and liberal technocrats, 80; political engineering of, 77;
  problems with military, 94; strategy for
  transition, 87, 88–89. *See also* conservative transition of 1979–82
Pzreworski, Adam, 16

Radical Party (Chile), 33, 34, 238 n. 8
Radical Party (UCR): and business, 161–
  63, 217; as Center-Right alternative to
  Peronism, 62–63, 126–27, 185–86,
  188–89; and CFI, 157, 185, 188–89;
  coalition building of, 63–64; and Concordancia, 59; core constituency of, 11;
  electoral coalition, 129, 130, 165, 167,
  169, 172; formation of, 37–38, 48;
  membership, composition of, 177; and
  1916 elections, 39; and 1983 elections,
  126–28, 130–32; and 1985 elections,
  165; and 1987 elections, 166–67; and